HOUSES VIRGINIANS HAVE LOVED

books by AGNES ROTHERY

Biography
Family Album
A Fitting Habitation
The Joyful Gardener

Juveniles
South American Roundabout
Washington Roundabout
Central American Roundabout
Scandinavian Roundabout
Maryland and Virginia Roundabout
Iceland Roundabout
Italian Roundabout

Essays and Travel
Houses Virginians Have Loved
New York Today
Rome Today
The Ports of British Columbia
Virginia, the New Dominion
Norway, Changing and Changeless
Denmark, Kingdom of Reason
Finland, the New Nation
Sweden, the Land and the People
Iceland, New World Outpost
Images of Earth: Guatemala
Our Common Road
The House of Friendship
A Garden Rosary
The Romantic Shore
Cape Cod, New and Old
The Coast Road from Boston to Plymouth
New Roads in Old Virginia
Central America and the Spanish Main
South America, the West Coast and the East

Novels
Balm of Gilead
Into What Port?
The High Altar
The House by the Windmill

A Play
Miss Coolidge

Photo by Dementi Studio

Built in 1735, Wilton was purchased by the Colonial Dames, who had it moved to its present site. Historically and architecturally, it is of ever-increasing value.

HOUSES
VIRGINIANS
HAVE
LOVED

BY AGNES ROTHERY

illustrated with photographs

BONANZA BOOKS · *New York*

for

WILLIAM EWART STOKES, JR.

and

VIRGINIA HARMON STOKES

This edition published by Bonanza Books,
a division of Crown Publishers, Inc., by
arrangement with Holt, Rinehart & Winston, Inc.

(C)

Copyright, MCMLIV, by Rinehart & Co., Inc.

Printed in the United States of America
All Rights Reserved
Library of Congress Catalog Card Number: 54-9125

foreword

Much has been written about old houses in Virginia.

Architects, historians, biographers and novelists have chronicled the most famous. Their ground plans and architectural details have been reproduced: their gardens have been analyzed and reconstructed. Artists have painted them: photographers have caught them. Truth and trash have accumulated around them.

This book mentions only a few—about a hundred—of these old houses. It touches only a few—less than a quarter—of the ninety-eight counties in the state. There is enough material left to furnish other writers with occupation until old age overtakes them. Furthermore, this book concerns itself only in passing with the technical discussion of architecture or resumé of history. It is chiefly concerned with stories, authenticated as accurately as possible, of less familiar places which have been lived in and loved and are thus infused with personal intimacy.

The houses chosen, while they include a few of the renowned shrines, are chiefly uncelebrated dwellings, regretfully omitting churches, courthouses, schools and public buildings. It is hoped that it will offer new objectives to out-of-state visitors.

It is also hoped, not so confidently, that it may stir the curiosity of Virginians who wave the flag—the Confederate flag in many instances—for Virginia, and yet are ignorant of any part of it beyond their own bailiwick. The inhabitants of Tidewater, while admitting rather vaguely that Southwest Virginia has glorious scenery and climate, are not only astonished but incredulous when they are told it also has some venerable and splendid architectural specimens. Countless complacent inhabitants of Piedmont have never set foot on the entrancing Eastern Shore. The people of Northern Virginia are not quite certain what comprises South Side Virginia. The Northern Neck is merely a confusing term to natives of the Shenandoah Valley. Virginia is a large state and a diverse one. Some sections have been overwritten, overdocumented and described, photographed and publicized. Others are almost unheard of beyond their immediate vicinity. It has been a fascinating pursuit to hunt out some of the houses which are less known, but not, therefore, less worthy or less loved.

contents

Contents

list of illustrations

Thanks to the Virginia Chamber of Commerce for permission to use prints 1, 2, 3, 4, 5, 11, 12, 14, 15, 25, 44, 49, 50, 63, 67, 69, 70, 71, 75, 76, 83, 86, 87, 90, 91, 92 and 93.

Thanks also to the Mount Vernon Ladies' Association of the Union for permission to use pictures 6, 7, 8 and 9, and to Colonial Williamsburg for permission to use pictures 94, 95, 96, 97, 98 and 99.

List of Illustrations

acknowledgements

I wish it were in my power to give more than gratitude to the members of the staff of the Alderman Library of the University of Virginia. Without their ever-ready and highly trained co-operation, I could not have compiled this book. Special thanks are due to the head of the Research Department, Mr. N. Harvey Deal.

Mrs. E. A. Ames
Mrs. Richard Baird
Mrs. Fredson Bowers
Miss Anna Barringer
Mrs. I. William Bagwell
Mrs. Frances Montague Balmer
Mrs. A. Caperton Braxton
The Honorable David K. E. Bruce
Mr. Charles R. Busch
Mrs. Carl Burger
Mr. Archibald A. Campbell
Mrs. Cathleen Campbell
Mrs. Demas T. Craw
Mr. William Garnett Chisholm
Mrs. Myrtle Conquist
Mrs. Grace Carnahan
Mrs. Clarke T. Cooper
Mrs. James Dillard
Mrs. Dixie Lou Fisher
Mrs. Ambrose C. Frost
Mrs. Garrard Glenn

Mrs. William H. Goodwin
Mrs. K. N. Gilpin, Jr.
Mrs. Garland J. Hopkins
Mrs. Margaret D. Hatch
Mr. Chester C. Hazard
Dr. Richard Nunn Lanier
Mrs. Rosa Tucker Mason
Mr. Arthur Pierce Middleton
Mrs. Harry Taylor Marshall
Mrs. John A. Mowinckel
Mrs. F. H. McKnight
Brig. General R. Latane Montague
Mrs. E. Walton Opie
Mrs. Philip B. Peyton
Mrs. Lillian Robey
Mrs. Henry J. Richardson
Mrs. Alma Lee Rowe
Miss Sara Jane Robinson
Dr. and Mrs. Harry L. Smith, Sr.
Mrs. John H. Stearns

Acknowledgements

Mr. and Mrs. William E. Stokes, Jr.	Col. and Mrs. C. J. Tucker
Mr. Curtis Thacker	Mr. and Mrs. Charles C. Wall
Mrs. Joseph A. Turner	Mrs. Robert H. Webb
	Mrs. Henry A. Wise

For Assistance in obtaining special photographs, I am indebted to:

1. Beverley Studio
2. Colonial Williamsburg
3. Dabney Studio
4. Dementi Studio
5. Ewing's Studio
6. Gene Campbell Studio
7. Gitchell-Lee
8. Greear Studio
9. Joseph W. Hazelgrove
10. Holsinger Studio
11. Howard E. Topping Studios
12. Hutchinson Studio
13. David C. Kent
14. Kiraly Studio
15. Mount Vernon Ladies' Association
16. Patterson Photo Service
17. Peters and Company
18. Thomas F. Scott
19. Lawrence D. Thornton
20. Winslow Williams
21. Virginia State Chamber of Commerce

HOUSES VIRGINIANS HAVE LOVED

Houses Virginians Have Loved

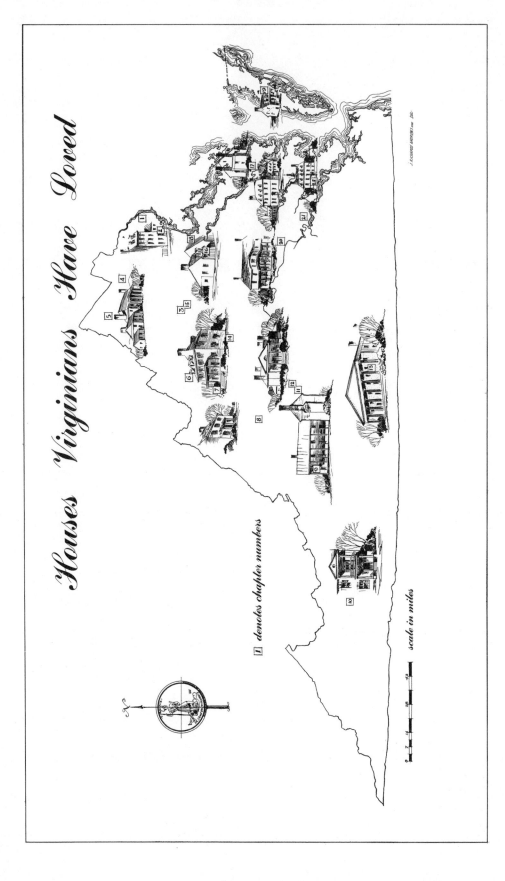

□ denotes chapter numbers

scale in miles

chapter I

TOWN AND COUNTRY

Alexandria: Carlyle House, Dulaney House, Lord Fairfax House, Geradus Clarke House, Emile Burn House, Dr. Brown, Dr. Craik, Dr. Dick Houses, Robert E. Lee House, Dr. Lanier Gray House, Gunston Hall, Woodlawn

Virginians have always had a passion for building houses.

Although none of them equaled Nero's Golden House, which was a mile long, quite a few managed to bankrupt their owners and clamp a mortgage on the family fortunes.

To be sure, most of the early houses were small—a few were handsomely large—but some of the smallest were enriched by paneled walls and hand-carved details and, large or small, each was set in as much land as was possible for the owner to acquire, often hundreds and not infrequently thousands of acres.

To a proper Virginian the acquisition of land is the breath of life. Maybe he wants to farm it, or raise apples or peaches or cattle or horses or turkeys on it. Maybe he merely wants to ride across it or sit on his front porch and look out over the surrounding acres and realize they belong to him. But land he must have, and to be land poor is an honorable predicament.

Obviously this meant that Virginians preferred to live in the country, and even today Virginia is a rural state with less than a dozen cities with a population of twenty-five thousand or more.

Alexandria, which is the point at which most visitors from

3

the North enter Virginia, has the distinction of having always been urban. Its site, at that time called Belle Haven, was chosen by the burgesses sitting in Williamsburg, and the town was launched with éclat. Of the eleven original trustees selected by the Assembly to lay out and found the new town, two bore titles (Lord Fairfax and Lord Stirling), and three were in direct line of succession.

The original survey of lots was made by John West, assisted by the young George Washington, then a lad of seventeen. When the lots were auctioned on July 13, 1749, the most important men in the colony came to purchase them, including Fairfax, Washington, Mason, Fitzhugh and Wormeley. Incidentally, the thirty-one lots sold at an average price of twenty dollars each.

With this head start, Alexandria was a town when Washington was an unmapped marsh.

The reason for its creation and subsequent prosperity was that the planters whose lands lay along the upper Potomac saw the need for a tobacco port and trading center. This need and its fulfillment resulted in a seaport larger than New York and a rival of Boston.

Sloops, brigs, barques and schooners no longer crowd her harbor, but automobiles by the thousand crowd her streets. For Alexandria, beside being a city in her own right, is a suburb—almost a dormitory suburb—and seems likely to remain so. It is quicker to commute to downtown Washington from here than to commute from uptown Washington. Furthermore, by living in Alexandria, one retains the right to vote, which is lost on taking up residence in the District of Columbia.

All of these factors are reflected in the houses.

From the days when Alexandria was a consequential seaport remain the narrow story-and-a-half and two-story buildings down by the wharfs, packed together like sardines. These served not only as shops and taverns and for offices dealing with all kinds of marine outfitting, commerce, etc., but as dwellings.

When the city grew richer, the wealthier men moved farther inland and built the large and beautiful mid-Georgian and early Federal houses, each in its garden, which now make the city a show place.

As Washington became more populous, people moved across the Potomac and apartment houses began to line the boulevards.

Thus the three layers of economic, social and political history are expressed in the architecture as a whole and more graphically in the individual houses which are the pride of residents and the delight of visitors.

The stranger on a first visit will probably be astonished at the number of large red-brick, white-trimmed mansions lining the streets, whose names—Prince and Duke, Queen and Princess and King—are reminiscent of days when the love of royalty was almost as strong on this side of the water as in the mother country. A little later the newer thoroughfares were to be named for Washington and Jefferson, Madison and Lee; for Wilkes, the member of Parliament who had suffered for the defense of the colonies; for Pitt, the Premier who loved liberty; and for the Bishop of St. Asaph, who is referred to in scholarly histories for his writings in favor of colonial independence. However, in Virginia, he is more cozily and approvingly remembered as the Patron Saint of Horse Racing.

Not only the streets but many of the houses are associated with famous names: the Washington and Fairfax families, George Mason and the Lees—both Light Horse Harry and his son Robert Edward—with Patrick Henry and John Randolph of Roanoke.

The visitor vows that when he gets home he will refresh his mind about these patriots who affected not only Virginia history but that of the whole United States. He may even take the trouble to learn the differences between Georgian and Federal architecture and the Greek Revival, all of which present excellent specimens in this well-preserved old city.

But even without such specific information he can put in an enjoyable half day or half a dozen days strolling up and down the streets, some of them still set with cobblestones, and by merely looking at the houses, formal in brick or quaint in clapboard, reconstruct something of the active and cheerful life which once surged up from the harbor and animated the narrow alleys and wide thoroughfares.

It is probable that he will be first introduced to the Carlyle House, a Georgian mansion built in 1752, which, with its gardens, occupied the full northern half of the block bounded by Fairfax, Cameron, Lee and King Streets, with the property falling away to the east to a private wharf, and a wide view of the Potomac.

5

FIGURE 1. The streets of Alexandria are lined with fine old houses, with curved flights of steps, graceful iron railings and delicately carved woodwork.

Its interior is on an equally grand scale with fine paneling and mantels and gracefully curved stairway. Although in 1820 the house was remodeled in the Federal manner and underwent many alterations—not entirely for the better—the historic Blue Room and the small adjoining library remain much as General Braddock knew them in 1755. The bold scrolled pediments above the doors and the superb chimney piece with its marble fireplace, the chair rail with a Greek key fret, and the cornice enriched with carved rosettes between the modillions, are typical of the best of the great colonial houses in the city.

With the refinement of its furnishings and its polished standard of living, it was the accepted center for social and political activities during the early crucial years.

At one time Henry Ford attempted to buy the mansion and

to move it to his transplanted Colonial Village at Dearborn, Michigan. He was not successful, and it is now owned by Lloyd Diehl Schaeffer, who operates it as a museum.

Handsome as the Carlyle House is, there are others which vie with it in architectural dignity and interest.

The house built in 1778 by the colorful Irish gentleman, Benjamin Dulaney, Sr., has been so carefully restored and furnished by its present owners, Mr. and Mrs. John Howard Joynt, that it is a practically perfect specimen of its period. Its quiet entrance and substantial walls face Duke Street, and the same air of elegance pervades the interior. Elaborately carved woodwork in mantel, stairway and cornice, the sumptuous yet restrained furnishings make it a place of unusual richness and dignity.

The Lauranson House is now known as the Lafayette House because Lafayette and his staff were guests there in 1824. It is considered the finest example of Federal architecture in the city.

And the visitor must not forget the brick town house of Dr. and Mrs. Lanier Gray, facing the cobblestones of Captain's Row— cobblestones which were brought in sailing vessels as ballast and laid by Hessian prisoners in the days when Alexandria was one of the largest ports in America. House, furnishings and walled garden in the rear make this a complete period specimen.

The three-story brick house of Lord Fairfax on Cameron Street is another outstanding example of the craftsmanship of the early builders. Low curving flights of steps, with a graceful iron railing, lead to the recessed vestibule with curved ends and an arched ceiling following the same curve. Delicately carved woodwork adds to the elegance of this vestibule, which opens into an interior with a spiral stair and elaborate gesso work around the doors and fireplaces—woodwork and trim being of Adam inspiration.

There are dozens of these houses—such as the ones associated with Dr. William Brown, one of the first surgeon generals of the Revolutionary Army, another with Dr. James Craik, the Scottish surgeon who accompanied Washington on his French and Indian campaigns and was in attendance at his death, and Dr. Elisha Dick, who was consulting physician during this last illness.

The two-and-a-half-story house of pink brick with white trim, to which Robert E. Lee's mother carried her young son to live, still stands in quiet dignity with its spacious side yard.

These, and many more, are described in books and pamphlets, with their ground plans, exteriors, interiors, the minutiae of their carving and paneling and every detail of their furnishing and finishing. While it is a mistake to make the extravagant claim that they are comparable with Georgian examples built in Britain for royalty and great nobles, it is true that the best of them hold their own with those of similar type in England, and they make Alexandria the most interesting colonial city in Virginia.

Besides the great houses, which are sometimes differentiated as urban or manorial, and which face the principal streets, there were the odd-looking "Flounder" houses whose truncated roof lines are visible in quite unexpected places. A "Flounder" house is a structure with a gable roof which seems to be split down the center along the ridge line, making half a house, with one flat windowless side. It is believed that this originated because of an early ordinance requiring that each lot in a new town be built upon by the purchaser within a stipulated time. Thus the rear wing was erected to validate the deed, but the main structure was never completed. Numbers of these remain, and in some cases they have been joined to the main house.

Neither the brick mansions nor the "Flounder" houses—which are sometimes of brick and sometimes of wood—present the whole story of domestic architecture in old Alexandria.

Down in the section of the old port are rows and rows of small houses—some of brick and some of clapboard—jammed together so closely that in some cases they can share a common attic, and one could not slip a piece of paper between their tiny gardens in the rear.

In the days when Alexandria was a flourishing seaport, exporting tobacco to England and bringing back portraits, brocades, silver and china, the water front was lined with wharves and warehouses.

Importers, sea captains, merchants and men engaged in all sorts of business connected with the ramification of seafaring activities, built themselves houses at convenient nearness, both for their business and their families. A usual plan for such a house, whose narrow width accommodated only one room, was to have the shop or office on the first floor, a kitchen in the rear, a family

Photo by Flournoy

FIGURE 2. A "Flounder" house has a gable roof which seems to be split along the ridge line. This makes actually half a house, flat and windowless on the lot side.

sitting room and a bedroom or two on the second. In the attic were stored goods for import or export or for trade, and here the apprentices were tucked away, one ventures to guess, on top of the goods.

In the early days, men of substance and standing chose to build their houses and live here, but gradually, as fashion shifted and wealthy men built their Georgian mansions and laid out their walled gardens farther up, this end of town fell into disrepute.

It became a hideaway for fugitives from the law, and it used to be said that it was possible for a person escaping from justice to be handed from one house to another through concealed doors or hidden and sliding panels, and thus pass undetected through the entire length of several blocks.

After it had been cleaned up legally as regarded law enforcement, and rather casually as regarded sanitation enforcement, it was more or less dropped from the minds of families living in the aristocratic houses on the principal streets. It became, briefly, a slum.

And then, about twenty-five years ago, artists, real-estate agents and victims of the Washington housing shortage began to discover the possibilities of these neglected buildings in an unfashionable locality.

Tentatively at first, and then with gathering momentum, the district was discovered and redeemed, like Georgetown in Washington and Greenwich Village in New York.

Although forced by irreducible measurements to confine themselves to hardly more than a dozen feet from side to side, they have resorted to a hundred tricks to make their bijou homes appear adequate, even commodious. The front door, which originally opened from the street into the shop or office, is sometimes removed, and a window substituted, and the entrance is effected from a side alley, thus giving privacy to the first floor. A parlor and adjoining dining room, a bewitching modern kitchen open in a long vista into the walled garden in the rear. A straight or a winding stair, maybe original to the house, maybe brought from some other old house, or salvaged from a wrecker's pile of debris, leads either from the front parlor or the dining room. Upstairs, what was once the family parlor, with a cozy fireplace and a touch of carving around the mantel, is the master bedroom or an upstairs sitting room. A bathroom is miraculously inserted, one bedroom or two are somehow contrived, and behold, a complete house, painted in Williamsburg colors or papered according to Williamsburg models.

Everything that could be salvaged from the past has been salvaged. If original doors are not to be found, new doors can be made from old wood. Antique locks and hinges are not too hard to come by, and if the floors laid in random-width pine seem to tip, and are so uneven that they suggest a slightly rolling deck, so much the better.

Thus a pre-Revolutionary Inn, in what is now Potomac Court, was so near the water that the river came up beyond the courtyard and was only stopped by a sea wall, part of which may still be seen. Coachmen stopping over night stabled their horses in the little brick houses across the courtyard. The hundred-and-fifty-year-old original part of the house has been remodeled and a wing added and a bricked and walled garden has been laid out in the rear. Here is the extraordinarily convenient residence of Mr. and Mrs. Gerardus Clarke, with Peale portraits, English pewter and Chinese chests—the cosmopolitan type of furnishing that has always been characteristic of seaport houses all over the world.

The house of Mr. and Mrs. Emile Burn consisted in 1800 of two rooms on the first floor and two on the second. A wing was added in 1870 and eventually the little house became a general store and a gathering place for neighbors who came to shop and to get water from the city pump across the street. The present owners added a third wing, made of brick to comply with the present building code; the old tin garage was torn down and a brick patio and walled garden took its place.

So ardent have the new owners of old places become in their search for old, suitable material to use in remodeling, repairs and extensions that they have ransacked junk yards, bought other old buildings and used their timbers, planks and hardware.

In many cases the restoration has been of such high calibre that the remodeled house appears even older than it actually is, so that its exact chronological period is unrecognizable except to experts—of whom there never is any lack in this city.

There are dozens of these reclaimed and deliciously remodeled old houses enjoying such rejuvenescence. Some are so narrow that it seems as if a shoehorn should be hung at the front door to ease one in, and yet, so cleverly have they been remodeled and so subtly has the scale of size been observed in the choice of furniture and its arrangement, that one is not primarily aware of the smallness, but of the charm.

When people from Washington began to discover the advantages of the old seaport and to take up residence there, the cave dwellers turned up their noses in a gesture universal to cave dwellers and spoke of the invasion of the "foreign legion," which seems to have dampened not at all the enthusiasm of the new owners for their new-old homes.

Whether we remember Alexandria from its big brick houses with their gardens, or from the crowded little clapboard ones near the water front, it was always, from the time it was laid out, considered a town, never a village.

Thus the wealthy men who sponsored its beginning and built residences there spoke of them as their town houses, and very convenient they were, in the center of the social and political and trading activity.

They were justifiably proud of these brick mansions, but this did not mean they cared to live in them the year round. The ambition of every true Virginian, even at that early date, was to be a country squire. They wanted a place in the country, with as large and fine a house as possible and with a good deal more land than we today would consider feasible or even desirable.

Thus the Fairfaxes, Washingtons and Masons who had been present at the first auction of lots in 1749 and who maintained houses in town had their large estates in the country and to them gave their liveliest interest and affection.

George Mason and Gunston Hall are typical.

George Mason (1725–1792) was the author of the Virginia Declaration of Rights, in which appear the words whose paraphrase is familiar to every American. "That all men are created equally free and independent and have certain inherent natural Rights . . . among which are the Enjoyment of Life and Liberty, with the means of acquiring and possessing Property, and pursuing and obtaining Happiness and Safety." It is the basis of the first ten amendments to our Federal Constitution—the Bill of Rights. He also wrote the Virginia Constitution, the first to be

Photo by Flournoy

FIGURE 3. The north porch of Gunston Hall is modeled after a design of a Greek temple found on an ancient Roman coin.

Photo by Flournoy

FIGURE 4. Gunston Hall has the first Chinese Chippendale room in America.

drawn up in the colonies, and the one which was used as a model for the constitutions of other states, since admitted to the Union.

These public contributions were made by a man without personal ambition or liking for official life who, after the Revolution, repeatedly declined public office. His reasons were entirely comprehensible to his friends and neighbors. He preferred to devote himself to the building up of his library, the furnishing of his house, and the cultivation of his gardens and orchards and fields. The management of great properties, which were similar to self-sustaining feudal estates, the overseeing of necessary exporting and importing, was recognized as a full-time business. A successful planter was a successful administrator.

Furthermore, it was one of the prerogatives of a gentleman to know something about styles of architecture, periods of furniture, quality of brocades, value of silver, china and glass. Domestic architecture and interior decoration had not, in those days, become the exclusively feminine concern which it is today.

George Mason began by looking around for the best architect procurable; and he commissioned his brother Thomson, who was in England, to find him such a one. Thomson Mason engaged William Buckland, who emigrated to Virginia under an indenture to George Mason. The original indenture papers are preserved and are now owned by Mr. Richard H. Randall, of Towson, Maryland. Buckland attained such distinction both as an architect and a craftsman, that Peale painted his portrait which hangs in the Yale University Art Gallery.

Gunston Hall was three years building (1755–1758). It is of brick, Georgian in type, with a steep pitched roof accented by tall chimneys, two at each end. It is not a large house or even an imposing one, but it has grace and dignity and the interior is surprisingly impressive. Here is the first Chinese Chippendale room in America, a famous Palladian drawing room and a north porch modeled after the design of a Greek temple found on an ancient Roman coin.

Like other gentlemen of his period, Mason took a keen interest not only in his orchards, fields and pastures, but in the landscaping of his grounds. He himself planted the box hedges, of the slow growing or suffruticose variety, which have now reached more than eleven feet in height in a two-hundred-and-fifty-foot

FIGURE 5. George Washington built Woodlawn for his step-granddaughter, Nellie Custis Lewis. The two thousand acres on which it stood were originally part of Mount Vernon.

allée marching from the porch to the lower terraces. Flanked by formal flower beds, outlined by lower hedges of box, the main walk leads to a sunken garden beyond which the pastures fall away to the river.

Originally there were two symmetrical structures to the north, flanking the main section—a plan typical of the middle eighteenth century in Virginia. There were the usual dependencies—the outside kitchen, the slave quarters, the blacksmith shop, the weaving house and the farm buildings, including the stables and carriage house, barns and granaries. None of these now exist.

The house and grounds which George Mason so loved, and which reflected the refinement of his tastes, remained in the Mason family until after the War Between the States. Then it fell into evil days, with wood merchants quartering their choppers in the

15

dormer-windowed bedrooms, Negro families squatting in the principal room on the ground floor, and mules stabled in the basement. It was rescued by a former Federal officer, Colonel Edward Daniels, who made it his home after the war. After Colonel Daniels the property passed through various ownerships, the last being that of Mr. and Mrs. Louis Hertle of Chicago. When Mr. Hertle died in 1949 he left the property to the Commonwealth of Virginia as a fulfillment of the wish of his late wife.

Feminine influence was rather in the shade during the life of George Mason, but the ladies now have their innings. Mr. Hertle designated the National Society of Colonial Dames of America as custodians of the estate. The Garden Club of Virginia has restored the gardens to the traditional eighteenth-century pattern.

While Gunston Hall is only about fifteen miles south of Alexandria, two hundred years ago this was a sufficient distance to insure the privacy of the country. And it was the country which most Virginians wanted then and which, incidentally, most of them want today.

George Washington was another man who maintained a house in town. It seems to have been a rather simple house with a stable, destroyed in 1854, and its site now marked by a garden. He lent or rented it to friends or kinsfolk when he himself was not using it, but his real interest was given to his plantation at Mount Vernon. He seems to have determined that other members of his family should share his love for the country.

When he made provision for the future home of his step-granddaughter, Nellie Custis Lewis, he saw to it that it was to be well away from the city where, incidentally, the Lewises had built and maintained Arch Hall, which still stands on Franklin Street.

The two thousand acres which George Washington set aside for Woodlawn were originally part of Mount Vernon, and the great mansion of Georgian Colonial with Classic Revival innovations cost no less than $140,000, a tremendous monetary expenditure. Dr. William Thornton, whose name is associated with the erection of the National Capitol, was the architect and he lavished his best talents upon it. The central unit, with brick walls laid in Flemish bond, rises two stories to a gable roof with hipped ends and a central pediment piercing the roof like a dormer. It is extended by balancing wings connected to the main structure by low galleries, and joined to outer outbuildings by a high brick wall, a type of manorial residence which became more or less a standard design in domestic architecture throughout Virginia.

This formal mansion passed from the Lewis family in 1848, was bought and sold several times, and is now owned by the Woodlawn Foundation and operated as a museum.

Alexandria remains a city of beauty, historical association and architectural distinction, but it was the plantations established at some distance from it, in Fairfax County and in adjoining counties, which give a distinctive character to the Virginia countryside.

Foremost among them is Mount Vernon.

chapter 2

MOUNT VERNON

Crowning a gentle elevation, Mount Vernon looks through the white columns of its long portico across a lawn down to the Potomac River.

It is believed that the nucleus of the present mansion may have been built by George Washington's father before he moved hither from Westmoreland County in 1735. In 1743, Lawrence Washington built here an eight-room cottage, and after his death in 1752 it became the property, with its accompanying two thousand, seven hundred acres, of his younger half brother George.

It was not until seven years later that this new owner began the first remodelings and additions and extension of the grounds, and found in these activities a satisfaction which was to continue through the rest of his life.

Our first President was a reticent man. He has survived the period of debunking, and no one seems likely to deny him the qualities of a noble character and a splendid mind. He awaits a biographer to endow him with personal magnetism. He himself must have been conscious of this lack when, as a youth seeking a bride, he was firmly refused by one young woman after another.

Even after his marriage to the Widow Custis, and his pleasure in the little son and daughter she brought with her from a previous marriage, his notebooks and diaries remain impersonal. His actions toward his adopted family were affectionate and generous, but it is chiefly through his feeling toward Mount Vernon that we catch the warmth and intimacy of the man.

Mount Vernon is a historical landmark and an architectural evolution. As a national shrine since 1858, it is known to hundreds and thousands of people. It was known to the British when their ships sailed up the Potomac to capture the Capitol. It was known to sight-seers who came by horse and carriage or by slave-propelled barge. In the early days it welcomed so many notable visitors that one of the first rooms which Washington added was a banqueting hall of stately proportions, pleasingly lighted by a Palladian window. Twelve bedrooms were also fully equipped.

Today hundreds of visitors roll up daily in cars and buses, while others arrive by the pleasant excursion boat from Washington. They are shown through the house, over the gardens and grounds, and led finally to the tomb of the first Commander of the Continental Army and the first President of the United States. With more than a million visitors annually, Mount Vernon is the most famous private estate in America.

Behind chronological records of campaigns in war and administration in peace: behind the serene façade and the tranquillity of the rooms, George Washington as a human personality has receded. The calm portraits, painted by Charles Willson Peale and Gilbert Stuart and a score of others, the marble bust by Houdon, present merely the impassive features of a man who, although he was born only a little more than two hundred years ago, is less real to most of us than Caesar or even Moses.

Something of that reality, almost obliterated by the thickly woven veiling of statistics, may, however, gradually reveal itself to those who seek it, not in a head-on assault, but indirectly at Mount Vernon.

Although, while still a bachelor, General Washington enlarged his house from a story and a half to two and a half, his first active interest in the plantation seems to have started at the time of his marriage to Martha Custis, when, like most newly married men, he began to plan for a future home.

Photo by Samuel Chamberlain

FIGURE 6. Mount Vernon, with more than a million visitors annually, is the most famous private estate in America.

He decided that the eight-room cottage on the banks of the Potomac must be overhauled, reroofed, resheathed, its foundation walls reconstructed, and two small wings added and connected to the cottage by open arcades. The frame timbers of the house are of hewn oak, mortised and pinned, and the sheathing is of longleaf pine, with rounded ends so beveled and painted with a sand finish as to give the appearance of stone. He found that many of the original cypress shingles were sound enough to use again, and, with characteristic frugality, he ordered them turned and put back. Some of them have been protected by the tin roof of the portico, where they are still in place and in good condition.

The bridegroom was detained at Williamsburg, where he had to remain a few months as a member of the House of Burgesses, and it was not until the spring of 1759 that the couple set forth for their future home, over which Washington had already assumed complete control. The day before he arrived with his wife, the steward received a note from him telling explicitly how to clean and air the house: saying what bedsteads to set up and make ready, admonishing that the tables and chairs and staircase must not only be thoroughly cleaned but rubbed, and adding that the larder must be stocked with certain provisions to be purchased in the neighborhood.

From that day until his death, forty-one years later, no detail in the house or on the grounds was too small to engage the master's attention.

If he was interested in every detail of housekeeping and hospitality, he was equally concerned with the building necessary for the great plantation he had in mind. There was to be a kitchen, outside the house of course, so no odors of smoke or heat could reach the dining room: there must be an office, a washhouse, a coach house, a spinning house, a storeroom and a greenhouse, to accommodate the tubbed and potted plants during the winter.

Many of these plans had to be executed when he was away. In 1775 he was called to the Continental Congress where he was unanimously chosen Commander-in-Chief of the Army, and he did not see his home again until 1781 on his hurried march to Yorktown.

Where absence prevented personal supervision, it resulted in a vast correspondence between himself and his kinsman, Lund Washington, whom he had engaged as manager. From these letters it is possible to see how carefully he considered every major change and every minor improvement. He chose a decorator to stucco the ceilings of the parlor and dining room and to attend to the paneling and papering of the other rooms. He was himself, happily, at home when the marble mantel arrived from Italy, and so he was able to oversee its unpacking and installing. He could not find the stone he wanted for the floor of the portico and ordered blocks of gray and red stratified sandstone from the west coast of England.

He decided on the laying out of the drives, walks, walls and gardens: the deer park and the bowling green, with its blind-ditch drain, and with his own hand drew maps to indicate the lay-

Figure 7. The reconstructed greenhouse overlooks the garden in which Washington set out a Palmetto Royal, Magnolia Live Oak and "sower" oranges.

out. He personally selected the trees and shrubs to be planted, and whenever he traveled collected nuts, seeds and scions. He even had a botanic garden back of the spinning house, where he analyzed soils, compounded fertilizer, tested seeds and propagated plants.

Although he seems never to have wearied of improving and refining the decorative features of the place, his interest was also utilitarian. Like other planters of the day, he was a practical agriculturist and regarded Mount Vernon not merely as a gentleman's estate, but a wealth-producing enterprise.

He kept adding to its area until it comprised eight thousand acres, and this in turn was divided into five separate establishments or farms, each with its laborers, each with its dwellings for overseers and laborers, stables for livestock, barns for the storage of hay and grain, also a well-ordered smithy and carpenter shop and a grist mill. His daily records show how closely he studied ways to expedite the sowing, planting and harvesting and rotating of crops and how carefully he inventoried his servants, livestock and all his possessions. He not only took justifiable pride in the rich yield of his fields, but it is pleasant to read of his gratification in being awarded a prize by the Agriculture Society of South Carolina for raising the largest jackass. In times of exigency on the farms he was surprisingly adaptable. Thus, if the market for rye was unfavorable, he had it hauled to his distillery and converted into whiskey, in one year producing twelve thousand gallons.

These varied and efficient activities are the more remarkable when we again recall how much he was obliged to be away from home. From 1789 to 1797, as President, he was obliged to live in Philadelphia, which was six days' coach journey from Mount Vernon. Since he could not personally supervise everything, he wrote detailed instructions, such as stipulating the "selected" bricks to be dug from his own kiln to line the well for the servants' use.

Thus his public life, which history has tabulated and recorded with more accuracy than liveliness, was accompanied by a private life filled with active planning and execution and administration. While most Virginia gentlemen of the period owned and managed their large or small plantations with varying degrees of efficiency, few were as efficient as this man who devoted to public service

FIGURE 8. In the library Washington received the reports of his overseers, made daily entries in his diary and posted his accounts.

energies which would adequately fill an average man's lifetime.

His impress was so strong and so evident in every detail of the mansion, in every outline of garden walk and wall, in the placing of their gates, in every ramification of farmland and forest land, that it might have been that even after his death this impress would remain indelibly fixed upon the plantation he so loved.

Such was not the case.

Although three generations of the Washington family occupied the mansion after his death, and although each did what it could to keep the buildings in repair and the fields in cultivation, the constant stampede of sight-seers, the prolonged stay of visitors became a burden which was too heavy for any private individual. Neither Congress nor the Virginia Legislature was willing to pur-

FIGURE 9. General Washington's bed, on which he died, is six and a half feet long. At its foot is the portmanteau bunk reserved for his personal use during the war.

chase the estate and make the necessary arrangements for its care.

The story of the Mount Vernon Ladies' Association is a long and admirable one. Under the leadership of Miss Ann Pamela Cunningham of South Carolina, representative women from every state were organized, and in 1858 the buildings and two hundred acres became the property of the Association.

The restoration of any old and neglected building requires not only a determined ideal but skillful advice and money: money for urgent initial repairs and more money for maintenance and improvement.

The devoted ladies raised the necessary minimum by efforts familiar to all women—from entrance fees and the sale of their own handiwork, and from donations solicited or voluntarily offered. During the years of the Civil War they managed to have the property recognized as "neutral territory" so that it would not be molested by either army.

What made these efforts unique was not only the gradual emergence of tumble-down buildings, overgrown walks, obliterated walls and rediscovered gardens, but the gradual emergence of the personality of George Washington himself.

The major repairs, such as leaking roofs and collapsing portico, had to be seen to immediately and required substance rather than sentimentality. But when it came to more intimate details, another factor began to be felt.

Small restorations followed in careful succession and with each one the presence of the original master of Mount Vernon took a step forward out of the fog which surrounds a figurehead into the light which reveals a human being.

After her husband's death, his wife divided much of the furniture among her four grandchildren, and it was carried away, scattered and lost track of. It was not easy to trace or to acquire all the pieces, but gradually many of them have been reassembled in their original places. In the dressing room off the bedroom is the marble-topped shaving stand purchased by the master of Mount Vernon from the first Minister from France, and in the linen room is the original washstand. Downstairs in the morning room is the table on which the General enjoyed playing Loo: in the library, the tambour secretary at which he wrote, and the terrestrial globe to which he referred. In the dining room stands the diminutive Windsor chair in which little Nellie Custis—and later her children—sat: in the music room is the harpsichord which her indulgent step-grandfather imported from England for her. Here, too, is his own flute which, incidentally, he never learned to play. On the stair landing the old hall clock still marks the hours.

The same fidelity of restoration has gone into clearing the gardens of weeds and repairing their walks and their borders of box. With each touch, the dim shade of Washington becomes more defined. The pedestal which has been elevated high and higher, so that the figure which tops it has become farther and farther away, subsides to more convincing proportions.

It is proper that continuous troops of school children should be shown how the history of Mount Vernon parallels the history of our country. Entirely proper that antiquaries and architects should be interested in particular aspects of the authenticity of this piece or the construction of that well.

But some Americans standing inside the rooms of elegance and hominess will realize almost with surprise that the owner who planned and furnished them with such thoughtfulness and taste is not merely a historical figure. For the first time they may think of him as an entirely human person who took pride in managing his farms and fields with intelligent energy and who loved his home with a simple and constant warmth.

chapter 3

MID PLEASURES AND POLITICS

Belmont, Rokeby, Oak Hill

The town, represented by Alexandria, was always on the boil with politics, for from earliest times Virginians were aware of their political responsibilities and prerogatives. In the country, hospitality and half a hundred sports vied with politics.

Loudoun County, which was cut off from Fairfax County in 1757 for convenience of administration, sustained both traditions. Dining, dancing, dicing, horse shows, racing, hunting—the entertainment of distinguished diplomats and an asylum in a time of crisis for state documents—these entered early into the life of Loudoun, and Belmont was one of its principal centers.

The brick Georgian mansion, about five miles East of Leesburg and set on a gentle elevation overlooking its farms and pastures, was the scene of such wide hospitality that the names of its guests read like a chronological history.

It was built in 1800 by Ludwell Lee (the son of Richard Henry Lee the Signer) and being not only commodious but conveniently near the capital, found itself well patronized.

In 1814, when the British burned Washington, it is said that President Madison took refuge at Belmont and stayed there while directing affairs of state. Lafayette must have been very willing to lay his head upon his pillow here after the day when he had entered Leesburg with President John Quincy Adams and ex-President Monroe, in a carriage drawn by four white horses—which become bay horses in some accounts—and accompanied by two troops of cavalry.

A salvo of artillery greeted the carriage and the roads were lined with ten thousand people, which was half the population of the county. Young ladies from the Leesburg Female Academy, dressed in white with blue sashes, and crowned with green garlands, and boys from the Leesburg Institute, with red sashes and black and white cockades, strewed laurel before the prancing horses. There was a banquet in the Court House Square and a double baptism of Elizabeth and Mary Mason, the two infant daughters of William Temple Thomson Mason of Temple Hall, and then a drive to Belmont for the grand ball.

At Coton, the neighboring estate, festivities continued that same night and the road between the two mansions was lined with a double row of slaves, each holding a flaming torch to guide the celebrants. The original house at Coton, which was built by Ludwell Lee, has vanished, but Mr. and Mrs. Warner Snider, formerly of Cleveland, have built and for more than thirty years have lived in a house on the twenty-five-hundred-acre estate.

A hundred years after Lafayette's visit we find Belmont still opening its gates to entertainment on a large scale. Mr. and Mrs. Edward Beale McLean—Mrs. McLean was the Evelyn of Hope diamond fame—built the ballroom in the rear. Later, the wings were added by one of the many successive owners.

For a while it was owned by Major General and Mrs. Patrick Hurley and the Loudoun Hunt Club was invited to hold its annual horse show there.

It must not be assumed that Belmont maintained such lavish hospitality unbrokenly for a hundred and fifty years. Less than a decade after Lafayette's visit in 1825 the plantation was, according to the diary of Miss Margaret Mercer, "a run down farm." It was because of its disrepair she was able to buy it for the purpose she had in mind—a school for young ladies.

And now, by a paradox, the rooms which had been the setting for balls and banquets stood in Spartan plainness. The grounds where thoroughbred horses had pranced were laboriously traversed by a few work carts. A small frail woman, burning with zeal to establish a better world, and to this end wholeheartedly devoting her fortune and strength and giving up everything which is usually considered personal pleasure, outshines the brilliantly costumed figures who had preceded her.

Margaret Mercer's name has been forgotten by most Virginians, and yet her personality still glows, obscurely but persistently, in the annals of the state.

She was born in 1791 in Maryland, where her father, a Virginian and friend of Jefferson, Madison and Monroe, was Governor. He was an able and liberal man and early recognized the exceptional mentality of his daughter. He taught her himself and gave her the range of his large and well-selected library. She plunged into the eager study of botany, gathering various kinds of wild flowers and painting and embroidering them with accuracy and taste. She showed equal enthusiasm for mathematics, Hebrew, metaphysics, literature and modern languages.

But although she had the intellectual taste and aptitudes of a scholar, she was possessed, in an ever-increasing degree, by the ardor of a reformer.

She began by visiting the sick and teaching in Sunday School and enlarged her activities when she undertook to raise funds for the Greeks who were, at that time, struggling for their independence from Turkey.

Fired by the conviction that not only the Greeks but everyone should have freedom, she threw herself into the American Colonization Society, whose object was to furnish the transportation of freed slaves to Liberia. She believed this would encourage manumission and ultimately lead to the elimination of slavery in the United States.

She did not confine her advocacy of emancipation to argument. She freed her own share of the family slaves and raised money to free as many others as possible. Neither did her efforts stop when her beneficiaries reached Liberia, but continued, as she raised money for educational work in that faraway land, where her name was better known and more deeply loved than in her own country.

In the meanwhile, having expended her entire personal fortune on these ventures, she decided to start a school, not only because it had now become necessary for her to support herself, but because she was inspired to spread enlightenment—moral as well as educational—to families nearer than Liberia.

She had, as a young girl, run a school in her home in Maryland—Cedar Park Institute—which was so successful she had been forced to build an addition to the house. She tried again in Franklin, near Baltimore, but decided it would be wiser to make a complete break and therefore traveled what was then the considerable distance to Virginia to investigate the possibilities.

Here she found and purchased the "run down farm" which had once been the scene of so many festivities, and was now falling into disrepair. Promptly she tackled the problem of first procuring teachers and students and then of arranging accommodation for them. These accommodations were far from luxurious, but Miss Mercer was never one to emphasize the gratification of the flesh. Where once pleasure and plenty had prevailed, austerity and hard work were the order of the day.

Some of the students paid for their board and tuition, but many were accepted without charge of any kind, and the children of the humble neighborhood were welcomed in free classes in agriculture, cooking and sewing, and grounded in the principles of personal cleanliness and, by no means last, Christian doctrine.

Miss Mercer was even then handicapped by the tuberculosis from which she was to die, but this febrile disease merely spurred her to greater activity. Her zeal was infectious. People from miles around tramped to her school and to the small chapel which she later built on the grounds, bringing her their problems. She wrestled with all the complications of maintaining her expanding family, procuring water, food, books and bedding. She listened to everyone and prayed with many. She gave popular lectures on ethics and wrote hundreds of long, loving letters—the hortatory passages well underlined—to dozens of her former pupils. She herself taught botany, chemistry, natural history, drawing, rhetoric, and superintended the plowing and planting.

In spite of the pressure of these driving duties, in spite of her prodigal expenditure of energy, she found time to give her warm personal sympathy to uncounted individuals, black and white, old and young, who came to her in sorrow or bewilderment.

31

Photo by Winslow Williams

FIGURE 10. A vault at Rokeby was chosen to hold our more important government documents when the British threatened to invade Washington. The Declaration of Independence and the Constitution of the United States are supposed to have been among these.

It is noteworthy that the school, which was the center of such strenuous propaganda and determined good works, should, according to the accounts of those who knew it, have been suffused with "a gentle, serene and kind spirit."

The little chapel she built may still be seen from the highway, but few pause to glance at it. The mansion of Belmont, enlarged by a succession of owners—its present ones being Mr. and Mrs. George C. Clarke—is no longer the scene of Spartan living and Spartan labor but has regained its old splendor.

From the highway one can see the red brick of its walls and the white of its shuttered windows, and the sweep of its drives and lawns and enclosing white fences. Probably Margaret Mercer, if she were to return to it today, would hardly recognize it.

And perhaps no one today would recognize Margaret Mercer if she should reappear, like a gentle and determined ghost, to sweep aside such evidences of comfort and luxury, and again endeavor to improve the state of the world.

While it remains debatable whether President Madison did or did not direct the affairs of government from Belmont, there is no question that the more valuable of the national archives were ordered to be removed from Washington for safer concealment. It was decided that a vault adjoining a bricked-in excavation under the front porch of Rokeby would be a suitable place. They were accordingly taken there.

Rokeby, on the old Caroline Road south of Leesburg, built of brick laid in Flemish bond, suggests an English manor, so that it is easy to credit the statement that it was planned and started by an Englishman. However, since Charles Binns was living there in 1754, it has been assumed that he completed it. Charles Binns was Clerk of the Court when Loudoun was formed from Fairfax County, and it is presumed that he had the vault built for his papers and records. It has two tiny windows with iron gratings, but its iron door was donated as scrap during the War Between the States. At all events, this was the vault which was chosen as a repository for our more important documents when the British threatened to invade Washington. It is said these included the Declaration of Independence and the Constitution of the United States. Possibly there was also a painting of Dolly Madison—then cut from the frame—now hanging in the White House.

Stephen Pleasanton, then a clerk in the State Department, was put in charge of the removal and he ordered a number of linen bags to be made to his specifications. So many books and documents were placed in them that some accounts say that twenty-two two-horse wagons were required for their transportation. Other accounts seem to think that four four-horse wagons were sufficient, while the most modest merely mention ox teams.

Whatever the number of horse-drawn or ox-drawn teams, the precious bags ultimately reached Rokeby safely, where Charles Binns, Jr., who, like his father before him, was Clerk of the Court, received them and stored them in the vault.

There they remained for two weeks, and when it was thought

safe to return them to Washington, they seemed none the worse for their sojourn.

After this brief and sudden adventure in importance Rokeby returned to its dignified English ways. It passed through several ownerships, and was purchased in 1886 by the family of the present owners, who built a large addition, conforming to the original type of construction. It is now owned by Mrs. John Hill Carter and her brother, B. Frank Nalle.

Rokeby was chosen as a safe place to hide the national documents because it is in the region of Leesburg, which is near enough Washington to be accessible and far enough away to offer privacy.

This used to be a long way from the capital, and young blades from Fairfax, driven by a coachman in a bottle-green coat with brass buttons, made a point of having him pause before they entered the town and announce their arrival by a blast on his trumpet.

And yet sometimes the journey was accomplished in jig time. The issue of a Leesburg newspaper on March 31, 1818, states that the Waggon Perseverance, laden with sixty-five thousand dollars in specie for the Branch Bank arrived in only two days from Alexandria.

Today the thirty-five miles from the capital are quickly covered by commuting automobiles. But although more and more people are discovering the charming countryside and exceptionally equable climate, Loudoun County is yet unspoiled and uncommercialized.

While some of the old buildings have been salvaged—the Mott House, once a hospital during the War Between the States, is now a small inn commemorating the Laurel Brigade—Leesburg has escaped being sweepingly "restored." A hundred years ago its population was 1,239. During the next forty years it grew to 1,700, and there it has remained despite the fact that some of the old houses have been beautifully restored and retenanted, and new ones have been built.

Such diverse people as General and Mrs. George Marshall and Mr. and Mrs. Arthur Godfrey have chosen to make it their home. The more or less accepted fact that President Madison carried on and directed the affairs of government while he was in Belmont and that Rokeby temporarily guarded the national archives, gave rise to the mild joke that at one time Leesburg "was once the Capital of the United States."

While this is hardly accurate, it is true that Loudoun County has had its share not only of political but of presidential association.

Like other presidents who were to follow him, James Monroe, while still in office, decided to build a dignified place for the years of his retirement. He owned a large tract of land on the Carolina Road, nine miles south of Leesburg, and on it his family had occupied a dormer-windowed cottage. He chose this spot, in 1820, to erect the large brick house which is the best known of the old homes in Loudoun County.

It took no persuading to get that indefatigable architect, Thomas Jefferson, to draw the plans for it, or James Hoban, who designed the White House and supervised the building of the Capitol, to oversee the construction. Monroe named the place Oak Hill in honor of the oak presented to the President by Congress from every state in the Union and planted on the wide lawn.

The central unit of the house, and part of the two wings are original. Later, fifteen feet were added to each of the wings and also the small porticos at each end. All of these are in such excellent proportion that there is no break in the continuity. Thus Oak Hill successfully exemplifies the adaptation of severely classical features to domestic buildings. The details of the north front, with its arched and recessed doorway, delicately traced fanlight and side lights, iron railings and double divided stair, are admirably simple.

The south, or garden, front gains both formality and intimacy from its portico with five thirty-foot Doric columns and a returning column on each side. As you look up at the porch from the garden or highway, you see only five of these. The usual plan calls for an even number of columns with a central doorway leading into the house. Here, however, the drawing rooms have four exits to the portico and enable a fifth column to be used—a design almost unduplicated in Palladian construction.

Monroe dearly loved the house, coming down from the Capitol as often as he could, his saddle bags stuffed with state papers. It was here, while he was President, that he wrote the message to Congress which embodies what has come to be known

Photo by Flournoy

FIGURE 11. President James Monroe built Oak Hill for the years of his retirement. Jefferson drew the plans, and James Hoban, who designed the White House, oversaw its construction.

as the Monroe Doctrine. It was here he entertained Lafayette, who had been a close friend since the days of Monroe's ministry to France. In memory of this visit Lafayette sent a gift of the two delicately carved marble fireplaces—not identical but similar— which face each other from opposite walls of the two drawing rooms.

There are a number of other association pieces in the lofty drawing rooms, with their deep cornices and crystal chandeliers: a Chippendale chair with a worn horsehair seat, which belonged to George Washington; another Chippendale chair, of maple, which belonged to John Adams; hurricane candlesticks once in the possession of Lord Fairfax, and a candlestick-stand which came from Monticello.

It must not be assumed that these have stood in their accustomed places for more than a hundred years. After Monroe's death in 1831, the place passed to various owners. First, to his daughter, Mrs. Gouveneur of New York, and then to Colonel John Fairfax, an officer on General Longstreet's staff. Colonel Fairfax set out large orchards of Albemarle Pippins and is said to have sent some to Queen Victoria, who pronounced them the most delicious she had ever eaten. There is some argument as to whether the apples which won the royal favor were from Colonel Fairfax's orchards at Oak Hill, or from the Green Mountain farm of Andrew Stevenson, the American Minister at the Court of St. James, or from the trees on the Redland plantation in Albemarle County. But in any case the result was a happy one, for the Queen promptly removed import duty on all American apples.

During the War Between the States, General Moseby used often to drop in at Oak Hill for a hospitable interlude, and even directed some of his raids from the great portico. Union officers came, too, and occupied it on occasion, although they seemed to have treated the place with respect. However, Mrs. Fairfax took no chances. Finding a handsome backgammon table with ivory playing pieces among the relics left by Monroe, she took the precaution of slipping her jewels between the wood and marble tops when the house was searched by Northern soldiers—so that years later, children hearing this story used to hunt for jewels, although they were rather vague as to who hid them and for what reason.

Colonel Fairfax sold the place to Dr. Quimby and he, after a few years, sold it to Henry Fairfax, son of the Colonel. And now it became a center for the two ruling passions of good Virginians—politics and horses. For Henry Fairfax was a beloved State Senator, and was also a breeder of Hackney driving horses, at times having as many as two hundred, some of them internationally famous. With twelve hundred acres of grassland, one can maintain quite a stable.

After him, Mr. and Mrs. Frank C. Littleton came into possession. It was they who extended the wings and, while sandstone was being quarried on the place, noticed certain strange imprints, which were subsequently pronounced to be dinosaur tracks—the first known evidence that such prehistoric creatures used to roam this section of the globe. The slabs with the faint monstrous imprints are now incorporated into the floor of a room opening out into the box-bordered gardens which drop down in terraces from the south portico. Others may be seen throughout the garden. After the death of his wife, Frank C. Littleton continued to live at Oak Hill, and for twenty-five years was so immersed in it that he became more interested in history and legend than in the years of his own reality. He was so attached to every stick and stone, every object and article, that when he was finally obliged to depart he would not leave behind a single piece of his beloved furnishings, and they were ultimately disposed of at Sloan's auction house in Washington, and the present owners—Mr. and Mrs. Thomas N. DeLashmutt—purchased some of them.

They have also furnished one bedroom completely with original Madison pieces, including Dolly Madison's massive four-post bed, with its original red damask hangings, her pier-glass mirror, dressing tables, etc.

House, grounds, gardens and furnishings are kept in perfect condition and set forth with a taste and suitability which would have gratified the builder, the fifth President of the United States.

chapter 4

HOUSES, HORSES AND HISTORY IN NORTHERN VIRGINIA

Oatlands, Gordonsdale, Rosney, Red Gate, Selma, Chapel Hill, Fairfield, Carter Hall, The Nook, Springsburg, Scaleby

Since Virginia is predominantly rural and not urban, it is the county and not the town which is politically significant. In the days of the horse and buggy, it was necessary to have the county seat within a day's ride of any point in the region it served. Twenty miles or so over the fearful roads was all a man on horseback could be sure of covering in a day, and that was why ultimately the state of Virginia found itself with a hundred counties, each with its courthouse and post office. Recently this number has been reduced to ninety-eight, but whenever further merging of administrative areas is advocated, local jealousies, to say nothing of local sinecures, raise such a protest that the matter is dropped like a hot potato.

Today, with automobiles and good roads, for the visitor the counties merge imperceptibly into one another, although the permanent inhabitants still take pride in emphasizing certain distinctions.

Loudoun County points to Oatlands as the traditional ideal of great Georgian mansions in Virginia, and it does indeed measure up to this claim.

Six miles south of Leesburg, of white stucco on brick, it has stood for a hundred and fifty years on an airy sweep of lawn, dappled by the shadows of a tremendous honey locust. A tall white portico with Corinthian columns rises before the central and highest unit, and the sides are extended in octagonal bays. Old prints show a cupola which has fortunately been removed.

Behind the imposing façade lies an equally imposing series of rooms, including a drawing room of the octagonal shape which Jefferson made so dear to Virginians. Two identical flights of stairs ascend from the two wings.

The plaster work on the ceilings—their cornices and rosettes —is intricate as deep lace. The woodwork is elaborately carved and over some of the doors appears the unusual motif of Indian feathers.

If the exterior and the interior are stately, the grounds more than supplement them. From the balustraded elevation of the lawn one can look out over a wide panorama, or down into a walled garden of complicated terraces united by a series of stone steps. The many gardens are divided by parterres of box, each garden individually treated, and yet combined to make part of a harmonious whole. Tree box frames a long vista traversed by an *allée* bordered by rare shrubs. Nothing is lacking. There is a bowling green and a burial lot.

The George Carter who designed and built Oatlands in 1800 also supervised its construction, which was done by his slaves. Neither did he trust his perfected handiwork to the care of any flibbertigibbet young bride. He waited until he was sixty and then cautiously ventured to introduce as his wife a widow of discreet years. This George Carter was the son of Councillor Robert Carter of Nomini Hall and great-grandson of the great "King" Carter. It must have been hard for him to leave the place which had been the source of so much pride and which had given him such an engrossing occupation with all its indoor and outdoor details. But part with it ultimately he was obliged to do, for at his death it passed, with three thousand acres and seventy-five slaves, to his oldest son—another George.

It is fortunate for those of us today who like to see what kind of house and what kind of life were enjoyed in Loudoun County a hundred and fifty years ago, that in 1903 Oatlands came into

Photo by Flournoy

FIGURE 12. Oatlands is considered the traditional ideal of great Georgian mansions and of early landscape architecture in Virginia.

the possession of Mr. and Mrs. William Corcoran Eustis. For they, like the original owner, delight in its handsome formality, which they have been able to restore and maintain. Thus it is that Oatlands can still hold its claim of being one of the most impressive examples of early landscape architecture in Virginia.

No visitor is permitted to leave Loudoun County without hearing of the duel associated with Selma, the estate which was once part of Raspberry Plain.

The youthful participants were near cousins, General Armistead Thomson Mason and Colonel John Mason McCarty. Both were already distinguished in public life—General Mason as United States Senator from Virginia, and Colonel McCarty as a lawyer. Political disagreements led to a quarrel, the quarrel to a

41

duel, and on a bitterly cold morning, February 6, 1819, the cousins confronted each other, standing so close that their "barrels almost touched." At the signal, both fired, and both fell, Mason dead and McCarty critically wounded.

Mason left a widow who, after her husband's funeral, locked the front door of Selma and never permitted it to be opened again until her son Stevens—an infant at the time of his father's death—came of age. McCarty, who recovered from his wound, married Ann Lucinda Lee of Coton and he also had a son.

The Mason and McCarty families, although living only a few miles apart, never spoke to each other, and when Colonel McCarty's son grew old enough to go hunting, he was scrupulous about never setting his foot upon the Mason property. One day, however, in order to get a better shot, he climbed a fence which marked the boundary and in some way his gun slipped and sent the ramrod through his head. He toppled over on the Mason side, falling upon the ground he had avoided all his life. At this moment, his cousin, Stevens Mason, happened to come riding by, and the dying lad was carried to Raspberry Plain, the birthplace of the man his father had slain.

Tradition has it that his father, overwhelmed by the double tragedy, became a haunted creature, who would wander away and after long periods reappear, his hair grown to his shoulders and his wild beard falling on his chest.

This true story, which reminds one of Scottish border ballads, has never been forgotten in Loudoun County, and although it is nearly a hundred and fifty years since the cousins faced each other in the fatal duel, it is still mentioned as though it happened yesterday.

After the tragic tales of Selma, the imposing formality of Oatlands, and the presidential facts and fancies of Oak Hill, Gordonsdale in Fauquier County, solid white-walled and unadorned, seems refreshingly restrained.

It is suitable that it should be unostentatious, for its tradition has been unbrokenly Scottish since the Reverend Alexander Scott came to America and took out the first grant for the property in 1726, paying "good and legal tobacco" for eight thousand acres.

His great-nephew, whose father inherited the tract, was sent back to Scotland when he was eighteen for having been implicated

Photo by Winslow Williams

FIGURE 13. Carter Hall in Clarke County is an immense mansion of light gray limestone. The joints of the mortar have turned cream colored and give a soft effect of plaster. The thirty acres of well-kept lawn sweep up to the main house and its dependencies.

in a duel. He took his degree as Master of Arts at King's College in Aberdeen, and while there met and married Elizabeth Gordon, daughter of the Provost. He brought her back to Virginia, which must have seemed wild and isolated to the eyes of the young girl; their first home was a log cabin on the original grant.

The log cabin is still standing, whitewashed and trim, and so are two slave quarters of stone, the last of thirty outbuildings.

To the young couple was born a daughter, Eliza, who married Doctor Chandler Peyton. He bought from the other heirs portions of the estate, and in 1818 built the big white house, an exact duplicate of the Provost's house in Aberdeen, which still faces King's College.

43

The rooms, with their seven original mantels and floors and early American and English furnishing, are in complete harmony with the unaffected exterior. On the shelves of a small hanging cabinet are arranged pieces of lustre which were so treasured that their mistress, traveling by oxcart from Connecticut to the Western Reserve, carried them by hand. Ultimately they were brought back east—not by oxcart—and now hang in the cabinet which is rumored to have a secret drawer.

The refinement of the house is further enhanced by the planting—said to have been designed by Major L'Enfant—with a garden which is green the year around, and with long narrow *allées* of tall clipped box. These *allées* run across the front, and encircling the rear are other box trees, whose immense slanting trunks made a Rackham forest into which many a child must have peered with delight.

Slipping across the invisible boundary line into Clarke County, the great houses like Carter Hall and Fairfield give grandeur to the Virginia scene. Carter Hall, a mansion of native limestone, overlooking a sweeping plantation of mighty oaks and gentle glades, has accepted as its due for a hundred and fifty years the recognition of being among "the most elegantly improved estates west of the Blue Ridge."

It has passed through various ownerships since Nathaniel Burwell built it some time before 1790. It has been enriched by additions and made more comfortable by modernizations, but it has always remained an architectural and historical landmark. William Thornton, architect of our national Capitol, is credited with having designed the handsome portico, seventy-two feet long and fifteen feet wide, its roof supported by thirty-foot modified Ionic columns with carved capitals.

Edmund Randolph, Governor of Virginia and first attorney general of the United States, died here in 1813 while visiting his Burwell cousins, and in the fall of 1862 Stonewall Jackson established his headquarters in the grove, politely refusing Mr. Burwell's invitation to transfer them to the house.

Fairfield, sumptuous in dimensions and magnificent with terraced gardens and blue-grass lawns, is also rich in historical associations. It was built about 1765 by Warner Washington I, first cousin of George Washington, upon a tract of sixteen hundred acres, which Warner purchased from his brother-in-law, Colonel George William Fairfax. Owned by Mr. Ralph R. Richardson, it is more impressive today than ever before, and would undoubtedly astonish and please George Washington who, with his wife and stepdaughter, arrived there for a visit in 1769.

These are indeed noble piles, but there are many smaller, more intimate ones, perhaps chronologically older and artistically as satisfactory.

Against the ancient walls and below deep windows with paneled inside shutters are antique pieces assembled and skillfully placed by their present owners. Fresh delicate colors in paint and hangings reflect the flower tints of the gardens lovingly tended by the mistress herself.

Such a one is Rosney, which belongs to Mr. and Mrs. Walter Lee, where the graceful balance of arrangement, the soft clear textures weave indoors and outdoors into a delicious unity.

Such a one is Chapel Hill, built about 1790, which is actually two stone houses which have been joined together to ramble along the garden and terraces. In one of the connecting passageways there shines a collection of horses' brasses—polished medallions which used to be hung on draft horses to indicate the kind of goods they were hauling, or the destination of such goods. Thus, the miller's horses wore a medallion with sheaves of wheat: an elephant meant the Indian trade: a kangaroo the Australian. This decorative and unusual collection is appropriate to a house built when beasts of burden were the only locomotive power on the land.

The reign of the horse is not over at Chapel Hill. Not only are the walls hung with men in pink coats leaping hedges, and hounds gathering, and foxes fleeing, but the portraits of children in riding togs bear witness to the tender age at which youngsters are still clapped on horseback in this part of the world.

Such a one is Red Gate, where the bricks which floor the entrance porch and make the walls—three inches thicker on the north side—were burned on the place about 1795. Cool, light colors on the walls and in the hangings, wicker furniture on the sun porch, with a picture window framing a wide view of the Blue Ridge Mountains and the Shenandoah River, impart a modern contrast to ancestral paintings and furnishings. The original house, built by Joseph Fauntleroy, whose sister Elizabeth was George Washington's "Lowland Beauty," passed through various ownerships before it came into the possession of its present occupants, Mr. and Mrs. Edward Jenkins, and its original name of Greenville became the present one of Red Gate.

Speaking of names, there certainly could hardly have been a more dashing one than that of the builder's son, which was nothing less than Daingerfield Fauntleroy. The young man seems to have been worthy of the name. Appointed by President Andrew Jackson as a purser in the United States Navy, he was Purser of the Fleet when he took part in the conquest of California. In recognition of his unexcelled marksmanship, Samuel Colt, the inventor and patentee of the Colt revolver, presented him with a pistol in solid gold. With it was a letter saying: "Understanding you are acknowledged to be the finest shot in the United States Navy, it gives me great pleasure to present you the finest pistol I am capable of making."

The young man, equipped with his spirited name and his gold-mounted pistol, must often have passed under the majestic oak on the front lawn, which stretches its mighty lower limbs at right angles to the trunk—a radical oak, defying tame convention and displaying its independence.

One might pass by The Nook, of white clapboard, close to the sidewalk on the main street of Berryville, without realizing it is the oldest house in town. For it approaches its two hundredth birthday without self-consciousness, comfortable, staunch and agreeably lived in.

It was built by Major Charles Smith shortly after the French and Indian Wars in which he served as an officer. The beams were hewed from walnut logs and the four corners of the house set true to the four points of the compass. Thus the sun shines in every room at some hour of the day, during every day—an accomplishment which might be profitably followed by modern architects.

Such an old house and such an old garden as the one which adjoins it have witnessed the coming and going of many generations, as new owners have filled the places of those who preceded them in unspectacular rhythm.

There is, however, in this simple home a collection which

Photo by Flournoy

FIGURE 14. Springsbury was built in 1792 by John Holker, the first consul general from France to the United States. It has been beautifully modernized.

would honor any museum, assembled and preserved by the recent owner, Mrs. Lewis Skoggs, for her own pleasure and amusement and willingly shared by her with visitors.

This consists of fascinating trifles in silver: one group, for instance, setting forth tiny chairs and tables, sofas and desk. There are oddities, such as a silver stopper and nipple for a baby's nursing bottle: many different types of silver spoons and ladles and snuffboxes and candlesticks. The history of transportation is illustrated by miniature vehicles of finely spun silver: sleighs and gondolas and even a wheelbarrow; a stagecoach, a reindeer sledge, a sedan chair. Under what Mrs. Skoggs called "occupational" are infinitesimal musical instruments, a windmill, a wellhead, complete with movable buckets, and matchboxes of various periods and workmanship. If you ask why matchboxes are placed with

47

occupational objects, you are reminded that smoking is really one of the pleasantest occupations that we know.

There is an astonishingly fine collection of Lowestoft china in The Nook; rare enamels, and a number of engravings of the Father of our Country.

But the fanciful silver miniatures, which one might expect to find in a fairy grotto or the dollhouse of a princess, give the four-square old house, built for the solid practicality of daily living, a delightfully impractical gleam.

Halfway between Millwood and Berryville, John Holker, the first consul general from France to the United States, built a brick house, Springsbury, in 1792. It consisted of a hall, with two rooms downstairs and two rooms upstairs. These five rooms, with their original floors and woodwork, were carefully preserved by the Williamsburg architects, Perry, Shaw and Hepburn, when, in 1935, they incorporated them into the present house. The central unit, facing the entrance court, is unusual with its two front doors, and it is connected to two new wings by glassed loggias, one of which serves as a breakfast room and one as a bird room.

In each of these loggias there is a rounded bay window lined with curved glass shelves on which are arranged one of the most pleasing and precious collections of glass in the United States. In the bay of the breakfast room are bottles and vases of blues and browns, greens and gray-whites. In the bird loggia, pinks and rose and ruby pieces predominate.

The loggias open into a bedroom suite at one end and into a dining room at the other, and on the walls of the dining room is one of those fascinating scenic wallpapers so prized in past centuries and in the present century regaining their proper appreciation.

In rich greens and blues it depicts the beauties of the island of Calypso: the grotto embellished with shells and pebbles, the crystal rivulets and meadows of violets and amaranth. The trees with golden fruit are outlined against the sea, limpid or turbulent; the mountains are festooned with vines and jeweled with purple grapes. According to the apochryphal story, as told by Fenelon, Telemachus, accompanied by Minerva disguised as Mentor, is shipwrecked upon the island of Calypso. Falling in love with him as she had previously with his father, Ulysses, for whom he is searching, the goddess Calypso strives to keep him with her, offering him immortality, beside the riches and pleasures of mortal life.

A procession of these riches and pleasures succeed each other around the stately walls of the dining room at Springsbury, where dancing nymphs and white-columned pavillions glint under the gigantic fronds of palm trees. They come to an end in the final scene, where Cupid is exciting the nymphs to burn the vessel which has been built by Mentor to rescue Telemachus from Calypso and carry him home. We see Cupid turning his winged back away from the ship, which is going up in billows of dark smoke, and we see Mentor, who has thrown Telemachus from a high rock into the sea so that he may swim to another vessel, herself leaping after him.

We remember how, at the departure of the young man, the goddess "regretted her immortality, as that which could only perpetuate affliction and aggravate calamity by dispair, for since the gate of death was shut against her, her grief would extend to the eternal ages."

The story of Telemachus on the enchanted island, tenderly told by Fenelon, appeared in 1699 and has ever since been regarded as a classic. The wallpaper, illustrating his adventures, printed by Dufour, appeared in 1825 and was one of the most popular in that period of fine wallpapers.

There are other original Telemachus wallpapers in this country, but probably none has, like their hero, passed through so many vicissitudes as this one at Springsbury. When Mr. and Mrs. Greenhalgh, the present owners, were restoring the old house, they found in South Carolina, tossed aside and abandoned in an empty building, a pile of torn rolls and fragments of paper whose worth they recognized. They brought the tattered pile of scraps—some no longer than the palm of a man's hand—to Springsbury and for more than a year watched them being matched and patched and fitted together until the design was discernible. After the paper was affixed, it took two artists six weeks to fill in the lacking spaces, and to cunningly blend their new paint with the old printing until the classic adventures were completed and revealed.

Neither is the unique dining room the only treasure of the

house. Georgian in feeling, the red brick, blushing through the white paint, blends with pinkish window frames and the soft hues of the slate roof. Wisteria, with extravagantly elongated blossoms such as might have graced the island of Calypso itself, are espaliered against the walls.

One should not leave Springsbury without seeing the great courtyard surrounded by stables where, once, as many as fifty thoroughbreds were kept for breeding and showing. In the tack room hang polished bridles and bits, riding crops and training whips, and behind the glass doors of two cupboards extending from floor to ceiling, are hundreds and hundreds of ribbons and rosettes, each one a memento of some triumph on race track or show grounds. In another cupboard are hundreds and hundreds more.

There are still thoroughbred horses at Springsbury, although not so many as once. The beauty of the place and its furnishings deepens with time. Only Telemachus, forever young, remains unchanged, and Calypso grieves for him, mourning that she is immortal.

And what about Scaleby—that twentieth-century palace, extending its buildings, lawns, gardens and glades; its pastures, woods, paddocks and stables over the rolling hills of Clarke County?

Handsome new houses, worthy to take their place among the handsomest of the past, are materializing all over Virginia, but few of these recent ones have so ancient a pattern and tradition as this Georgian mansion, begun in 1908 by Mr. and Mrs. Henry B. Gilpin.

It took three years before the eight-inch impregnable walls, the portico with its tremendous columns of Carrara marble and a bas relief by Daniel Chester French sunk in its floor, before the staircase of royal proportions and the sumptuous rooms, opening into vistas, were completed. More years were to pass before all the portraits and costly furnishings were assembled or inherited—years in which weddings were celebrated, children born, visitors welcomed, while down in the stables were bred and trained horses famous in the racing world.

There are numbers of big places in this section of Virginia

Photo by Flournoy

FIGURE 15. Scaleby is named for the Gilpin ancestral home in England, where Cowper was visiting when he wrote his famous ballad.

which have been the scene for similar social and sporting pleasures. But Scaleby has its distinction in being named for the Gilpin ancestral home in Cumberland County, England, and for preserving unique family mementos. There hangs in the dining room an oil, painted on wood, depicting a young Gilpin who, in 1215, killed the last wild boar in England. There he stands, in doublet and hose, bracing himself as he thrusts his spear down the gullet of the tusked boar, who obligingly holds his mouth open while dogs leap upon his back to harry him. This was painted in 1790 by a kinsman, Sawry Gilpin, President of the Royal Academy, and commemorates the event which resulted in the King knighting the hunter and giving him the manor of Kentmore—a name preserved in the manor house on this present Virginia estate.

Visitors of the generation which was brought up on books

instead of television, may find themselves recalling still another Gilpin—John—who set forth on a pleasant ride from Cheapside to join his wife and children—who had preceded him by chaise and pair—to celebrate their wedding anniversary at the Bell at Edmonton. The ride which began with a trot accelerated into a gallop, accelerated until the rider's hat and wig went sailing through the air, the two stone bottles of wine bobbing at his waist, banged and burst, and his red cloak streamed behind, while he clung manfully to the horse's mane. Dogs barked, children screamed, windows flew up and the turnpike men flung wide their gates as the horse with smoking flanks tore through the narrow streets.

Meanwhile, Mistress Gilpin and the others of the wedding party, waiting on the balcony of the inn at Edmonton, spied the disheveled figure wildly galloping by.

> "Stop, stop, John Gilpin! Here's the house"—
> They all at once did cry.
> "The dinner waits, and we are tired;"
> Said Gilpin, "So am I."

The horse, alarmed by the shouts, gathered fresh speed and shot into Ware, coming to a sudden halt before the house of his owner, who rushed out amazed to see what all the clatter was about. He could not persuade his travel-battered friend to dismount.

> "Said John, 'It is my wedding day
> And all the world would stare,
> If wife should dine at Edmonton
> And I should dine at Ware.'"

He consented, however, to borrow a wig and hat from his friend, and turned back toward Edmonton. Once again his steed snorted and bucked and tore through the streets. Once again hat and wig went sailing through the air, and once again the distracted Mistress Gilpin saw her bareheaded husband appear and disappear. Upon her urging, a postboy was dispatched to stop him, which merely quickened the excitement and spurred other riders to join the pursuit, shouting, "Thief and Highwayman!" Never once did the villainous horse stop until he had landed Gilpin at his own steps from which he had mounted that morning.

It is a jolly old ballad, written by Cowper when on a visit to Scaleby Castle and it is possible that it may be read and laughed over when the voice of the radio has been pushed aside for some newer invention.

Should it occur to a visitor to Scaleby to inquire if the luckless hero from Cheapside was kin to this Gilpin family in Clarke County, he will be assured that such indeed was the case. In fact, the breathless gentleman, hatless, wigless, cloakless, but game to the end, has been affectionately remembered down the generations, so that it is possible today to shake the tiny hand of a grandson of the house, who is no less a person than a properly and proudly accredited John Gilpin.

Thus it is that Scaleby, although not an old place as compared with many others in Virginia, maintains a remarkable continuity of name and story. These may be traced from the exploit seven hundred and fifty years ago of a young Gilpin who killed the last wild boar in England, through the enforced gambols of a bareheaded rider on a runaway horse, down to today when his distant namesake gravely acknowledges the greeting of visitors.

chapter 5

WINCHESTER'S WARS AND ROSES

*Thornhill, Hackwood, Abrams Delight, Rose Hill Farm,
Holly House*

As might be expected in the oldest Virginia city south of the Potomac and west of the Blue Ridge, Winchester is well supplied with antiques, including a number of buildings associated with the Revolutionary and Civil Wars. George Washington lived here while surveying for Lord Fairfax and also had his headquarters here during the erection of Fort Loudoun. Later William McKinley and Rutherford B. Hayes fought here during the Civil War. Sheridan and Jackson had their headquarters a block apart. During this war seventy-two battles were fought in the town which changed hands three times in one day.

Such reiterated and violent conflicts left their mark upon private as well as public buildings, and some of them which were deplored as defacements are now proudly pointed out as historical souvenirs. Such a one is the Cannonball House which was struck by a cannon ball fired from one of the forts northeast of Winchester, probably during the battle of June 4, 1863. There is a black mark painted on the north wall to show where the ball entered and in the south wall the missile, which passed directly through the house, is still embedded.

Other traces of the great conflict are still being discovered.

Thornhill, a handsome house near the center of town and belonging to Dr. and Mrs. Monford Custer, has been recently restored and redecorated. It is a spacious house, well back from the street, whose main section was supposed to have been built in 1787. The fine carving around the mantels and doors is credited to those Hessian workmen who remained in this country after the war for which they had been hired by the British. There are a good many other houses which are fortunate enough to have samples of Hessian carving in their mantelpieces and around their doorways, but Thornhill is perhaps the only one which for almost a hundred years has unknowingly concealed a traitorous document. The white painted framework of the door which opens into the front hall is topped by a lintel with a bull's eye carved in a block in each corner. In the process of repairing, one of these blocks had to be removed. The workman, turning it over in his hand, was surprised to see a penciled message scrawled on the back. On examination this was deciphered as a message relating to the movement of the Union troops in the vicinity. We do not know if the message was ever received or acted upon. But at any rate, for ninety years it stayed hidden, within hand's grasp, over the doorway through which hundreds of people must have passed.

At Hackwood near Winchester there was no attempt to conceal the penciled scrawls. Northern soldiers scratched their names and initials all over the house—which was used as a hospital—and many of these can still be seen. For good measure, they tore out the paneling in the hall and principal rooms and used it for firewood.

In spite of such vandalism, Hackwood remains one of the most imposing residences in Frederick County. It was built during the latter part of the Revolutionary War by Major General John Smith, who was a member of the Virginia legislature and later a congressman. General Smith was made the custodian of three hundred Hessian prisoners interned at Winchester, as well as fourteen Quakers suspected of pro-British sympathies. When the Hessians were finally released, many of them settled in the valley, where their skill as masons and carpenters was soon recognized.

Everything about Hackwood, inside and out, is so peaceful and prosperous today that it is hard to realize that so many

55

FIGURE 16. Northern soldiers scrawled their names on the interior and exterior walls of Hackwood, and even tore out much of the paneling for firewood. But one wonders if the woodwork was any finer in proportion and workmanship than the present, particularly the doors in the central hall.

soldiers from Vermont were killed here on September 19, 1864, that General Thomas erected a monument for them—difficult to believe the old story that the fields were so strewn with dead bodies that one could walk over them from here to the Berryville Pike.

As though there were not enough carnage among enemies, there had to be a duel between former friends. Peyton Smith, a son of the house, and Joseph Hughes had just opened a law office together. Accused by a United States recruiting officer of violating some code of honor, they felt themselves forced into a duel. In order to be outside Virginia, they crossed the border to Maryland, took their positions and fired, and Peyton Smith fell dead. Long afterward the story was retold of how Peyton Smith's young wife brought home his body, and how, as the carriage neared the house, all the slaves came out to meet it, slowly waving lighted funeral torches and chanting a funeral dirge.

This bloodshed, which looks so unnecessary in the perspective of years, was one of the cases which finally brought about a change in the dueling laws of Virginia.

Of course Hackwood has its ghost—a wispy little old lady in gray, whose inoffensiveness is only equaled by her persistence. She was seen first a long while ago when a visitor arrived at Hackwood and found the family were away at a party. The servants, however, showed him to a guest room and when he went in, he saw a little old lady in gray sitting in a rocking chair. Thinking the servants had shown him into the wrong room, he politely backed out, and not knowing where else to go, came downstairs and bunked on a sofa in the parlor until the family returned.

They had never heard of the little old lady and probably assumed their visitor, like them, had been to a party.

But plenty of people have seen her since, and even the present cheerful owners, Dr. and Mrs. George H. Smith, admit that every now and then they are conscious that just as they enter the hall someone is disappearing through a door into one of the parlors.

Another strange figure was more than once seen at Hackwood, although this was no ghost, but a flesh and blood man—or what was left of one. He had served in the Union forces and lost an arm and during the time Hackwood was a temporary hospital had convalesced there. When the war was over and he had returned home, he had taken the long journey back to Hackwood, politely asking permission to hunt for the spot where he believed his arm was buried somewhere on, or in this case, in the grounds.

Neither the phantom of the little old lady in gray nor the forlorn one-armed soldier seem to have affected the health or morale of the household. General John Smith lived contentedly here to his ninetieth year and slept quietly in the family burial lot, until his body, and that of his wife, were removed to Mt. Hebron Cemetery.

Photo by Peters and Company

FIGURE 17. Abrams Delight, the oldest house in Winchester, has recently been acquired by the Winchester-Frederick County Historical Society. Before the War Between the States it was a center of hospitality and handsome entertainment.

The depredations of the Union soldiers no longer distress anyone. Their initials scratched on the stone walls of the portico are even pointed out as curiosities. The original paneling may have been used for firewood, but one wonders if it was any finer in proportion and workmanship than the present doors—particularly those in the central hall.

Outside as well as inside there are no intimations of mortality. In fact, wild ducks have found a small lake at the foot of the hill so peaceful that they have settled permanently in it as a sanctuary. They evidence no apprehension at the bullets and Minie balls occasionally turned up in the nearby fields, and they never did display the slightest interest in the old lady in gray. Children in the neighborhood still search sporadically for buried treasures, although they are vague as to what treasure and what spot it might be in. But the Union soldier has given up his search for the grave of his buried arm.

Featherbed Lane, Petticoat Gap, Shirt-tail Bent, Apple Pie Ridge—in a vicinity so decked with odd and pleasing names, it is appropriate that the oldest house should bear the quaintest one of all.

When Abraham Hollingsworth first saw the 583 acres he afterward acquired, he declared them a delight to behold—as they still are—and the name thus suggested, Abrams Delight, was so felicitous it has persisted since that time.

Abraham Hollingsworth was an adventurous pioneer and a squatter in this region before George Washington was born. He built a log cabin on this site and afterward his son Isaac constructed upon the same place a two-story limestone house, affixing under the gable in the east wing a stone bearing the date—1754.

It is a plain and sturdy house with limestone walls about two feet thick. There is a center hall, with a good stairway, and with a room on each side. Beyond the room on the east is a third, in the east wing, with its own enclosed stairway leading to the floor above. The upstairs rooms of the main section and the addition are not connected. There are simple fireplaces in all the downstairs rooms and in most of the upstairs ones. The woodwork is plain, with merely an indication of carving at the doorways. In the basement in the east wing is a large fireplace, in what was probably the kitchen.

Strangers in Virginia are often puzzled to hear a dwelling of such modest dimensions and unadorned workmanship referred to as a mansion. They forget it was so described when log cabins were the usual homes, and when Indians and buffalos roamed over the wilderness taking turns in attacking the settlers. In such an environment the substantial stone house was conspicuously grand, and in it were entertained Washington, Lafayette, Fairfax, Morgan and whatever other notables were passing through.

On all sides were evidences of the thrift and prosperity of the Hollingsworth family, who were members of the Society of Friends. Abraham built the log cabin and his son Isaac built the

Photo by Peters and Company

FIGURE 18. A two-story limestone house took the place of the first Abrams Delight, which was a log cabin. Under a gable in the East Wing is a stone with the date when it was built—1754. The ancient construction may still be seen in the rear.

stone house. Jonah, the son of Isaac, erected and operated a flax-seed-oil mill, a carding mill and a factory for building carding machines. He also rebuilt the grist mill. After Jonah's death, his son David inherited the house. As is often the case in the sequence of generations, we find a father who devotes his energies to industrial projects followed by a son with aesthetic tastes. David, after marrying a cousin who brought him an inherited fortune, re-decorated the house and took great pleasure in making it a center of hospitality and entertainment. He built a dam which enlarged the mill pond into a lake spreading toward the east, and this was used by the family and their friends for pleasure boating.

With David's death the house passed to his children who

witnessed the Civil War sweeping away most of their money, so they were obliged to sell some of their land and buildings. The last sister, Miss Annie Hollingsworth, left the ancestral home and moved to Winchester, where she died in 1930.

Thus the long history of Abrams Delight, which received its name in 1735, came to a close as a family home nearly two centuries later. The house, which up to that time had been occupied only by members of the Hollingsworth family, was closed and vacant until 1943, when it was taken over by the city of Winchester. Later it was turned over to the Winchester-Frederick County Historical Society.

Now the Historical Society is restoring and repairing it and opening it to the public, and the grounds and gardens are being replanted.

To visit an old place like this is like turning the leaves of a book in which is written not only the history of the family but the history of an era. In the name we have the record of Abraham who bought the land nearly two hundred years ago. In the house we have the visible evidence of his son, Isaac. The mills and factories expressed the ambition of the grandson, Jonah. The beautification of house and grounds was contribution by the great-grandson, David. Finally, the Civil War lays its stamp upon it and ultimately enforces the desertion of the place by the last remaining member of the once dynamic family.

Throughout Virginia there are repetitions and variations of this story on grander or lesser scale. It might seem that they will be less frequent as time whirls rapidly by. It is no longer taken as a matter of course that the son will inherit his father's house and continue to expand his father's business in the place his father chose to live. As for grandsons and great-grandsons, they scatter like seeds before the wind.

For this reason Abrams Delight, presenting its historical and industrial sequence so compactly, and under the guidance of wise restoration, is of special interest and value.

The story of the Hollingsworth family is not confined to Abrams Delight. Rose Hill Farm, on Featherbed Lane, is believed to be part of the original Hollingsworth grant. It passed by inheritance to the descendants of Isaac and subsequently on

FIGURE 19. The dignified door and wrought-iron entrance gate of Holly House open into one of the most delightful houses in Winchester.

down to the present owners, Mr. and Mrs. Edward W. Barr.

It is not definitely known who built Rose Hill Farm or who gave it its name, but it is generally believed the wing was built before 1790 and what is now used as the main section about 1815.

Such age has been honored by retaining all the original floors and woodwork, with the exception of the floor in the old kitchen, which is now used as a den. The woodwork in the wing is of pine and very plain compared to that in the main section.

Much of the furniture and the silver and china belonged to the Hollingsworth and other ancestors and is displayed to the best advantage.

The Barrs found the dining-room cornices stowed away in the attic and have replaced them in their original position.

It is a charming house of brick painted white, and an old brick kiln recently uncovered suggests these were made on the place. The light façade contrasts with the solid dark-colored shutters and is led up to by a front walk which is unusual in incorporating glaze brick.

As so often happened with the most commodious houses in this vicinity, this one was used as headquarters by both Union and Confederate troops. The inevitable destruction accompanying such occupation has long since been repaired, and purebred Herefords graze peacefully on the 179 acres once torn by and tramped by fighting men.

In a world which has seen so many more recent and more far-flung conflicts, the Civil War is gradually receding in the memories of both Northerners and Southerners. But it was a vital factor in building our national heritage and it is proper on occasions such as a visit to Rose Hill Farm to recall it.

One of the most beautiful houses not only in Winchester but in northern Virginia holds a place of composure on the corner of two of the principal streets.

Every passer-by can see the dignified façade and the wrought-iron work of Holly House, and those who peer through a grill in the high white garden wall can see one of the most successfully planted and prettiest gardens imaginable.

However, only those who are invited inside may gaze at the array of polished antique furniture, at the silver and the portraits:

FIGURE 20. In the dining room in Holly House is an iron fireback which belonged to Lord Fairfax and bears his coat of arms. It was made in the old factory at Marlboro (1773–1777) and is unusual in being brilliantly painted.

may see for themselves in the dining room an iron fireback which belonged to Lord Fairfax and bears his coat of arms. It was made in the old factory at Marlboro (1773–1777) and is unusual in being brilliantly painted.

This is by no means Winchester's only memento of the misogynist who, after he was jilted, nursed such bitterness toward all women that he refused to invite even one to his lavish entertainments. Paradoxically, his name has been given to a school for young ladies and to garden clubs composed chiefly of the hated sex.

After a long life of contentions and complaints, he finally decided when he heard of the surrender of Cornwallis that it was time to die. He could not, however, conform to even this last earthly obligation without making a certain amount of trouble. He was buried in the old church in 1781 and the exact location was forgotten. In 1926 a Winchester lawyer employed the Negro sexton to hunt for the bones. He hunted and hunted without success and finally the lawyer ordered the digging to be discontinued.

Reluctantly the sexton stopped the work, which, although it had been unprofitable in one sense, had been highly profitable in another. The next morning he returned and explained that the location had been revealed to him in a dream.

"If I find de bones, Boss," he promised, "you pay me. If I don't, you don't."

He was permitted to resume work and the bones were found with rather amazing promptness, and reburied in a crypt under the floor of Christ Episcopal Church.

Thus the proprietor, who was once the master of five million acres, has finally come to rest in this narrow but sufficient space.

chapter 6

UP THE SHENANDOAH VALLEY

Fleur-de-lis of the Valley, The Racing Parson

The way from Winchester up the Shenandoah Valley was first broken through and then followed by German pioneers who came pushing south from Pennsylvania, for in the valley of the north-running Shenandoah, you go "up" the valley as you head south. The permanent evidences of that migration remain in the names of places and people, and in the prosperity of the farms and houses which border the modern highway.

There are evidences, too, of other early settlers, in the not infrequently met covered buggy drawn by a plump horse and carrying a Mennonite family, with the women and even the littlest girls in identical black bonnets and identical dresses, made without buttons or buttonholes. There is an occasional Mennonite church, and barns and farm buildings displaying a Hex sign.

People of German descent, of Dutch and Scotch-Irish descent, have long been an integral part of the Valley population. Lutherans, Baptists, Catholics and even Swedenborgians have been free to build their churches.

These racial elements have been generally and widely recognized, but a great many Virginians have never known about

66

the pungent French infusion whose flavor still persists in a certain section of Rockingham County a little south of Newmarket.

For more than two hundred years Toll House Farm has stood upon its present site, shaded by giant cottonwood trees, with the road passing by the front and a series of small ponds sparkling along the side. The meadows with their outcroppings of limestone which turkeys and sheep find so much to their liking were probably more or less as they are now when the property was granted Valentine Sevier by the King of England some time before 1746. Valentine Sevier's father had emigrated from France to England, and his son from London to Baltimore, and then to the Shenandoah Valley. The five-room house which he built was quite a different affair from the present spacious white clapboard residence which incorporates the original section with added rooms and porches and the luxuries of modern living.

Valentine Sevier's house was surrounded by a hive of small buildings, whose foundations indicate that here was a complex and self-sustaining plantation, with its own tool house, cobbler's shop, countinghouse, stables and cabins for slaves, for this French household, unlike those of the Germans and the Quakers, who did not believe in owning slaves, had plenty of that convenient commodity.

Most of the outbuildings have disappeared. The new ones for sheep and hens and twenty thousand turkeys are at some distance from the house, but one stone building has been preserved which testifies to the ingenuity of its early owners. The building is small, but it was large enough to hold four important rooms. In one of the upper ones the ice which was cut in winter was packed in sawdust and preserved throughout the summer. As it melted, the water ran to the floor which sloped toward the middle, into a beam which was hollowed. The water trickled along this, dripped through a hole and fell into a trench in the room below which served as a dairy—thus accomplishing two things, draining the ice and cooling the milk. The huge fireplace in the room adjoining the dairy could be so regulated that its smoke was confined in the attic above to cure the hams hanging there. Finally, there was a place for the cool spring water which flowed constantly and still does.

Today the fireplace is used for a barbecue and near the little

Photo by Gitchell-Lee

FIGURE 21. Few Virginians know about the French families who settled in the Valley. Their original homestead, "Toll House Farm," is the birthplace of John Sevier, founder of the state of Tennessee. It is splendidly restored with extensive boxwood planting and a series of trout pools.

old stone building is an out-of-door dining pavilion. For Toll House Farm is now the hospitable home of Mr. Thomas Heitz and Mr. Lloyd S. Keehan, who bought it in 1941, and have not only remodeled and refurnished the house, but have transformed the grounds into parklike beauty. The box gardens and rose gardens, the formal and the green gardens, the beds of exotic and tropic flowers are irrigated by pipes concealed in trenches, and these same trenches carry the wires which give electric lighting in such a way that each garden is illuminated as if it were a separate room, even more romantic by night than by day.

Another truly lovely feature of the grounds is the series of clear trout pools, crossed by footbridges and rippled by cascades fed by the spring.

Toll House Farm is more than a handsomely restored old plantation. It is the birthplace of John Sevier, who was born here September 23, 1745, and whose achievements and personality made him one of the best-known men of his day. He was the eldest son of Valentine Sevier—there were subsequently half a dozen more—and he began his career laying off lots in what is now the town of Newmarket, and selling them, establishing a tavern there and giving the Baptists a site for a church.

But trading and farming were too tame for the lively young man who, by the time he was twenty-eight, was married and the father of seven children. He crossed the Alleghenies to the Watauga settlements and for seventeen years kept moving up the Valley with the advancing frontier. At King's Mountain (1780) he won fame by leading two hundred and forty men across the Smokies to victory against the British, and a year later he fought under Marion and was made a brigadier general. Three years later he founded the independent state of Franklin and accepted the office of governor. When this state was dissolved and became part of Tennessee, he was elected its first governor and served three successive terms (1796–1801). Although this was as many as the constitution permitted, he was persuaded to serve three more (1803–1809). He also served in the State Senate and was a member of Congress.

Whatever his other duties, he continued to speculate in land and to fight the Indians, regarding his last activity as a public service, but not less exciting on that account. His Gallic daring and personal magnetism made him immensely popular, and he spent the last years of his life moving in polite society, drinking tea at the Governor's house, dining out, attending balls and playing whist.

The pronunciation of his name has been so Anglicized that many people forget its French derivation, just as they forget or never knew the French manners and customs which made Toll House Farm unusual among the German and Dutch farms in the Valley.

For when Valentine Sevier sold the place—the deed which gives the date as March 19, 1777, and mentions that the tract is "commonly known as the place where Valentine Sevier formerly lived" hangs in the walnut paneled library—it was to another Frenchman, Michael Bowyer. Bowyer was one of a group of French Huguenots, and when, in his turn, he sold the farm, it was to a compatriot, Sabastian Marché.

Marché was a yeoman under the British Colonial Governors, and collected tolls from passers-by and from this came the name of the farm.

The plantation remained in the Marché family until 1877, although by that time the German neighbors had corrupted the name to a spelling and pronunciation easier for them and called it Martz. The French tradition was broken when it was bought by an Englishman, James Bradford, who added a wooden wing to the original brick section.

But until Mr. Bradford's day Toll House Farm maintained its Gallic liveliness, so that it was natural that a certain French nobleman, traveling up the Valley, should choose it as a place to ask for a night's hospitality, which was most cordially granted.

Before he had settled in and was strolling around the place a clumsy farm hand bumped into him and the fiery Frenchman thereupon instantly challenged him to a duel. Naturally there were no dueling weapons at hand, but the nobleman seized an axe handle, the astonished countryman a pike, and a crowd gathered to watch the fun. The old countinghouse, where the present barn now stands, was the stage for this combat, which the Frenchman, deftly wielding his axe handle, won and thus saved the honor of France.

The French strain continued through the five sons of Sabastian Marché, one of whom, Michael, lived on a hill near Toll House Farm and bred Lipizzans, those extraordinary horses, which are born brown or gray and take four to six years to turn white. Sired from Arab and Berber stallions and Spanish mares, they can be trained to the most precise pirouettes and courbettes— a series of forward jumps on the hind legs—and leavades, holding a pose of 45°. Doubtless Michael Marché knew that in 1564 the Emperor Maximillian II of Austria had founded a royal riding school of Lipizzans, but it would have taken someone with the gift of prophecy to know that in 1945 General George Patton would personally intervene to save the eighty stallions and also the brood mares and foals which were in Czechoslovakia, from falling to the Reds.

There is no record to just what point of perfection Michael had brought the training of his Lipizzans, but there is a record that when he was dying and his family asked if there was anything he would like, he said yes, he would like to see his Lipizzan stallion. So the noble creature was led to his master's bedside and stood there as motionless as a marble horse while his master murmured adieu.

There is another story about another grandson of Sabastian, who, during the war of 1812, was coming home with his wife from the Island of Martinique. Looking over the side of their ship they saw bits of wreckage floating past and on one spar what looked like a living creature. They came about and managed to scoop up a tiny child, whom they brought home to Toll House Farm. They gave the little boy the affectionate pet name of the Sea Urchin and here he lived, as a member of the family, until he died twenty-five years later, and was buried in the family graveyard.

In this spot, surrounded by a high iron fence with an ornamental gate, there are a number of gravestones—one of them so old that a tree has grown up around it and embedded it until only a few inches of the stone are visible.

One of the gravestones might puzzle visitors who do not know the story of the shipwrecked baby, his unknown origin, his miraculous escape from the ocean and his acceptance into the Marché family. Upon it is lovingly engraved a little sea urchin.

In the enclosure lie various members of the Marché family and one notices that they finally conceded to the Germanization of the French name, and on this final testimonial permitted it to be spelled Martz. But one notices, too, that over the Germanized name is engraved a symbol which needs no translation. It is composed of the petals of a spreading French fleur-de-lis.

The passion for fine horses and fast horses swept up the Valley. One did not have to be French, one did not have to be a country squire to devote what might be considered a disproportionate amount of time and money to this fascinating pastime. In fact, the first race track west of the Blue Ridge was laid out seven

FIGURE 22.   From "Meadow View" one can look toward the first race track in Virginia. It was laid by the Racing Parson.

and a half miles southeast of Harrisonburg, near Cross Keys, about two hundred years ago. With it is associated the story of the racing parson.

The Reverend John Hindman had been a Presbyterian minister in what was then Augusta County and is now part of Rockingham County. The Reverend John loved horses: he loved horse racing. He indulged himself so freely in this sport that the Presbyterians at last excommunicated him for his unseemly behavior.

The Reverend Mr. Hindman thereupon went to his friend, John Stephenson, who lived on what was then and still is called Meadow View Farm, to ask advice.

The advice came promptly and, furthermore, Mr. Stephenson implemented it with hard cash. He financed the Reverend Mr. Hindman on a trip to England, where he took the requisite studies and courses and returned to the Shenandoah as an ordained clergyman in the Church of England.

Now John Stephenson loved horses, too. He laid out a race track across the crest of a hill not far from his home, cutting a wide swath through the timber to make the course level and straight. Warmly he welcomed the Reverend Mr. Hindman when he returned from England. Ardently the two friends gave themselves over to their favorite diversion. When Mr. Stephenson was not supervising his thousand-acre farm and when the Reverend Mr. Hindman was not preparing or delivering sermons in the church to which he had been assigned, the two gay fellows were in the stables or up on the track.

This hilarious heyday was cut short by the untimely death of the Reverend Mr. Hindman in 1748. The effects which he left —with what varying degrees of reluctance we can only surmise— consisted of his divinity books, his vestments and wigs, his jockey coat and cap and twenty-three race horses—probably a unique estate for a clergyman.

John Stephenson's large white frame house with two enormous chimneys stands upon the present farm of Meadow View and is used as a tenant house. The handsome brick house near the highway was built about 1870 by Edward S. Kemper, with the stone for the foundation quarried nearby and the bricks made and burned in the field beyond the present road. Every room had a fireplace and each fireplace had a separate flue. The woodwork was native yellow pine cut nearby.

The modified Georgian house, with twelve rooms and an English type basement, now belongs to Mr. and Mrs. D. C. Stickley who have modernized it discreetly and furnished it with greatest care. The big square rooms are furnished with family heirlooms and antiques and with excellent handmade reproductions constructed from cherry and walnut cut on the place. Many of the pieces of furniture and much of the china have been in use through succeeding generations of the family, and some of the silverware, which dates to 1790, was carried by the wife of Colonel Charles Tyler when she accompanied him across the continent in a covered wagon. The colonel's small army field desk, which he used throughout the Civil War, is also treasured.

The race track where Mr. Stephenson and the Reverend Mr. Hindman spent such grand and glorious days can be pointed out from the Stickley's house, but there are no stables for race horses any more on Meadow View Farm. The old stone icehouse does very nicely as a garage for swifter transportation. But one notices that the handsome brass doorstop in the front hall is in the shape of a horse.

chapter 7

STAUNTON

Kalorama, Stuart House, A Presbyterian Manse

At 19 South Market Street in Staunton there stands an enormous white brick house, set well back from the street behind a terraced lawn. Over the front door is a wide arched fanlight, and under the four front windows on the first floor are small iron balconies.

For more than two hundred years this building—undergoing various changes—has been a Staunton landmark, and although it has not always been as we see it today, the principal rooms remain as they were when they were planned and erected by William Beverley, loyal Tory and indefatigable colonizer.

It is hard to realize that the Shenandoah Valley was practically a wilderness when William Beverley received from Governor Gooch a grant of 118,491 acres "in consideration for inducing a large number of settlers to the community." Augusta County was not to be formed for two years more, 1738, and the present city of Staunton would not be named until 1761. The settlers who had already arrived were putting together cabins of chinked logs and stone.

In the midst of this pioneer region William Beverley began

to build what was called a "Manor Mansion House" which amazed his neighbors who, unless they had traveled across the Blue Ridge Mountains to Tidewater, had never seen such magnificence before.

The wide hall had a great staircase. The four rooms—two on each side—were twenty feet square and lofty in proportion. There were paneled wainscotings and windows with deep embrasures.

To be sure, colonial law ordered that a man must build a dwelling on his land, but there was no law or precedent for a dwelling of such dimensions. Furthermore, it was remarkable that William Beverley should want such a house, for he already possessed his large manor of which he was extremely fond, named Blandfield, in Essex County.

It was a long rough ride on horseback from Essex County to Augusta County, and Beverley's velvet riding coat was often streaked with perspiration and his white wig pushed back on his forehead when, accompanied by a group of friends or perhaps only by a servant or two, he would arrive to visit his new domain and oversee the construction of his house.

After the manor was completed and settlers began to acquire more farmlands and build more cabins, Beverley did not make the journey so often. His bailiffs and commissioners conveyed the parcels of property to be purchased following the old English custom called "Livery of Seizin'." This meant that as the commissioner handed the buyer his deed, he would pick up a handful of earth from the property being conveyed, and pour it into the outstretched hand of the new owner.

There is some argument as to whether Beverley intended to live in his grand new house. There is a record of a paper dated July 1739, written in his own hand, to go by the next vessel sailing to England. In it he orders the following:

> "10 gals. Linseed Oyl in jarrs
> ½ Qt Wte Lead
> ½ Qt. Red Led
> ½ Qt Spa Blue and

as much paint of a deep olive colr ready ground with linseed oyl as will paint 200 yds of wainscott."

Photo by Howard E. Topping

FIGURE 23. When William Beverley built Kalorama more than two hundred years ago in what is now Augusta County, it was the handsomest residence west of the Blue Ridge.

Whether this was for Blandfield in Essex County or for his Manor Mansion in the Valley is not certain. But at all events the new house was very grand indeed for that time and place, and it is still impressive after more than two centuries of various usage.

William Beverley's only son Robert inherited his father's Valley holdings in 1756, but although he came frequently to Staunton he apparently preferred to lodge elsewhere than in the huge, echoing house. But his son, Carter, seems to have inherited his grandfather's interest in the old place. He rented it from Daniel Sheffey, who had bought it in 1805, and accumulated suitable furniture for the big square rooms, and the best English silverware and glass and china he could find, for entertaining on a lavish scale. He stocked the roomy stables with blooded horses and his guests were free to follow the chase or ride over to Waynesboro where there was a level race track.

As elsewhere in Virginia, the love of horses was accompanied by the love of dancing, and when three of the big rooms in the Manor Mansion were thrown together, they made a tremendous ballroom, which never lacked couples in silks, satins, brocades and fine broadcloth.

This period of gaiety was followed by one of more subdued decorum, for at Mr. Sheffey's death in 1830, his widow and two daughters opened a school for young ladies in the mansion house and changed its name to Kalorama.

It was an excellent school and became popular throughout the Valley. Then the Staunton Episcopalians decided to organize a church school of their own. Although they gave it what was doubtless considered a most alluring name—The Virginia Female Institute—they were obliged to wait for suitable buildings. At this point Mrs. Sheffey offered to accommodate it along with her own and she was thereupon made co-principal with the Reverend James McElroy. The Virginia Female Institute later became Stuart Hall, so named in honor of the widow of Jeb Stuart, the beloved Confederate cavalry officer.

After Mrs. Sheffey's death, the Beverley Manor Mansion passed through various hands, at one time being a rooming house. Finally, Mrs. Edmonia Bell Bayley bought it (1886) and took great pleasure in its restoration. The big square rooms with their graceful mantels and matching cornices again stood forth in dignity as they had in the days of William Beverley and later of his grandson, Carter.

Mrs. Bayley and her family enjoyed the old place for many years and later her daughter, Mrs. Fannie B. King, gave it to the city to be used as a public library (1941). Even after it was converted, there were rooms reserved upstairs and in the frame extension for members of the family and their friends.

It is interesting today to step inside the old building and see and admire the proportions of the wide hall and the principal rooms, which lend themselves very well to library use.

The Manor Mansion house must have been astonishing when it was erected in a semiwilderness, where log or fieldstone cabins

FIGURE 24. Stuart House, with the Chinese Chippendale gate, was among the first of the fine houses in Staunton. Jefferson drew the plans and presented them as a wedding present to the Archibald Stuarts.

were the usual habitations. It is still a dignified landmark in a city of many handsome buildings and long and honorable history.

The beautiful and beloved Stuart House holds itself well above the level of Church Street in Staunton. A white picket fence and an unusually graceful Chinese Chippendale entrance gate heighten the air of aristocratic exclusiveness. One must mount a few steps from the sidewalk to the gate: ascend a sloping brick walk lined with box, and climb two more flights of steps before reaching the white portico with its four tall Doric columns and railed upper gallery.

Although the delightful red brick mansion was built fifty-four years after Kalorama, it was one of the first of the fine houses in the Valley, and its hospitality was enjoyed by whatever distinguished men came to the pioneer settlement.

Its builder was Archibald Stuart, who was a member of the Virginia Convention which ratified the Constitution of the United States, and who served for thirty-nine years as Judge of the General Court of Virginia. When he was a young man, he had studied law in Jefferson's office and had asked his help with the plans for the house he hoped someday to build. Jefferson, who was never too busy to get out his drawing board, not only drew the plans with pleasure, but presented them to the Archibald Stuarts as a wedding gift.

It was, and is, a fine example of the best work of the eighteenth century, with its emphasis on classic balance, and its use of all three Grecian types of columns. On the façade these are Doric, in one parlor they are Corinthian and in another, Ionic. The entrance hall is a spacious one, with a plaster ceiling painted to suggest marble. The rooms, too, are spacious and high ceiled, with hand-carved mantels and hand-carved details over the doors, which still display their original brass locks and hinges. Many of the panes in the long windows are the original ones. The carved wooden ornament used in the woodwork throughout the lower floor is not the usual urn or pineapple, but a twisting flame.

There have been no alterations in the course of more than a hundred and fifty years, the hall and two downstairs rooms and the four upstairs rooms being part of the original building. In 1844 the Honorable Alexander H. Stuart, son of the judge, added a wing which was hardly a wing at all, but a quite separate and complete house, without any connection between it and the main dwelling—an inconvenience now rectified.

The necessary modernizations have been carried out so quietly that one hardly notices that the elaborate black bronze chandeliers are fitted with electric lights: or that the bells which hang in the pantry—each of which once had its own colored attendant who recognized its individual tone—are no longer usable. The long, gold-framed mirrors, standing on their gilded consoles, the portraits, the rugs, the furniture are all family pieces, for some member of the Stuart family, with their alternating Archibalds and Alexanders, has lived here since the house was built in 1791. The present owners, who belong to the fourth generation, are Mr. and Mrs. Peyton Cochran.

One of the upper chambers is called Jefferson's room, for this was where he chose to sleep on his frequent visits. His bed, with a trundle bed underneath, was so high it necessitated a pair of steps to climb into it, but it is now replaced by another with the delicately turned posts and spindles called "teardrop." Under a rug the floor boards show where there was a secret hiding place for the family silver during the War Between the States.

A piece of furniture which has a special association is a secretary with a secret drawer. When Archibald Stuart was a student at the College of William and Mary, he was elected Vice President of the Phi Beta Kappa Society, the first Greek letter society in this country. Although still highly honored, it is no longer a secret society, and its gold key is worn, sometimes a bit too ostentatiously, by women as well as men, not only as a mark of scholastic attainment, but for various kinds of merited distinction. But when the Phi Beta Kappa was founded in 1776 in the Raleigh Tavern in Williamsburg, its members numbered only a handful, and its secrets were jealously guarded. Young Archibald Stuart, on the approach of the British, snatched the new seal of the new society and spirited it home to Staunton. Here, fifty years later, it was discovered by his son in the secret drawer of the secretary.

The Phi Beta Kappa Society at William and Mary was promptly notified, but, oddly enough, was not interested. Mr. Stuart then notified the Beta Chapter at Harvard University, which sent a special emissary posthaste to receive the precious symbol. With due reverence he carried it back to Harvard and there it remains, and it is possible that the Chapter at William and Mary may sometime rub its eyes and wonder how such things can be.

On the deep window sills in the lower hall used to stand the white marble busts so admired by previous generations. They have disappeared, but lying casually on one of the sills is a small, boat-shaped basket of leather, filled with thick, heavy and ancient keys.

It was the custom in old Southern households for the mistress to keep the provisions for the dining room and the rations for the kitchen well locked up. Every morning she would measure the sugar and the lard and whatever was needed for the next meal or for the day, set it out for the cook and then lock the storeroom door.

It took a good-sized storeroom to hold the barrels of flour, and molasses, and sugar, and all the other staples needed to feed a dozen or more in the dining room and a score in the kitchen. Today we empty a small box of sugar into the sugar bowl and leave a small can of tea unguarded on the pantry shelf. There is no danger of any one pilfering, for probably the mistress of the house is also the cook, and if her cupboard space is limited, she does not buy in bulk but goes shopping any day, or even twice a day if she pleases.

The little old leather key basket is quite a curiosity to such modern housekeepers, whose idea of provisions is not to keep them at all, but to use them up as expeditiously as possible, or to stow them in the deep freezer without measuring, weighing or counting.

Everything changes with the revolving years, but the old key basket still stoutly holds the keys entrusted to it, although no one knows what locks they fitted, and can only surmise what casks and kegs, what bags and barrels they once faithfully protected.

For almost a hundred years the corner of Coalter and Frederick Streets has been accented by a plain, square and flat-roofed brick house, painted white. Like many other houses in this city

FIGURE 25. Woodrow Wilson's birthplace has been made into a shrine, and the garden restored by the Garden Club of Virginia.

of hills, there are two stories on the side facing the street and three on the side facing the garden.

There is no special architectural distinction about the building, which is of the type called Greek Revival. It was built in 1846 as the manse for the First Presbyterian Church, which was only a short walk's distance through what is now the garden. There was probably no special distinction about the furnishings, since Presbyterian ministers are usually more noted for their treasures in heaven than on earth. On the ground floor there are the dining room and the brick-floored kitchen with its huge fireplace. On the floor above, two bedrooms and two parlors. On the floor above that, two bedrooms, a study and small museum.

The reason the house is famous is because on December 27, 1856, Thomas Woodrow Wilson, who was to be the twenty-eighth President of the United States, was born there.

He could have had little childhood remembrance of the

house, for his parents—neither of whom were Virginians—moved away from Staunton with their family before he was two years old. When he was a student at the University of Virginia, and his sisters were at Mary Baldwin, he visited his birthplace several times. He returned to see it in the summer of 1911, and again on December twenty-eighth, when he was a house guest at a home-coming celebration.

It is, therefore, entirely fitting that the place should have been purchased (1938) by the Woodrow Wilson Birthplace Foundation, and that President Franklin D. Roosevelt should have dedicated the restoration in 1941.

To be sure, the deceptively simple interior decoration, and the elaborately landscaped grounds as they now stand, are a far cry from the plain old manse and yard Stauntonians remember.

Precisely how it looked when the third child of the Reverend Joseph H. Wilson was born here is a matter of conjecture. But the Foundation has done a truly admirable job in converting it into a national shrine, suitable to commemorate a famous man.

With impeccable taste the walls have been hung with a quiet gray, small-figured paper. Furniture which belonged to the President or to his family has been re-assembled and repaired and put in place in the various rooms.

On the left of the present front door is the room where the infant was born, although the tremendous mahogany four-poster is not the actual bed, but one which did later belong to the President. In back, in the nursery, is a crib used in the Wilson family. Across the hall in the front parlor, a violin lies on the piano, although Wilson never learned how to play it, and near it is his mother's guitar. Upstairs are furniture and pictures which he had during the two years he spent at the University of Virginia, and during other years at Princeton—plain pieces of value only through their association.

Whether the rooms look as they did at the time when the baby Thomas was born and when the two older children raced— or paced—through them is really not important. The air of gentility which pervades them is a reflection of an ideal Presbyterian minister's household.

The garden is something else again. No ministers, Presbyterian or otherwise, in Staunton—possibly no one at all in Staunton a hundred years ago—ever imagined such an intricate arrangement of bowknot flower beds and box-edged paths of the terraced garden, the gift in 1933 of the Garden Club of Virginia. It cannot be called a reconstruction, for it is an entirely new creation. But it is an extremely effective Victorian garden, scrupulously cared for and properly admired.

There is inevitably something static about a "shrine" and there are always arguments about authenticity of details. But this has the distinction of being the only birthplace of a President of the United States which has been preserved as the original house, and dedicated as a shrine. And there can be no argument that the restraint, the good taste and careful maintenance of this house and garden are a tribute to the twenty-eighth President and to the Woodrow Wilson Birthplace Foundation.

chapter 8

IN AND AROUND LEXINGTON

Col Alto, Spring Meadows, Greyledge

For a hundred and fifty years the wide driveway enclosing a circular forecourt of box in front of Col Alto has symbolized the hospitality of this well-known and well-loved landmark. The warmth of this welcome is repeated in the depth of the front portico and in the wide entrance hall.

When the big brick house was built early in the nineteenth century by James McDowell (Governor of Virginia 1842–1846) its grounds sloped down without a break to the town of Lexington. Much of the original ground has been sold and today there are many houses between the mansion grounds and the town. But there are still plenty of lawns and gardens and walls around the grand old place to give it privacy.

Governor McDowell wanted a manor in which he could entertain with openhanded ease, and everything about Col Alto fulfills this ambition. On the left of the front door there is a series of four large, high-ceiled rooms, opening into one another through double doors and running the entire depth of the house. As you stand in the first parlor you look through the other rooms which terminate in the dining room where there stretches a gleaming

85

dining table which can seat twenty-four people without crowding. On the other side of the hall are several rooms where smaller groups can gather.

If Governor McDowell planned the arrangement with hospitality in mind, Mr. and Mrs. Henry St. George Tucker, who bought the place about 1900, carried on the tradition with remarkable grace. The special gift for attracting interesting visitors has rarely been better exemplified than in the Tucker regime which still persists in the present owner, Mrs. Rosa Tucker Mason.

Not only distinguished strangers passing through, not only friends and neighbors and townsfolk, but a great clan of kinsfolk have been drawn into this magnetic orbit. Neither have they merely made a brief appearance and departed, but so many of them are remembered in the oil portraits, in the engravings and photographs hanging upon the walls and standing upon the mantels and tables, that one seems continually surrounded by mutual friends who once moved familiarly through the halls and rooms, up and down the stairs, and across the lawns.

The first of these to greet us, in a three-quarter bronze bust, is General Albert Sidney Johnston in Confederate uniform. In days when men were not embarrassed to possess beauty, or artists timid about doing justice to manly comeliness, the features of this revered soldier offered an irresistible subject to sculptors and painters. Edward Valentine, who did the recumbent marble statue of Lee in the Memorial Chapel in the nearby college of Washington and Lee, gave his all to the General. And yet it seems that the noble regularity of the features was not exaggerated, and that character was their worthy accompanist. The Tucker family have produced—and continue to produce—an amazing number of distinguished Virginia names. Albert Sidney Johnston was one of them, and the bravery of his death fitted the bravery of his life. For it was at the Battle of Shiloh that, hearing of the agonizing casualties among the Union troops, he dispatched his own personal physician to tend to the wounded enemy. Shortly afterward he himself received a wound which appeared at first to be merely superficial. But in the absence of a physician the General bled to death—thus laying down his life for his enemies in tragic literalness.

Other kinsfolk of the Tucker family are remembered and

Photo by Ewing's Studio

FIGURE 26. Col Alto was designed for hospitality and generous entertaining, and for more than a hundred years it has maintained the tradition.

honored in Col Alto. An engraving of John Randolph of Roanoke looks down on the long dining table, once belonging to him. It extends to a paradoxical length for the table of a man who preferred to live in a log cabin for a winter house, a four-room clapboard cottage with an outside stair for a summer house, and who had a one-room clapboard building for a library—none of which could possibly have accommodated the generous length of this magnificent board. Near the John Randolph hangs a portrait of his half brother, Henry St. George Tucker, while gentlemen in wigs, ladies in turbans, children in fitted bodices, young men in stocks, statesmen with flowing mustaches and in frock coats, brides in bustles and dowagers in trains, maintain their individual permanence in the Tucker genealogy, with a mezzotint of George Washington and steel engravings of Henry Clay, Daniel Webster and John C. Calhoun thrown in for good measure.

In spite of the multitude of names and faces which have

passed from the living scene, Col Alto is by no means a mauso-
leum. Members of the Tucker family still overflow the many
bedrooms during the summer, strangers from various parts of the
country stop by to pay their respects to the present hostess.
Townspeople look toward the house on the hill as a center of
hospitality. All of them look through the four great rooms which
open one into another, climaxing in the dining room where so
many have gathered around John Randolph's table.

Today we take it as a matter of course that we can hear voices
and see faces from the other side of the world. Perhaps tomorrow
there will be another invention by which faces and voices lost for
hundreds of years on the other side of time may be recalled.

Then what excitement among the social historians who are
at present forced to piece together informal conversations from
diaries and letters! What ripples of laughter, what compliments,
what decorous jokes—when there are ladies present—what clink
of wine glasses and clatter of dishes, what slap of cards and
rhythm of dancing feet will fill the rooms at Col Alto!

If we are ever able to see as well as hear these scenes of days
that have passed, the bustles behind the slender waists of the
ladies and high stocks and swathing cravats around the necks
of the gentlemen may look surprisingly becoming.

And should General Johnston appear in the doorway, we can
verify the features of the bronze bust in the hall, and admit that
it was not only comprehensible but practically inevitable that
maidens should swoon frequently in an era when cavaliers were
so beautiful.

One of the attractions of any university town is that not only
the faculty belong to the town as well as the gown, but that people
from other parts of the country choose such a community to
settle and live in, thus bringing a touch of cosmopolitanism to
places which may be geographically remote from any large city.

This is especially true of Lexington, which has not one but
two academic centers—Washington and Lee University, originally founded under the name of Augusta Academy on a different
site in 1749, and the Virginia Military Institute which opened
in 1839.

The lovely pastoral region around Lexington seemed, until

comparatively recent times, located in exasperating inaccessibility. The automobile has changed all that. Lexington today is far from provincial. A stream of visitors finds its way to this prettiest of towns, and some of them, captivated by the tranquil elevation and airy vistas, relinquish the title of visitors, and renting, buying or building large houses or small, become permanent residents. Retired professors decide not to retire at all, but to continue their activities along different lines, and become orchardists, breeders of horses, cattle, poultry. Alumni who come back to make sure that the scenes they remember from undergraduate days are really as lovely as nostalgia whispers, find they are even more lovely, and decide to go no farther to find a place to live and bring up their families.

Thus one discovers in the town and on the outskirts and well beyond the outskirts, half hidden in the county, all sorts of delightful old houses which new owners have remodeled and furnished to suit their tastes, and where they enjoy whatever degree of social life or seclusion they choose.

Such a place is Spring Meadows, a little south of Lexington in Rockbridge County, on land which was originally part of the Thornhill estate of General John Bowyer.

General John Bowyer obviously appreciated a fine site, including great stretches of meadowland, lying under a wide, wide sky and encircled by mountains, not formidable but protecting.

So did Matthew White appreciate a fine site, for in 1859 he built on it the present house for which, according to tradition, he used some of the timber from the dismantled post-bellum Plank Road which ran from Washington to Memphis and passed in front of the farm.

The property changed hands a number of times and in 1924, most happily for house and grounds, was purchased by Colonel and Mrs. George A. Derbyshire, who have made it into one of the most successfully productive farms in the Shenandoah Valley.

Successfully productive farms are not unusual in this fertile region, but a house like Spring Meadows is. To be sure, the approach through an avenue of Chinese elms, the façade of old brick with white trim, the box trees and box walled garden and the pool with water lilies, are according to Virginia tradition. But as soon as you have stepped across the threshold you have one foot in Virginia and the other firmly placed in New England. Mrs. Derbyshire, who came from Hingham, Massachusetts, has achieved this paradox.

Spring Meadows insists that it is just a farm, not a plantation or an estate; that its yard is not a lawn, and the house is not a mansion or a manor but a farmhouse.

When the Derbyshires acquired the dilapidated place and carefully rebuilt the house, a local observer admitted, "A heap of folks said they couldn't make a house of that old thing, but I'll be god damned if they ain't done did it."

It was Mrs. Derbyshire who done did it. With the background of her birthplace in her mind's eye, and rooms full of Massachusetts heirlooms on her hands, she has brought a New England feeling into a Virginia setting.

The cozy, low-ceiled rooms are furnished with comfortable chairs and sofas, reading lamps, books and pictures. Beside the fireplace in the book-crammed library hang two leather fire buckets with painted designs familiar to all proper New Englanders of previous generations. On the mantel is the equally familiar black marble clock. Here is the roundabout chair in which Mrs. Derbyshire's grandfather sat during his undergraduate days at Harvard. In one of the several parlors is a pair of whale-oil lamps, and a Chinese lacquered tea chest, such as seafaring men from the New England coast used to bring home from their Eastern voyages for their wives to place in neat, unused parlors.

In the dining room is a silver tankard made in 1695 by John Coney, to whom Paul Revere's father was apprenticed, and also many other silver pieces which, due to New England providence, have been kept intact, and, due to New England diligence, have been kept polished for more than two centuries. The many ancestral pieces, from the Cushing, Thaxter and Quincy families, consort amicably with antiques picked up at nearby auctions.

Everything about Spring Meadows is unaffected and friendly. It may not boast the most elaborate woodwork in Rockbridge County, but the interior doorframes indicate that the local carpenter took pleasure in his handiwork.

North and South associate in unforced amity in the farmhouse which refuses to be a mansion.

The Derbyshires have done did it.

Photo by Ewing's Studio

FIGURE 27. Spring Meadows brings a New England atmosphere to the Derbyshire farm near Lexington.

Greyledge begins to extend its charms as soon as one turns into the grounds from what was called the old Plank Road between Lexington and Salem in Botetourt County.

The winding, well-kept gravel driveway leads past groves of forest trees, under the dappled shade of century-old hemlocks, past a ten-acre lake; leads on and up until the panorama of mountains which encircle the entire horizon opens to reveal a great clearing. Through the branches of tremendous elms, its long rectangular mass crowning a plateau, its gray painted bricks blending into the shadows cast by the trees and half lost in the vines which muffle it, Greyledge mistily appears.

The house is massive, but it is so veiled it seems elusive, and after you have crossed the threshold, the rooms, connecting with one another, seem elusive, too. There are so many of them and they are furnished with such a profusion of furniture, mirrors, bric-a-brac and pictures; there are so many windows, half revealing, half concealing the outer vistas which extend on every side, that the whole place seems half real and half legendary. As you pass from room to room, it is almost as if you were not walking but floating through apartments which might vanish behind your back and disappear into space as you leave them.

On land granted in 1740 to Henry Cartmell, two Cartmell bachelors conceived the idea of building this great house on this site, with the Alleghenies sweeping into the Blue Ridge and Purgatory Mountain as a backdrop. Contentedly living in their log cabin in the forest, they took their time to build according to their ideas, which were sturdily masculine. The bricks were made on the place and used to make the inner walls as substantial as the outer ones. The timber was cut and left to season five years before it was used. It is not recorded that the two bachelors ever lived in the house they so obviously enjoyed planning and seeing rise on the cleared plateau, although a Cartmell niece, Anne Sission, owned it briefly. It was rented, bought, and changed hands frequently until in 1895 it was purchased by the Jameson family, and Mrs. Sydney Jameson still owns it, happily using the dining room, parlor, library, study, living room and various sitting rooms. She has even added a sun porch at one end to be sure of having plenty of space.

It is an incredible, an enchanting place, with such an accretion of heirlooms and such a blend of traditions that it would take weeks and months to sort them all out. Where else can one find such an array of Waterford glass, and a complete dinner set of hundred-year-old Meissen ware? Where else can one find in comfortable juxtaposition a mirror which hung in the bedroom George Washington used when he was in Philadelphia, and a Windsor armchair of Benjamin Franklin, and mementos of a family ancestor who was no other than Percy Bysshe Shelley?

Where else can one find not only the descendants of Richard Brinsley Sheridan, but a portrait of one of them by Sir Peter Lely? This three-quarter painting hangs over a mantel in one of the parlors and shows Lord William Russell magnificent in furs and laces, in brocade and velvet, his long brown curls framing his manly face. It is such a proud and handsome head that even after two hundred and thirty years it gives us a pang to remember that it was destined to be chopped off by the executioner's axe.

Sir William Russell was accused, unjustly, it is now believed, of conspiring against James I, and was tried by a jury of his peers and sentenced to death. A courtier of power and of distinction, he was only forty-three, the surge of life at its highest, his chief sorrow when he faced death concentrated in the parting from his wife, whom he loved with a peculiar and single devotion.

The portrait was painted by Sir Peter Lely, who must have delighted in the clear gaze, the exquisite hands and sumptuous robes of his sitter. Lely was frank in his admiration of sitters who were aristocratic and beautiful, and in Sir William he found both characteristics.

The portrait alone is worth a trip to Greyledge, uniting as it does the skill of a famous painter and the countenance of a famous man. But it is supplemented by another picture in an adjoining room—a large steel engraving depicting the trial. Sir William stands, erect and composed, facing the circle of his peers. At a small table on a level below sits his wife, who, besides being one of the great beauties of the day, was one of the first women in England ever to study and practice law. The engraving shows this young Portia, clad in white, a pen in her hand, defending her husband. Near her their youthful son, Lord Wriothesley, is lifting some documents from a small coffer to hand to her.

A friend of the Jameson family, familiar for years with the Lely portrait, came across the engraving in a tumble-down cottage in the country and recognized the central figure. She could learn nothing about it except that it had been brought from Scotland long ago and could be had for a dollar or two.

Lord William had stood for many years in his rich robes, looking out upon the descendants of the Sheridan family. Now the engraving brought the sequel. Lord William, his lady and their son were easily recognizable, but the jurors were merely a sea of faces. It was not until inquiries were made at the British Museum that the key to their identity was found.

In the bouquet of memories, legends and heirlooms which permeates all the rooms, there is another special and delicate scent from Great Britain and royalty. It drifts from one of the smaller parlors, upon whose walls hang framed and glassed panels displaying a collection of fans. Here is one of carved blond tortoise shell, another of lacelike ivory; others of camphorwood, of mother-of-pearl, of silk and paper whose painted design can be traced only with a magnifying glass. The fans are old and fine, and so is the crimson velvet on which they are mounted. For it was cut from the costume of a page of the Duchess of Somerset when she attended the coronation of Queen Victoria.

Greyledge is large and solid and it might seem heavy if it were not for an animation, a gaiety which is created by the realization that all the many rooms are lived in and enjoyed. The historic chairs extend unaffected hospitality to callers; the historic tables offer smooth sleeping space for a cat of immense composure. The garden flowers which grace every room during the spring and summer and fall are replaced in winter by potted plants on the window sills.

The same grace touches the outdoor panorama, whose majestic mountaintops might be almost too overpowering if it were not for the perpetual shift of light and color, almost too close if it were not for the open sweep of lawn and meadow in front of the house and airy terrace in the rear. Grace touches the elms whose spreading branches rise high above the roof of the house: it glints on the lake embowered in green and stretching tranquilly at the foot of the slope.

The long winding driveway leads away from the enchanted spot, leads down past the forest and beneath the dappled shade of the hemlocks. You look back from the highway and nothing of it is visible, and you find yourself wondering if it really ever existed. You wonder if Sir William Russell, draped in his furs and laces, still looks down into the pleasant parlor, unaware as yet that his proud and beautiful head is destined to topple in the dust.

chapter 9

ROUND ABOUT ROANOKE

Monterey, Greenfield, Lone Oak, Fotheringay

Just north of the city limits of Roanoke, in the county of the same name, is one of the most unusual and pleasantest old houses in Virginia.

This is Monterey, which appears, as one approaches it from the front drive, to be a one-story pretty brick pavilion, with a deep veranda running the length of the front to insure shade. Everything about it, from the overhang of the cornice and the large front door, topped with a transom and having side lights which can be opened to insure ventilation, and broad, three-sashed windows with sectioned shutters, suggests not Virginia but the deeper south of Louisiana.

On walking around to the rear, one is surprised to find two full stories above the ground level, a long gallery above the first level and a basement partitioned in the same plan as the main floor. If it is a surprise to find that what appeared a one-story pavilion is actually a two-story house, the surprise is reversed when we step across the threshold of the front door and see that all the principal rooms are on the main floor. Thus, paradoxically, we return to the first impression of a one-story house. The rooms are high-ceiled and unexpectedly spacious. Each has its own fire-place and although all the fireplaces are identical, each has its separate chimney, giving distinction to the roof line.

Good architecture is always adapted to climatic and social and economic conditions. Monterey exemplifies this perfectly and unobtrusively. Originally the kitchen was a separate log cabin, a little distance from the main house—an arrangement extremely popular in a hot climate where it was desirable to keep the heat and odors of cooking as far as possible from the dining room. If we, today, wonder how the food reached the table piping hot—as it certainly did—we can remember that not only the dishes but their tightly fitting covers were thoroughly heated before they were seized by butlers, maids and pickaninnies and rushed in unbroken procession to the dining room. Dating from those days, it is the saying that all waiters were required to whistle during their journey from one building to another, to make certain they did not pop a tempting morsel into their mouths.

At any rate, the many dishes were spirited back and forth with astonishing celerity, and whether they were borne through underground tunnels, like those at Monticello, across passageways open at the side and roofed overhead, or directly across the yard between kitchen and house, it was taken as a matter of course that whatever the weather—snow, rain or hail—they would arrive promptly and at the desired temperature.

All of this, of course, depended upon an army of slaves, of both sexes and of all ages.

At Monterey, as in other Virginia houses throughout the state, the kitchen was finally moved to the basement, where it required merely one butler with perhaps a maid to run up and down the stairs with the dishes which the cook, who was a stationary fixture, prepared over an open fire with an array of spits and cranes and kettles.

As the slaves became servants, it seemed expedient to lighten their labors and to move the kitchen once again—this time out of the basement and up to the same floor and as near the dining room as possible—a procedure which was followed at Monterey.

To be sure, as the kitchens have come closer the cooks have receded. In fact, they have disappeared entirely in some very grand houses, and it is no longer a colored hireling who sits before

Photo by Joseph W. Hazelgrove

FIGURE 28. While Monterey appears from the front to be a one-story pavilion, it drops in the rear to make two full stories. Each room has its fireplace.

the smoky cave arranging the soot-encrusted kettles, but a white mistress who manipulates the electric stove and deep freezer and automatic washing machine.

The Virginian home, like its counterparts in the Middle and Far West and in the North—albeit a decade or so later—is reluctantly approaching the servantless era. The long mahogany dining table, burnished to mirrorlike brilliance, which used to accommodate twenty people, now holds only a vase of flowers and the family gathers around a plastic-topped chromium dinette at one end of the kitchen, presided over by the wife and mother of the household.

But the spacious parlors with their family portraits, the chambers with their high-posted tester beds, the immense wardrobes which served in lieu of clothes closets, the many open fire-places with needle-point screens and brass implements, still give a gentle traditional formality to rooms which do not acknowledge any kinship with those in Western ranch houses or New England cottages.

Monterey is such a home. It was built about 1840 on a large tract of land which was originally patented by Israel Christian of Augusta County and of which, in 1773, he gave a section to his son-in-law, William Fleming. Fleming built a large, comfortable log dwelling on a knoll and named it Belmont after his ancestral home in Scotland. While part of this original structure still stands, Monterey is on a different although equally airy site, and its name has superseded the old one of Belmont.

The present owners, Mr. and Mrs. Frank W. Read, have re-tained within its walls an air of elegance, and beyond them, in well-kept farm buildings, pastures and gardens, an air of abun-dance and established prosperity.

The small boy who laboriously wrote for a history paper that "the Sallic law means that no woman or descendant of a woman is permitted to occupy the throne" might have applied the phrase to Greenfield. For this has been a predominantly masculine house since it was built as a stockade against the Indians by Colonel William Preston, down to the present day when it is owned and occupied by W. Alfred Preston of the eighth generation.

Colonel Preston, who was a son of the Scotch-Irish im-migrant, was granted a hundred thousand acres by King George III in recognition of his military services on the frontier. He chose for his house a site with a spring of water nearby and on high ground from which any approaching Indians could be seen from whatever side they might emerge from the densely wooded moun-tains. Norborne, Baron de Botetourt, appointed Preston as colonel of the militia of Botetourt County—and this commission duly framed hangs on the wall in the library at Greenfield.

Colonel Preston had his hands full. In a letter of his, dated 1754, he speaks of the Indians as being on the warpath and adds that within the walls of Greenfield were eighty men, forty guns and by the grace of God he hoped to hold the fort.

Mrs. Preston, one of the few women who appear in annals

FIGURE 29.   Greenfield was built in 1762 to serve as a stockade against the Indians. The present owner is the eighth generation of Prestons to live here.

chiefly about men, also found her hands full. When a twelve-year-old boy came running from a neighboring farm, crying that Indians had attacked his family, it was Mrs. Preston who insisted that every man and boy at Greenfield rush to the defense of the Cloyds, while she alone kept guard over the stockade.

The rescuing party was too late. They found only the scalped bodies of every single person who had been on the Cloyd place. Mrs. Preston as best she could comforted the boy who had raised the alarm, and she and her husband brought him up as their own son. Years later he was to save Colonel Preston's life at the Battle of Guilford Courthouse.

The oldest section of the Greenfield we see today is that behind the white columns, where the weather boarding and the old logs are still intact. The front section is a later addition.

Inside it all appears equally old and equally firm in its tradition of masculinity. Guns, pistols and sabres hang on the walls, sharing the space with hunting prints and pictures of horses, and scenes of duck shooting, fishing, etc.

There is, of course, a good deal more than Indian arrowheads in the ground and firearms in the halls of Greenfield. There are furniture, books and portraits accumulated through nearly two hundred years. While there are a great many of these heirlooms, it is possible to use and enjoy them. But in the attic there was, until twenty-five years ago, an accretion of letters too numerous to be enjoyed or even enumerated. It seemed an excellent idea to accept a modest offer for them. So they were bundled up—letters from Patrick Henry, Richard Henry Lee, Lord Botetourt, Lord Dunmore, and all the other men of importance with whom Colonel Preston, when he was in charge of the militia, had correspondence. There were six hundred pounds of them, and when they were examined and classified they were clapped, very properly, into historical collections.

Greenfield does not seem to miss them particularly. Its rooms are still full of valuable and valued articles. Its orchards are heavy with apples, its pastures thick with blue grass and the long drive from the highway is traversed by plenty of visitors.

It is not traversed as often as might be wished by colored people ready to find work. For there is a rumor that the ghost of the old Colonel can be heard on certain windy nights stamping all over the house, opening doors and slamming them with a great hullabaloo. Native labor—or would-be labor—is proverbially wary about a place which harbors such goings on.

In the spring in the old terraced garden to the south are daffodils, and under the ground are Indian arrowheads, and on every side are the wide meadows and pastures and orchards protected by the encircling mountains. Colonel Preston chose a good site and built a good house and both indicate they are ready to enjoy the next two hundred years.

Fotheringay is the debonair name of what was once one of the finest houses in Southwest Virginia. Its balconied portico, its wallpapers, its carved mantels and cornices, its furniture and family portraits were among the proudest traditions of the region which lies about fifteen miles west of Salem.

General John Hancock selected a site which embraces a panoramic sweep of mountains, and on it he built, some time before 1780, the house he had long dreamed about and planned for. It became the stage for many conferences during the Indian Wars, at one of which the plot to kill General Washington and his two aides, General Andrew Lewis and Colonel Preston of Greenfield, was frustrated.

The road which had been beaten up from the valley toward the west was a rough one, but nevertheless there was no lack of visitors in those days, and those who could not be accommodated at the great house could find a bed—or some part of a bed—in the tavern at the foot of the hill.

General Hancock loved his handsome manor and took great pleasure in supervising the fine reeded carving of the front doors —these were duplicates, one on the first floor and one on the second—and in the placing of the marble steps. In fact, he was so reluctant to leave it, even after death, that he arranged to be buried upright in a tomb on the hillside overlooking the house and garden, although some of the slaves whispered that this was so he could keep an eye on them and make sure they were continuing to do their work properly.

The tomb still glints in the sunshine and the General presumably still stands upright within it. But there are no slaves for him to supervise and unless radical renovation begins shortly there will be no Fotheringay. The Edmunson family, who were kin of General Hancock, purchased the place from him in 1810 and with the death of Miss Anne Edmunson in 1953 the old place has slipped into ever-deepening desolation. The marble steps are broken and the tall pillars which support the balcony are decaying. Wind and rain have left only the faintest indication of the reeded carving around the lower side door. The upper side door, placed in an arrangement identical to that of the upper door on the front, is blocked out.

Yet even in its dissolution there is something rather splendid about Fotheringay. The shadows from the ancient trees flicker across the brick and half conceal the ravages of neglect and half reveal the fine cornicing of gable and eaves.

There are plenty of old houses in Virginia which have been rescued from even worse plight. Brick and wood, stone and paint can all be repaired, restored, or, in extremis, replaced. Even traditions can be salvaged.

The lofty and generous topography of Southwest Virginia, its fertile fields and pleasant towns are being discovered by surprised strangers and by equally surprised Virginians, from other parts of the state. Fotheringay may be due for a new lease of life. If so, General Hancock will feel recompensed for standing upright for a century and a half, and there is no doubt he will make sure the restoration is done in good and proper order.

Another house which was built, in 1767, with an eye to the Indians is Lone Oak, with a basement dug for this protection. Colonel Thomas Tosh acquired the original grant, which included several thousand acres of land on the Roan Oak—now Roanoke—River, from the Crown in 1748. Today the city of Roanoke stands upon part of this land, but Lone Oak, although within the city limits, maintains a five-acre tract.

Colonel Tosh took ten years to construct the house, as the brick had to be brought by canalboat from Richmond to Buchanan and hauled from there by oxcarts, a procedure whose slowness and laboriousness we can hardly visualize.

Oddly enough, after all the precautions against the Indians, and even though the house was used as headquarters by General Andrew Lewis and conferences were held there by him and fellow officers during the Indian Wars, Colonel Tosh seems to have remained on remarkably friendly terms with the red men. They visited him frequently and there is no record of any one of the household ever having recourse to the shelter provided in the basement.

It was the first brick house in this region and perhaps its grandeur appealed to a certain widow who, to assuage her grief over her recent bereavement, was traveling from Alabama to visit friends in Richmond. Her carriage got stuck in the ford nearby and she appealed for help to Jonathan Tosh, who had inherited the mansion. Mr. Tosh hospitably brought the widow into the shelter of his home so she had an opportunity to see the inside as well as the outside. It evidently pleased her, for she proceeded

Photo by Joseph W. Hazelgrove

FIGURE 30. General John Hancock built Fotheringay before 1780 and is
buried, standing upright in his tomb, on the hillside in the rear.

no further on her journey. She married Jonathan Tosh and at his death inherited the house—basement and all.

The place has undergone a number of alterations and modernizations, and changes in ownership and even in name.

It was originally called Rock of Ages in reference to the rock ledges on which it stands. Afterward it was called Big Oak for a magnificent oak near the driveway. It remained in the Tosh family and in the Lewis family—Elizabeth Tosh married a nephew of General Andrew Lewis—until 1901, when it passed into the hands of a kinswoman of the Lewises, Mrs. Lawrence S. Davis. It was Mrs. Davis who changed the name to Lone Oak.

The oak has been blown down. It was a mighty specimen, measuring more than twenty-five feet around the trunk, with branches reaching two hundred feet into the air, and yielding, when it had fallen, thirty-two cords of wood.

The tree might have seemed considerably more substantial than a mere name, but the latter seems destined to remain and is the one used by the present owners, Colonel and Mrs. Lucien D. Boothe.

No ghosts are reported from Lone Oak. The widow who married Jonathan Tosh apparently rests in peace. There is no echo of anyone lurking in the basement, which was to serve as protection against the Indians, who proved themselves friends instead of enemies.

chapter 10

SOUTHWEST VIRGINIA

An Unknown Architect of Pulaski. Wytheville, Abingdon

To the fertile uplands of what is now Pulaski County, there came shortly after the Revolution a Hessian named John Swope, to recuperate from wounds he had received in the war. It may be that he was directing his steps toward the West, but when he reached this extraordinarily welcoming region, with its rich and rolling fields and its great trees and clear streams racing over limestone beds, he went no farther. For this the people not only of Pulaski but of Virginia should be grateful.

For John Swope was an architect of exceptional ability as is proved by the houses he built, which are testimonials to his craftsmanship and good taste.

When he arrived in these airy highlands—for Pulaski County is about two thousand feet elevation—most of the dwellings were log cabins, and numbers of them may still be seen, still serving as outbuildings in back yards of later and larger houses, and even incorporated into them. Their builders were the Scotch-Irish who had come up the valley and who in 1738 sent a petition to Governor Gooch, asking that a settlement might be made in these remote parts by the Church of Scotland. Governor Gooch gave

Photo by David C. Kent

FIGURE 31. Back Creek Farm, designed and built by John Swope, was the home of the Cloyd family from 1742 to 1930. The front door, with its unusually graceful fanlight, is duplicated on the side.

ready assent, since he realized that such sturdy pioneers, who were soon joined by other settlers of German descent, were the most effective kind of buffer against the Indians.

The first log cabins were constructed with the purpose of withstanding Indian attacks, and even when the settlers began to build houses of brick and frame, it was a long time before they lost their uneasy sense of the menace of the red man.

For this reason Back Creek Farm is of twofold interest.

It was, in a way, a fortress with its barn having iron bars chiseled into the rock and with portholes narrow on the outside and widening toward the inside. In the house itself the solid front and back doors were reinforced with bolts of iron against possible onslaught, with huge locks inside and neither lock nor knob outside. These necessities of primitive defence did not prevent John Swope from designing a house of unexpected excellence.

Back Creek Farm is a little distance from the highway which continues to White Sulphur Springs. When you turn into the drive, you pass through two entrance posts, each bearing a large stone pineapple—that immemorial symbol of hospitality. On the stone gate nearer the house is affixed a marble slab with a list of the Cloyds who, from 1742 to 1930, have lived here.

The red brick house under its great trees and overlooking a clear stream, while old enough to be interesting—it was built in 1742—is sufficiently modernized to be livable.

Whether you enter by the front door or the one at the side, you will be struck immediately by their extremely beautiful woodwork—a little more elaborate in the front—and by their identical and exceptionally graceful fanlights.

The massive front door opens into a central hall. There is a large square parlor on the left with a hand-carved mantel. Indeed there are hand-carved mantels in all the principal rooms—which are generously proportioned—each one unlike any other. The interior partitions are of brick eighteen inches thick. The two stairways are of walnut.

Everything about the interior and everything about the exterior reveals a genuinely good architect. The outbuildings, such as the slave quarters of patterned brick with detailed cornices, are models not only of splendid brickwork, but of first-class architectural proportion and design.

Despite the impregnability of the doors and the portcullis slits in the barn walls, little remains about the place to remind us that it was a stockade. There is nothing to suggest that the meadow across the creek was once an Indian encampment or to recall that on it raged the Battle of Cloyd's Farm.

At this time the routed Confederates were saved from almost total annihilation by troops under the command of General John Morgan. The troops arrived too late for battle, but took up a position across the turnpike in woods near the New Dublin Church. At this point Morgan's men—there were only five hundred of them—held the Federal forces in check for more than two hours and thus saved the Confederate troops and the town of Dublin.

Today Back Creek Farm is owned by Mr. and Mrs. George Clayton Farris, who, like a good many other inhabitants of Pulaski County, have recognized its potentialities for raising cattle, and who run a dairy farm with three hundred registered Angus and Herefords.

Photo by David C. Kent

FIGURE 32. Springfield, built by John Swope, shows lintels of finely finished native dolomite, and unusual ironwork.

Photo by David C. Kent

FIGURE 33. Stairway detail, of black walnut, with fresco painting of mountain scenes. From Springfield, built by John Swope.

FIGURE 34. Brick detail of hexagonal smokehouse at Whitehorne in Pulaski County. Another example of John Swope's work.

FIGURE 35. The Cowan Homeplace on the horseshoe of New River between Pulaski and Montgomery Counties.

John Swope did well with Back Creek Farm, but he outdid himself with Springfield. The front door sets the tone. Its lintel and the bases of its frame, as well as the lintels over the windows, are of finely finished native dolomite or limestone. The wrought-iron railings, set in lead, on either side the front steps, are comparable to ironwork anywhere in the state during this period.

Inside the house the mantels and bookcases bear the unmistakable stamp of Swope's design and execution, as does the black-walnut stairway, with its twisted newel post and with fresco painting of mountain scenery running along the walls. Unfortunately, Springfield burned and we have only photographs to prove the unquestionable value of its workmanship.

Swope was a busy man. The recessed front door of the Cowan birthplace—sometimes called Buchanan's Bottom—is another example of his refined design, as are the several eight-sided smoke-houses whose walls reveal a perfection of brickwork.

Neither was he the only skillful and industrious foreigner to leave a stamp upon Pulaski County. Two German-Swiss, Peter Rife and Peter Whipple, who came to this country about the time of the Revolution, made clocks—Peter Rife doing the wood joining and marquetry and Peter Whipple the brass works.

One of their masterpieces which survives is a tall grandfather's clock, made basically of mahogany, laid and interlaced with 365 different woods, one for every day of the year. Rife procured imported woods from Richmond, and also used some from native shrubs and trees, such as rhododendron and boxwood, dyeing certain pieces with indigo. He also obtained and incorporated bits of ivory and ebony. Every now and then someone starts to count the different pieces of inlay. One such computer reached 22,779 pieces, then lost track and gave up.

The clock was made for Sebastian Wygal, in 1809, when he lived at Sinking Springs Branch, south of the present town of Dublin on the old Richmond-Nashville road.

Mr. Wygal kept a tavern, which was a dividing point of the road, and maintained a line of wagons running to and from Richmond, transporting freight and supplies, and doubtless, during the time Peter Rife was making the clock, choice bits of cabinet wood. Mr. Wygal's daughter married James Miller, who was an ancestor of the present owner of the clock, Professor J. S. Miller of Charlottesville.

Photo by David C. Kent

FIGURE 36. Two German-Swiss artists in Pulaski County made this clock, with 365 different kinds of wood and between 20 and 30 thousand pieces of inlay.

It has survived many vicissitudes in nearly a century and a half. It has been used to store eggs. It has been knocked over and suffered various bangs, bruises and breakages. It has been painstakingly repaired and now stands in Professor Miller's hall, without a visible flaw or even a scratch—an aristocratic refutation to those Virginians who like to believe that all elegance in houses and their furnishings stopped short at the Blue Ridge.

Back Creek Farm is only one of the handsome old houses in the vicinity. Dobyns Farm is another. It is reached by a long drive which winds along a willow-bordered stream until it arrives at the house whose immediate grounds are encircled by a brick wall.

The rectangular red brick house has a long double gallery—the upper one screened—and the residence, gardens and prosperous outbuildings—including the original brick meat house with its walls slitted for ventilation—and all the farm buildings are in apple pie condition.

It took about four years, 1845–1849, for Colonel Joseph Cloyd to build Dobyns Farm on land once granted from the Crown; since that time only three families have lived in it. During the Civil War it was used as a hospital for Confederate soldiers and in a room on the lower floor, called the dungeon, Confederate soldiers, escaping from the Northern army, were hidden. There is a small house beside the main one where the slaves who were used as house servants were quartered. The other slaves were quartered over the barn.

The simplicity of John Swope's designs did not appeal to the wealthy men who, a few years later, began to purchase the temptingly rich lands and to erect their more pretentious dwellings.

Such a one is Rockwood, a big square red-brick house with tall white columns and elaborate wood trim, set in a grove of oaks amid a thousand acres. It was built in 1876 and its original, intricately laid parquet floor in the hall is still in perfect condition. The immense rooms, with their heavy cornices, opening one out of another, are furnished with old-fashioned marble-topped tables, and embellished with the gleaming silver and sparkling cut glass characteristic of this period.

Rockwood is now a dairy farm, with one hundred and seventy-five Guernseys, but there is a man in Pulaski who remembers it before it was given over to its present use. At that time there puttered around the place an old colored man with a name which might have come from an English comedy, Charlie Lumpkin. Poor Charlie had lost his mind and either for this reason or some other had been locked up for ten years in the penitentiary. When he got out, he found the odd jobs at Rockwood not too much for his capacity, and also found himself a favorite with the children. The gentleman who recalls those days was a small boy at the time and one of his tasks was to read the Bible in the evening to the other children and to Charlie Lumpkin.

The elders were gratified at the quietness which prevailed during these sessions, and it was not until years later that they discovered that instead of the little boy instructing his younger brother and sisters in Holy Writ, they were all absorbed in listening to tall tales—much taller than the Biblical ones—told and retold by Charlie Lumpkin. Even today some of those children remember his story about a little boy who lived at Rockwood, and who went into the stall of the stallion and was killed by the fierce creature.

The small ghost used to come back at night and Charlie often heard it crying, and the children listening to Charlie and then straining their ears for the eerie wailing, were sure they heard the crying, too. At any rate, the Bible lay open and unread while they listened to Charlie's interminable recitals.

The name Pulaski was given to the county in 1839 when it was created from Montgomery and Wythe counties. It was in honor of Casimir Pulaski, a Polish Count (1748–1779) who was at one time Commander-in-Chief of the Polish patriot forces. Driven into exile about 1772, Pulaski came to America and joined Washington's army. He distinguished himself at the Battle of Brandywine, and was made a brigadier general and chief of cavalry by Congress. He raised a mixed corps, called the Polish Legion, and won further distinction in the southern theatre of war. He was mortally wounded when he fought for the colonists in the Siege of Savannah and died on board ship. Lafayette laid the cornerstone for a monument to him, which was completed in 1855, in Savannah.

It is fitting that the Polish Count should be remembered when the syllables of his name are uttered thousands of times every day in Pulaski.

It will be fitting also when, someday, we find out more about the Hessian architect and builder who left an enduring contribution to the countryside which gave him asylum and which he came to love so dearly.

As the Scotch-Irish pioneers pushed up the Valley, a trail was definitely opened over which they would reach the wilderness, conquer it, build log cabins and establish schools and churches of the Presbyterian faith. This road was first known as the Buffalo Road, and then as Warrior's Road, then as the Great Road which merged with the Wilderness Road. It was to become the main thoroughfare through Southwest Virginia into Tennessee, Kentucky and the Far West.

It was no wonder that many of these pioneers stopped and

settled in Wythe County. They found here mountains rolling away to the horizon: they found, at an elevation of more than two thousand feet, the potentialities of rich pasture land with brilliant streams cascading through them.

As early as 1757 the discovery of lead mines of New River facilitated the development of the region, and Colonel John Chiswell, who made the discovery, built the first frame house west of the Alleghenies. Fort Chiswell, which was first a fort and then a tavern, became the focal point of religious and social and political activity.

Before Colonel Chiswell built his house, cabins of squared logs sufficed. Such a cabin stands in the rear of Bowling Green, and another, about fourteen feet square, is incorporated into the house.

Bowling Green, behind a white picket fence, and shaded by great oaks, overlooks a sparkling creek, as do so many houses in the county. It was owned by the Kent family and its alterations and additions and extensions make it a palimpsest of many generations. Approaching it from the rear one can see what looks like five or six separate houses huddled together while seven chimneys are visible.

Inside, the houses are joined and divided with a bewildering series of doors and partitions. One section is reached by a well-constructed spiral stairway, unusual in this region.

Bowling Green was given its name from a clearing on the farther side of the stream, which suggested a natural place to play bowls. It was also a natural place for horse racing, an advantage which no Virginian—even if recently a Scotch-Irishman—was likely to overlook. Indeed, Andrew Jackson, riding by, was so taken with it that he stopped, dismounted and promptly entered his horse for a race.

One wonders how Andrew Jackson happened to be near enough to see Bowling Green, for it is a full two-mile drive from the road and hidden by the folds of the hills.

However, travelers in those days, as night came on, looked about for any path which might lead to a place where they could get lodging for themselves and for their horses, and although politely asking hospitality as a favor, nevertheless expected to receive it as a matter of course.

Photo by Greear Studio

FIGURE 37. Bowling Green, in Wythe County, is a palimpsest of many generations. Andrew Jackson, when he was passing, stopped long enough to enter his horse for a race on the other side of the stream.

It was in the early 1800's that Dr. Johann Van Haller, from Philadelphia, in search of a location where he might establish himself in practice and build a house for his bride—when he had won her—arrived late one night at Bowling Green, which probably looked very much as it does today under its trees and beside its stream.

He drew rein and paused, waiting for the welcome customary in such remote places, when the door was flung open and a gentleman, rushing out, waved his hands and shouted, "Go away! Go away! Don't come near the house!"

The traveler explained with dignity that his horse was unable to go farther that night, and he was asking hospitality. The owner of the house continued to gesticulate and urge him to flee, and

115

finally from his confused protests Van Haller learned that there was some sort of dreadful epidemic raging. Not only were the slaves dying, but members of the family were stricken and it was for his own safety the distracted gentleman was urging him to get away as speedily as possible.

Dr. Van Haller quietly dismounted and said, "I am staying. You see I am a physician."

Into the plague-stricken house he went, and immediately recognized typhoid. He stayed not only that night but enough nights to rout the dread disease, contributing his own medicines and enforcing certain sanitary rules, incomprehensible at that date. He had lime scattered freely about the place, forbade anyone to drink milk or eat butter, and after long and laborious ministrations, led the household out of danger.

When he left Bowling Green and saw more of the glorious countryside, he was convinced God had shown him his future home. Thereupon he rode back to York to tell the future bride to prepare for the wedding.

Catherine Goering was sixteen and she was terrified at the thought of leaving home and going with a husband into the wilderness of Virginia.

Her father had no sympathy with her notions. He commanded her sternly to go to her room and pray for guidance, which she presumably did, for in the course of time she made her appearance and told the doctor she would marry him and travel with him to the savage and unknown country. She did marry him, but she could not quite make up her mind to travel with him without other company, and persuaded a young friend to come along— on the wedding trip—a trio which recalls Shelley and Mary and Claire Clairmont on their trip to France.

At all events, the three of them set forth on the journey and when they came to Wytheville, they stayed at the Cross Roads Tavern while the doctor—who had changed the spelling of his name and was now John Haller—began to build a house.

Cross Roads Tavern was a stop for stagecoaches and it had its flurry of excitement during the Civil War. A battle was being fought on Tazewell Street and Mrs. Gibboney, who had just given birth to a baby, was carried by her twelve-year-old son—the eldest male present—out to the yard for safety. It seems a rather

Photo by Greear Studio

FIGURE 38. The old Rock House in Wytheville. German influence up the Valley and toward the southwest can be traced in houses of native stone, like the stone houses of Pennsylvania.

odd way to insure it, for the Northern troops flocked in and camped at the Goodwin House, only a mile away. The mother and grandmother and four young daughters stayed up all night baking biscuits for the hungry Union soldiers and using up a whole barrel of their precious flour. The next morning the Commander came to express his thanks, and as a token of his appreciation presented his sword to the prettiest daughter. Cross Roads Tavern is now the charming remodeled home of the three Lacy sisters, and behind the door in the living room hangs the Yankee sword.

Dr. Haller built Rock House of native stone, very like the stone houses of Pennsylvania. Indeed, the infiltration of the Germans up the valley can be traced to this day by similar stone houses from York, Pennsylvania, to Hagerstown, Maryland, to

117

Harpers Ferry, Winchester and the Shenandoah Valley to Abingdon.

Dr. Haller's house was and is attractive and substantial and when it was finally completed people came riding and driving from sixty miles around to admire the wallpaper in the dining room and to gaze at the furniture which had been three months on the road from Philadelphia.

The little bride remained captious. Ultimately she did permit her girl friend, who was Harriet Clark, daughter of General Clark of the Lewis and Clark expedition, to leave her, but when kinsfolk from York and Philadelphia were passing through and dropped in—it is incredible how many people took these rough and interminable journeys—she was so ashamed of her house in the backwoods that she used to hide under the bed and refuse to come out.

Ultimately the doctor brought her around and they happily produced and raised a large family, and one of their descendants, Mrs. Cathleen Campbell, still lives in the old Rock House, part of which she uses as a gift shop.

There are other eighteenth-century houses in Wytheville, but one which is held in great esteem is of later date and more magnificent style.

This is Loretto, which was built in 1830, of gray painted brick with white columns, topped with a mansard roof and with added sunrooms and baths. It is a huge period piece, from an era when a handsome house had large rooms and plenty of them and, it may be added, plenty of slaves to take care of them.

Anyone who is past fifty and steps inside Loretto steps back into his childhood, when there was usually in the community one such testament of wealth at which the inhabitants of lesser domiciles peeked with awe.

It is all here—the polished hardwood floors, the Oriental rugs and the gold-framed mirrors. The walls are hung with steel engravings of the Castle of St. Angelo, with the angels of Fra Angelico in their twisted gold frames, and with Guido Reni's Aurora marching toward the dawn. The young people of this age who have never eaten a meal except in a dinette at the end of the living room or at a counter in the kitchen, look with amazement at a house which possesses not only a dining room, but a parlor;

Photo by Greear Studio

FIGURE 39. The stair of Rock House is, like the exterior, sturdy, simple and in excellent taste.

not only a parlor, but a drawing room and a library. They may even have to be told that the covered extension over the driveway at the side of the house is a porte-cochère, the most convenient arrangement imaginable and now presumably lost forever. To children who have been born and brought up in apartments, or even in ranch houses, such an establishment seems more curious and archaic than Rock House or Bowling Green.

Loretto doubtless took advantage of the new illuminating fuel which was advertised in 1858 by Andrew Boyd. The advertisement first lists "a large stock of Kerosene Lamps of various styles which Ill sell very cheap for Cash. The attention of the public is called to Oil—it is the cheapest and most popular light ever produced being equal to 6 candles at the cost of half a cent per hour."

Loretto has been the home of the Campbells and Stuarts, whose names are synonymous with Wytheville, for more than a hundred years.

Here, during the summer of 1855, a son was born to William A. Stuart, and a young uncle, on leave from the Military Academy at West Point, came for a visit. He chose the room in which the baby was cozily asleep in his cradle to demonstrate to his sister-in-law the manual of arms. To his horror, the sword flew out of his hand, passed over the cradle, and struck in the floor, having narrowly escaped poniarding his small nephew. The baby, Henry Stuart, lived to become Governor of Virginia, and the swordsman, who was no other than Jeb Stuart, became the beloved Confederate General who dashed through his campaigns singing "Old Joe Hooker" and wearing a rose in his buttonhole and with a wreath of flowers flung around his charger's neck.

Wythe County, with its immense riches of grain and cattle above the ground and its wealth of iron and lead below, has attracted men of enterprise ever since Samuel Crockett, who died in 1749, arrived here with a four-horse wagon bountifully supplied with household furniture and kitchen utensils.

Another enterprising gentleman, of later date, was Major Graham, who had acquired large holdings of lead and iron ore. He had to transport his products to Baltimore to be smelted and at every overnight stop was obliged to put up his horses and drivers. He decided this was poor economy, so at each stopping

Photo by Greear Studio

FIGURE 40. Loretto, home of the Wytheville Campbells for more than a hundred years, is a period piece from another era.

place he bought a farm which became an overnight station for travelers, and he himself was able to commute from one to another, not paying for accommodation, but making money out of it.

In the early days the settlers of German descent did not mix readily with the Scotch-Irish whose language and religion were so dissimilar. They established St. John's Lutheran Church as early as 1776 and persisted in giving their sermons in German for a long time afterward. As late as 1912, they engraved their tombstones in Latin or German.

If we do not usually think of Lutheran ministers as figures of romance, we must make an exception of the first one to arrive at Wytheville. Pastor George Flohr had been a friend of Marie Antoinette and had obtained the melancholy privilege of being near her when she was beheaded. As her blood splashed, he fainted, betraying his loyalty, and thereupon Robespierre exiled him from France. By what highways and byways he came to Wytheville has to be documented, but come he did, and this serenely remote region must have been welcome to eyes which had witnessed the horrors and terrors of the French Revolution.

The log cabins of Bowling Green (built before 1750), Rock House (built in 1815), Loretto (built in 1830), and the Old Tavern (remodeled in 1855), present a sequence of Wytheville domestic architecture.

The brides of today—unlike little Catherine Haller who was ashamed because her husband's home was not as grand as her father's had been—are proud of their pretty little brand-new ranch houses and Cape Cod cottages, complete with every convenience, perched on the sides of hills.

Fashions in houses change and apparently the once-admired timidity of brides changes, too. But there seems little doubt that the wide skies and rolling miles of Wythe County will convince many young couples, as they did Dr. Haller, that God has shown them their future home.

When General Francis Preston and his wife, Sarah Buchanan Campbell, built their house in Abingdon it was the most costly residence in Southwest Virginia. This was in 1830–1832, about a hundred years after their ancestors had emigrated to America from Ulster Province in Northern Ireland and settled in Augusta County, Virginia, at that time a wilderness with only a few white settlers.

The house so proudly erected and regarded, was the first of any pretension in Abingdon, which was the county seat of Washington County, and the first incorporated town west of the Alleghenies. The excellence of its architecture is immediately recognizable in the central unit which was at one time part of the Martha Washington College and is now part of the Martha Washington Inn.

To be sure a hundred years before Dr. Thomas Walker had surveyed for himself nearly seven thousand acres of land where the town of Abingdon now stands, and in 1753 had obtained a patent for it. And to be sure in 1760 Daniel Boone with a companion struck camp at the spring a little to the south where they

Photo by Patterson Photo Service

FIGURE 41. When General Francis Preston built this part of what is now the Martha Washington Inn, it was the most costly residence in Southwest Virginia.

were attacked by a pack of wolves which killed several of their dogs and thereby gave the locality its first name of Wolf Hills. "The Cave" near the Barter Theatre where actors and audience gather after the show also recalls this incident.

Abingdon today is an exceptionally pretty town, but although there are a number of pleasant old brick houses lining its streets, it is too animated to seem antique. The animation comes from the Barter Theatre, a venture which was started in 1932 when Robert Porterfield collected and engaged a band of about eighty actors, technicians, directors and playwrights and invited them down for the summer to produce and give plays during the off season.

They used the buildings of the former Stonewall Jackson College and accepted local produce such as hams, chickens, eggs, vegetables, et cetera, at the box office in lieu of cash.

Those days are past. Today the company has its own theatre in the town, often visited by New York stars, and charges conventional admission.

So successful has it become it also keeps traveling companies for six months a year touring Virginia and nine other states. It is incorporated as a nonprofit educational organization and since 1944 has received ten thousand dollars annually to make it the State Theatre of Virginia—the only professional theatre in the country receiving such aid.

All of this is a far cry from the days when General Francis Preston was building Preston House and David Campbell, Governor of Virginia, was (1837–40) building Montcalm. For its site he chose a hilltop south of the town and overlooking a magnificent view with White Top and Mount Rogers, the two highest points in Virginia, plainly visible.

It may be presumed that Governor Campbell decided upon this name to commemorate the Heights of Abraham in Quebec where the French General Montcalm lost his life. Governor Campbell had been an officer in the War of 1812 and had seen service in Canada under General Alexander Smythe for whom Smythe County is named. At this particular time we were at daggers drawn with Britain and bosom friends with France—all of which doubtless influenced Governor Campbell in his selection of a title for his home.

At all events he built a handsome house which is still in excellent preservation, with large parlors where public receptions were held and with a spiral staircase winding from the first floor to the third. The giant white pines he set out with his own hands and attached to each a hollowed gourd, which a small Negro boy was ordered to keep continually filled with water—such a commission being typical of the days when there were so many slaves of all ages and both sexes on any plantation that it was not unusual to appropriate the full time of one of them to a single task.

Such a multiplicity of hands was bewildering to visitors from the North. "What is your special job, Auntie?" said one of these to a placid old Negress who was sitting in the sun with her hands folded. "I picks the chickens, sah," she answered with the complacency of one who has earned a good night's rest after a good day's work.

At all events the gourds and their attendant seem to have provided an effective watering system judging from the size of the white pines today.

FIGURE 42. Aklin, the headquarters of General John Morgan during the War Between the States, is a little way outside Abingdon.

More than a century has piled up the stories and legends of Montcalm. Such a story concerns Mrs. Campbell's bed.

This was a carved tester affair so high it was impossible for the lady to get into it without assistance, so when she was ready for sleep she dispatched her maid, who called a certain stately manservant. He came with a ladder which he placed with extreme care so that she might make the ascent safely—a process repeated in reverse the following morning. Possibly like the small boy with the gourds and the old woman who picked the chickens, this was his one and only duty.

Governor Campbell died and Montcalm became the property of his brother William Campbell, Governor of Tennessee, and after that it was rented by Judge John A. Campbell, for there has never been in this region a dearth of Campbells conspicuous in high offices.

Big as the house is, as the family grew, a Montcalm Junior

was built nearby as bridal cottage—and even a Montcalm Third, as a playhouse, afterward moved to the side of the river. The house is creditably old, as houses go in Southwest Virginia, but there has always been plenty of fresh life around it. One of the prettiest expressions of this occurred only a few years ago when the daughter of Mr. and Mrs. Wilton E. Mingea—the present owners of the house—decided upon her wedding dress.

Since she had been a little girl she had loved to dress up in a family heirloom which was an elaborate embroidered frock with a full overskirt. It was older than Montcalm itself and had been worn to a garden party in Buckingham Palace.

This she chose for her wedding dress and in it she was painted and the picture hangs on the wall in the parlor which has been the scene for so many distinguished gatherings.

The children of Abingdon are particularly fond of a story about the wild and wicked Indians who were a constant threat to the town in its early days. In 1776, a band of them appeared in the neighborhood of Blacks Fort, scalped and killed Frederick Mongle and attempted to capture the Reverend Charles Cummings, William Creswell and others. They did catch and kill Creswell and his grave may be seen in the Sinking Springs Cemetery, but the Reverend Mr. Cummings was too fleet for them. He was wearing his fine white wig, and as he ran through the brush it caught on a twig. The pursuing Indians, seeing the waving white curls, leaped upon them and applied their tomahawks, to find to their disgust that their quarry had escaped and that they possessed a scalp without a head.

Another house Abingdon is proud of is two stories and of red brick with white trim a little way east of town on a hill. This is Aklin, which, during 1864, was the headquarters of General John Morgan—not to be confused with the more famous Daniel Morgan, but nevertheless a noted Confederate Cavalry leader in his own right.

John Hunt Morgan (1825–64) was born in Huntsville, Alabama, and grew up in Lexington, Kentucky, where in 1837 he organized the Kentucky Rifles. But since his father was a Virginian and he himself joined the Confederates in 1861, and many of his most spectacular forays were on Virginia soil, he is more or less claimed by the state, and particularly by Abingdon. It was he

Photo by Patterson Photo Service

FIGURE 43. The Bank Preston House was built in late 1840 as a residence and also as a bank. The old bars at the windows and also the vault have been kept in the present dining room.

who with only five hundred men swept down on the Federal forces in the Battle of Cloyd's Farm in Pulaski, and held them in check for more than two hours, thus saving the Confederate troops and the town of Dublin.

So bold was he in decision and action, so devoted to the cause and successful as a raider that he was made Brigadier General of a Cavalry Division. His military career was a series of hairbreadth escapes. When his cavalry division was destroyed and he was captured and imprisoned near Cincinnati, he escaped and was then assigned to command the Department of Southwest Virginia.

His apparently charmed life came to an abrupt end when, attacking the Federal forces in Knoxville, he was surprised and killed. He was buried in Sinking Springs Cemetery in Abingdon, although afterward his body was moved to Richmond and finally, for the last time to Lexington, Kentucky, where it now is.

But the peaceable-looking house which served as his headquarters is still pointed out from Abingdon, and the bridge opposite it bears his name.

If Sinking Springs Cemetery sounds a bit damp and forbidding, it is only one of a number of curious names applied to sacred soil. For the Virginians, who have always had a felicitous flair in titling their estates, occasionally went to the opposite extreme with their churches. Thus we find Slash Church and Frying Pan, Crooked Run, Tinkling Spring, Hickory Neck and Goose Creek Meetinghouse, Timber Ridge and even Cat Tail— where pictorial rather than pious description seems to be the objective.

One of the most attractive homes in Abingdon is the Bank— built in the late 1840's with one side to serve as a bank and the other as a residence. Today, the two are thrown into one, the old bars in the windows of the main room of the bank, still remaining in the present dining room. The original vault is a closet.

In the rear the big old house extends out through a garden, and is converted into apartments of exceptional charm.

The Union forces, looking for gold, raided the Bank several times. Probably the treasures of the present owners and occupants, the William Alexander Stuarts, are far more valuable than the money once locked up here, but no one in the pleasant old town thinks of robbers any more and any invaders are probably merely arriving to attend a new play at the Barter Theatre.

chapter II

LYNCHBURG

Poplar Forest, Point of Honor, Quick House

Thomas Jefferson was the most hospitable and generous of men and Monticello was constantly filled with visitors who came for a night or a week or a month: with his children and grandchildren and with strangers from abroad who appeared on the doorstep with letters of introduction.

But in spite of his social resilience, the statesman, agriculturist, writer and architect sometimes admitted to being too hard pressed by conflicting demands upon his time, attention and strength. He needed a place to which he could escape the ever-mounting flood of callers, kinsfolk and admirers. There had come to him through his wife's estate four thousand acres in the neighborhood of Lynchburg, and he decided to take this and build on it a very specialized kind of retreat for his own pleasure and privacy. It was an unique and in many ways a truly fascinating place.

He had once designed an octagonal house to be built for his daughter Maria on Pantops, one of his estates near Monticello. Maria had died, but he still had the plans and he decided to use them.

The central room was twenty-foot square, two-storied, and lighted by a glass roof or skylight with sixteen panes of glass. Fitting into this central square are three long rooms with octagonal ends. Four chimneys on the diagonal walls make possible a fireplace at every end of the outer walls. There are porticoes at the front and at the rear, the latter dropping down to two stories with a basement arcade.

Thus in a rather small compass Jefferson incorporated a number of favorite architectural ideas: the octagonal pattern, the front façade to suggest a one-story pavilion and the rear façade of two stories with a basement arcade. The placing of the outbuildings and the planting all emphasize the octagonal composition, concentric with the house.

There are plenty of pictures and sketches to show how Poplar Forest looked when, after three years of building, it was finished about 1809, and Jefferson used to come riding the ninety miles from Monticello to find here a recess from people and politics. In those days the flattened roof bore a skylight and the pediment a balustrade. Kitchens and Jefferson's office were in separate buildings a short distance from the main house.

Jefferson dearly loved Poplar Forest and was never tired of improving and refining it. He spoke of its "tranquillity and retirement much adapted to my age and indolence." He loved every tree he planted, including the thirteen poplars in front, representing the thirteen colonies. No detail was too inconspicuous to escape his caressing touch. Thus, even the two privies, one to the east and one to the west, politely called "necessary houses," were built in octagon shape with high brick walls supporting domed roofs. Since these little buildings escaped the fire which gutted the main house in 1845, we can still see that their cornices, doors and interior trim are of Georgian detail. When Jefferson removed earth to allow the main house to drop two stories in the rear, he had it piled as a modest screen in front of the "necessary houses," planting willow trees on top and aspens at the base.

The restoration which followed the fire altered the original appearance, and not for the better. The skylight was taken out of the roof, and the balustrade removed from the parapet. Dormer windows were inserted and other windows bricked up. A corner of the square dining room was abruptly partitioned off to allow

FIGURE 44. Poplar Forest was designed and built by Jefferson as a retreat to which he could escape from visitors at Monticello. It is one story in front and two in back.

for a stairway to the attic and another to the basement or ground floor.

In 1947, when the place came into the possession of Mr. and Mrs. James O. Watts, Jr., there began another and this time a felicitous restoration, which has resulted in house and grounds more nearly as they were when Jefferson knew them than they have been for a hundred years.

One enters the grounds through a broad alley bordered by hedges of English tree box, opening out to form a forecourt encircling a maze of English dwarf box. From this point the house appears as Jefferson intended—a one-story pavilion with a portico upheld by four slender brick columns painted white, and a perfectly proportioned fanlight in the pediment.

Beyond the central room—no longer a dining room—one

passes into an eight-sided parlor running the length of the rear and overlooking the gardens. This bright and enchanting room has had restored to it an elaborate handmade cornice of precisely the same dimensions and design as the original. It has its original white marble fireplace and it is furnished with the unpretentious elegance and modern livability which Jefferson, always receptive to the combination of the best in what is modern with the best of what is classical, would have approved.

Appreciation of Jefferson's intention has guided the Wattses and kept them from being mere copyists. Just as Jefferson was not afraid of innovations which made for pleasure or comfort, so the Wattses have not been afraid to build a new brick wall—with one end serpentined—around the rose garden. They have not hesitated to bring the kitchen into the house, and put the dining room and pantries near it, in the basement. The small buildings which were formerly kitchen and Jefferson's study are guest houses.

Perhaps the first thing which attracts even a stranger is the consciousness of the affection out of which the retreat was engendered and through which it was enjoyed. The second thing is the awareness that it is still, in a most remarkable way, being loved and enjoyed.

It was more than two hundred years after Jefferson's birth that Poplar Forest came into the possession of its present owners. and yet such is the power of Jefferson's enthusiasm and personality that these two young people have dedicated themselves to the restoration and rehabilitation of the place with an ardor comparable to that of Jefferson himself. They have studied every plan, weighed every alteration, engaged the highest architectural assistance and spared neither patience nor energy in bringing to life not only the same details, but the same spirit which animated their creation.

Jefferson put his architectural pencil in the plans for many a residential pie. He made rough sketches and even completed the plans for homes for his friends and neighbors. He never wearied of building, and although he had a predilection for certain effects and devices, and used them so often that they became his sign manual, he was always working out ingenious novelties and always willing to adopt modernizations when he recognized them as improvements.

Photo by Gene Campbell

FIGURE 45. In the rear, Poplar Forest drops to two stories. The dining room behind the brick arcade is on the ground level.

Poplar Forest is instinct with his vibrant, outgoing personality. This is partly because it is not only smaller than his public erections, but more intimate than most of his residential ones.

The Wattses have become imbued with this sentiment and infected with this zest. They reverence what is worthy in the past and open their hearts and minds to the exhilaration of the present. Poplar Forest is not a shrine, carefully comparing chronology and weighing the authenticity of every piece of furniture and every fixture before admitting them. It is a loved and lived-in home, as it was during the days of the builder.

It belongs to the Wattses and not to Jefferson, although there is no doubt that the sage of Monticello, who would have adapted himself without hesitation to the twentieth century, and maybe outstripped it, would feel as much at home in it today as he did a hundred and fifty years ago.

On a hill overlooking the James River, in what is now one of the poorer sections of Lynchburg, a large house of stuccoed brick extends its impressive length. It is a shabby old place and there are plenty of native Lynchburgers who cannot direct a stranger to it, or tell him anything about it, although one might think that its spirited name, Point of Honor, would have found lodgment in their memories.

George Lynch, founder of Lynchburg, deeded the land to Dr. George Cabell in 1792 and on it, about 1806, Dr. Cabell built a house which he took pride and pleasure in making one of the handsomest in Lynchburg.

Around the front door with its lunette is finely carved reeding. Over the interior doorways and on the stair ends—the stair rail is solid mahogany—are festoons tied with bowknots. The parlor, with heavily carved paneling, has five tall windows with carved frames, and a mantel, across the entire length of which there runs a mirror, adorned with a vase of carved fruits and with large pineapples over each of the fluted side columns. The dining-room mantel is simpler, with a cup of plenty in the center. Upstairs the bedrooms have mantels ornate but in excellent taste.

During Dr. Cabell's day the lawn swept down to the river, and there were gardens with summerhouses and arbors, and walks edged with box. Around the garden was a wall over which grew roses and English ivy, and toward the river were terraces, planted with spring bulbs.

During this time Point of Honor was one of the most fashionable places in Lynchburg. There were dances in the parlors and mint juleps on the porches, and across the sloping lawn and through the gardens strolled the beaux and belles.

It was more than a mere social center. In the library gathered the most eminent men of the city and county to discuss politics and the problems of government. Finally, it was the favorite place for young blades to settle their differences in a duel. It was one of these which gave it its name.

The story runs that Dr. Cabell received a challenge from Captain Samuel Wiatt, a tobacconist of Lynchburg, who had in 1812 commanded the Lynchburg Rifles. The message was delivered by Henry Scaisbrook Langhorne, but Dr. Cabell, for personal reasons, refused to fight Captain Wiatt. Thereupon

FIGURE 46. Point of Honor, overlooking the James River in Lynchburg, was once a center of fashion and hospitality. It is now a much-needed recreation center, with extensive playgrounds.

Langhorne, who would ordinarily have acted as second, declared he would fight the Captain.

The duel was forthwith fought, but terminated without bloodshed. When it was over and the combatants parted, Dr. Cabell shook hands with Langhorne and said, "Thank you for giving me the name for my home—Point of Honor."

Dr. Cabell died in 1823 and the house he had been so proud of passed to his descendants, and in it was born in 1839 Mary Virginia Ellet Cabell. In her memory the Lynchburg Chapter of the Daughters of the American Revolution has placed a plaque at the entrance to the grounds. Subsequently this property was purchased by Mr. James R. Gilliam who, with his wife, Nell McClure Gilliam, gave the major portion of the land to the city of Lynchburg to be used as a playground, and lent the house as a recreational center.

This recreation center and playground have proved of so much value to the community that a few years ago the city purchased the house and the remaining land so they could always be used for this admirable purpose.

One cannot imagine a better use for the old place. As many as eighty children a day swarm through the rooms, playing ping-pong, poring over books and magazines, painting pictures, contriving dollhouses, making cakes and cookies, and cutting and sewing costumes for parties and plays. They race and chase across the grounds, under the eye of a trained supervisor who is helped by students from Randolph-Macon College as part of their curricula.

There are recreation centers in other cities in Virginia, but the reason Point of Honor is of special interest is that it suggests a vital use for certain large houses which in increasing numbers are problems, architecturally and economically.

Motoring through the state, one ponders the fate which has overtaken so many of the once-handsome old places. The neighborhood in which they were built has changed; sometimes real-estate values have increased so that the land is untenable for residential purposes. Or real-estate values have deteriorated, and cheap buildings crowd the boundaries of the once exclusive properties. Or the whole region may have become deserted, so that the house is practically inaccessible. Such establishments are expensive to maintain—in fact, impossible to maintain without servants, whose scarcity is only equaled by their cost. Because of historical association or architectural value, it may be shortsighted to raze them.

A few ancestral places are bought by descendants who have made a sufficient fortune elsewhere in the world to be able to retire and indulge a sentimental nostalgia. Others are purchased by strangers from the West and North, who hope to purchase sentiment with real estate. A few are being bought and redeemed by patriotic or shrewdly commercial groups and made into shrines.

But there still remain many outmoded mansions, impractical for modern living, whose remodeling would be prohibitively expensive.

For this reason it is heartening to visit Point of Honor.

It is no longer a gathering place for fashionable society or for earnest political groups, or for hot-blooded duelists. But it is a gathering place for those members of a coming generation who need guidance and recreation. Its very location is in its favor, for it is immediately accessible to the community it serves.

Thus, in a quiet way, the old house with the shining name offers its individual answer to a question which must often occur to people motoring through a state whose present and potential prosperity must be viewed against the enhancement of its historical and architectural background.

It would be impossible to find a residence of more decorous appearance than the Quick House, three and a half miles outside Lynchburg.

Of substantial red brick, with the usual white trim, it stands not far from the Amherst Road where it was built almost a hundred and fifty years ago by Edward James Hill. To be sure, at that time the grounds ran from the house down to the James River, but the knoll was the same and so was the view toward the west. A good many generations of Hills lived in it, but it took its name from the Quicks who held it for briefer tenure.

Excellently constructed, embodying the proportions usual in a rectangular, two-story house for the period, it is rather handsomer than most of its neighbors. With its vines and shrubs and formal portico, one cannot imagine its conducting itself in any way unseemly to a proper colonial residence.

The interior is equally reassuring. A central hall opens to the usual rooms, finished in cherry wood, with the carving around the mantels and at the stair ends nicely executed. The original basement kitchen is now a furnace room, the basement dining room a playroom, the old wine cellar a storeroom. Nothing could appear more normal and less fantastical. And yet around this composed exterior and pleasant interior swirl a persistent series of legends and echoes of the supernatural.

There is one room in which a window refuses to stay up. There is another where, if a candle is lighted, it immediately goes out. A cradle rocks and a sewing machine whirrs without being touched by visible hands, both of which might have advantages for a busy housewife. One can go out, leaving everything securely locked, and come back to find rooms in disarray, while footfalls on the stair and a woman's sobs outside the door can be heard almost any old time. Such stories do not bother the present owners, Mr. and Mrs. Edward Woody. In fact, they cheerfully declare they have never heard or seen anything which could not be explained by some natural cause. They discount the children's stories about a riderless white horse galloping around and around the house on certain nights. Of course they cannot get a servant to stay on the place, but that is by no means a unique inconvenience these days.

The stories which have accumulated during the years vary with various tellers, but there is one which has persisted more or less along the same lines.

It is concerned with a rich and beautiful and, as it subsequently transpired, wicked young woman, who, through her fiendish jealousy and rages, had driven her husband to suicide. As a bereaved widow, and accompanied by a friend, she took a trip by stage and rail to St. Louis and thence by steamer to New Orleans for Mardi Gras. In those days one of the diversions of such a holiday was to stroll back of the old St. Louis Hotel to attend a slave auction and to shop around for a pleasing purchase.

The widow was so taken with an exceptionally lovely young girl, dark and timid and speaking French, that when she was put up on the block, she purchased her immediately to be her personal maid.

She brought her back to Quick House and found her both skillful and gentle. But she also found the girl's beauty a threat to her own, and expressed her jealousy by brutal whippings for any slight mistake and even for no mistakes at all. George Landrum, an eligible and handsome young bachelor, enters the story at this point, coming to court the widow. If he himself did not realize that he was moved by the dark, unearthly beauty of the maid, her mistress realized it, and every time after Landrum left the whippings were more violent and prolonged.

One evening when Landrum was coming to call, he dismounted at the gate and started to lead his horse up the graveled drive. He heard the sound of running footsteps, and a young girl rushed into his arms and clung to him, too frightened to move.

After a gasp, she freed herself and whispering, "*Ah, c'est vous, Monsieur; pardon je vous prie,*" pulled herself away and sped toward the house. Her entrance was met by a whiplash so savage that Landrum, sickened, went back to the gate, mounted his horse and rode away.

He had no inclination to see the widow again, but after several months yielded to her importunities and accepted an invitation to tea. On his way up the drive he heard the sound of sobs, and listening, found it came from the summerhouse. He stepped inside and found the slave girl weeping on the floor. Seeing the compassion in his face, she clasped her arms around his knees. He loosened them gently and with reluctant feet proceeded to the house, making excuses to leave as soon as possible.

He rode down the drive and turned into the road and there he was overcome by a presentiment of evil so overpowering that he turned and went back. Before he had time to dismount at the gate the slave girl came running wildly to meet him.

Frantic with fear, she told him in a jumble of French and English that as soon as he had left and she had come in from the summerhouse, she found her mistress waiting with a long table knife. Out of her senses with fear, the girl managed to evade her and, as she darted through the hall, seized a pair of garden shears lying on the table. Grasping them with the primitive instinct of self-protection, she rushed upstairs to a room where the wind immediately snuffed out the candle. This is the room where, since that night, no candle will stay lighted. Into the darkness crept the mistress, uttering horrible snarls of rage, and finally springing with her drawn knife at the cowering victim. The girl, beside herself with terror, struck with the shears, felt them pierce soft flesh and heard her mistress fall with a scream. The girl had torn out of the house and met Landrum coming up the drive.

Realizing the dreadful sequel to such an action on her part, he caught her up and held her beside him as he turned his horse and galloped down the road. But the scream had been heard, and the servants and neighbors were after him. The fugitives were caught, and Landrum contemptuously dismissed. The girl was dragged into the house and locked in one of the downstairs front rooms.

What fate awaited her she did not dare to think. She tore at the window sash until it gave way, and then raising it without a sound, slid to the ground and fled down the path which led to the river. She reached the boulder which can still be seen jutting out over the water and leaped. Two days later her body was found floating in the eddy below the dam.

The widow was recovering from the wound when a white-faced woman arrived from New Orleans and hunted out George Landrum. To him she told her story. A Creole slave who had just died, had confessed that the drowned girl was the daughter of indiscreet and youthful parents who had tried to hide her unwanted birth by giving her to a trusted slave to bring up. When that slave died, the girl had fallen into the hands of the trader who had put her on the auction block. Meanwhile, the guilty parents, repenting of their act, had been hunting in vain for their child, and had only now traced her to the house of the widow in Virginia. Both parents were from the first families of New Orleans.

This is the reason there are sounds of a woman's sobs, of running footsteps and a galloping horse. This is the reason candles are blown out in a certain room, although the rocking cradle and whirring sewing machine do not fit precisely into this story—which, incidentally, is sometimes altered to have the slave girl an Indian and not a Creole.

The only concession the Woodys make to the unusual concerns the windows. When the western sun strikes the windows in front of the house they turn to gold, and the children gather to wonder at them. Occasionally passing motorists, catching the strange gilding, stop, too, and some of them explain that the glass must have been made with peculiarly yellow sand.

Nothing untoward has occurred at Quick House for a long time. But the windows turn gold with every setting sun, and the Woodys can't get a servant to stay on the place.

chapter 12

BELLE MÈRE

Winton

Personality, intangible and invisible, may be more enduring than bricks and stone, mortar and wood, permeating a place and affecting the lives it touches. While biographers try to explain it in terms of attributes or accomplishments, the explanations remain and the personality escapes.

In the small town of Clifford, twenty-five miles north of Lynchburg in Amherst County, there is, set comfortably back from the road in landscaped grounds, a spacious white clapboard house named Winton. It was built by Colonel Samuel Meredith in 1770 for his bride, on a grant of land received from King George III. It consisted originally of four well-proportioned rooms, each with a fireplace, the overmantel in the principal room being of exceptional interest. Like so much of the best wood-working in Virginia, it is attributed to Hessian prisoners, and they certainly spared no labor to make it as impressive as possible. Deeply and delicately incised, it gives great dignity to one whole wall and, indeed, to the whole room.

Since Colonel Meredith built Winton, it has passed through various ownerships and undergone various enlargements and alterations, culminating in the present farm and residence, belonging to Mr. and Mrs. V. V. Kelcey, and one of the handsomest estates in Amherst County.

In one hundred and eighty-four years many family stories and legends have become associated with it, like the one of the Beasley family. Shortly before the War Between the States the father of Mary Susie Jennings bought Winton and presented it to her as a wedding present. Her husband presented her with another present—five small stepsons who made it lively for all concerned.

When it was rumored that Northern troops were approaching, Mrs. Beasley hurried out to the smokehouse, pulled up some floor planks and hastily concealed treasures which were, according to a scale of evaluation which is still respected today, a number of hams and the household silver, in that order. She shoved these back under the flooring, replaced the planks and drew the door shut.

When the Northern troops did arrive, one of the small Beasley boys courteously inquired if they were looking for the hams his mother had buried. On being assured that this was the case, he obligingly led them to the smokehouse and explained just where they could be found. The smokehouse still stands, its battered door revealing the intrusion, but what happened to the small boy who was so eager to be a hospitable host is not reported.

However, the chief legend of Winton, which had its inception long before the house was built, is quite another sort and has nothing to do with buried treasure or raids. It has to do with Mrs. John Syme, the widow of Colonel Syme, who died in 1731, leaving her with one child.

It was during her rather brief widowhood, before she came to live at Winton, that we first hear of Mrs. Syme, and from that first word until the last pronounced over her grave, her unique personality is immediately felt.

In those days, when taverns were far apart and uncomfortable, it was customary for a gentleman traveling through the county to accept the hospitality of one of the plantations, even if he knew his host or hostess merely through mutual acquaintance.

Thus it was that the wise old William Byrd was introduced to Mrs. Syme and accepted her invitation to stay at her house

Photo by David C. Kent

FIGURE 47. The fireplace at Winton, where Patrick Henry's mother lived, is credited to Hessian prisoners.

while in that vicinity. In an entry in his "Progress to the Mines" in October 7, 1732, he records the visit thus:

"The lady, at first suspecting I was some lover, put on a gravity which becomes a weed, but as soon as she learned who I was, brightened up into an unusual cheerfulness and serenity. She was a portly, handsome dame of the family of Esau, and seemed not to pine too much for the death of her husband, who was of the family of the Saracens. He left a son by her, who has all the strong features of his sire, not softened in the least by any of hers.

"This widow is a person of a lively and cheerful conversation with much less reserve than most of her countrywomen. It becomes her well, and sets off her other agreeable qualities to advantage. We tossed off a bottle of honest port, which we relished with a broiled chicken."

On the next day he adds:

"I moistened my clay with a quart of milk and tea, which I found altogether as great a help to discourse as the juice of the grape. The courteous widow invited me to rest myself there that good day, and go to church with her, but I excused myself by telling her she would certainly spoil my devotions. Then she civilly entreated me to make her house my home whenever I visited my plantations, which made me bow low and thank her very kindly."

It is, to be sure, only a brief entry, and yet there is something about it which catches and warms the imagination. One sees "the portly and handsome dame" and the sophisticated master of Westover, chatting with greatest liveliness over a bottle of "honest port" and broiled chicken. Colonel Byrd, a connoisseur in such matters, does not imply that the "weed" of Colonel Syme was young or beautiful, but she was evidently so thoroughly magnetic and so thoroughly companionable and delightful that he saw fit to devote these pages to his recollection of her.

Not long after his visit, Mrs. Syme was married to Colonel John Henry and the only distinction usually given her in histories is that her second son—she had two sons and seven daughters—was Patrick Henry (born May 29, 1736). It is possible, however, by bringing various oblique rays into focus to obtain a more definite image.

Photo by David C. Kent

FIGURE 48. Mrs. Beasley hid hams and household silver under the floor
of this smokehouse at the approach of Northern troops. But her small step-
son, reared in the tradition of hospitality, showed them the place and invited
them to help themselves, which they did.

After one of her daughters had married Colonel Meredith, Mrs. Henry came to Winton and lived there until her death in 1784. It is believed that her room was above the parlor on the left and could be reached by a private stair. One finds mention of her "remarkable intellectual gifts" and "unusual command of language": that she united "firmness with gentleness" and her "fervent piety" is frequently commended. But admirable as are those qualities of character, they do not necessarily make a woman fascinating.

And this is what Mrs. Henry must have been. Just as she had charmed William Byrd, she continued to charm everyone she met. Thomas Jefferson, on his way to Poplar Forest, made a point of stopping off to see her; her son Patrick sought her out in times of stress.

Foremost among her admirers was her son-in-law. So completely did he capitulate to her that after her death he arranged that he should be buried at her feet.

She died on Christmas Day, 1784, and before the tremendously ornate fireplace she lay in her black walnut coffin made by the plantation carpenter, its silk lining quilted by loving black hands, and under her head a tiny pillow of choicest "goose tender."

There was such a heavy snow that Patrick Henry, one hundred miles away in Richmond, could not get to the funeral. But there were plenty of hands to hold the flaming torches as the procession wound its way to the family burial plot not far from the house. Here Colonel Meredith himself fashioned the brick arch, the length of the grave, to protect it against wild animals and wild elements. As he laid the last brick, he stood at the end of the grave and said: "When I die, lay my body just here, so that for all time I may lie at the feet of the deeply venerated and beloved mother of my wife."

This request—surely unique—again sets us to speculating just what made Mrs. Henry irresistible even in death. The customary eulogies, doubtless sincere, do not enlighten us. One may offer respect but hardly emotional devotion to a woman because of her "good sense," "amiability" or "piety which is a blessed example" or because her "reception into the heavenly mansions is exalted."

It is impossible for us to put a finger on the quality of this unusual mother-in-law, which drew to her men as well as women, black as well as white.

The family burial ground is fenced in amid the pleasant pastures, perfumed by lilacs in the spring and covered with myrtle the year round. From it one overlooks a superb sweep of the Blue Ridge Mountains, and near it stands as a sentinel the last of the white pines which were part of the virgin forest. A sign placed by the Daughters of the American Revolution at the entrance to Winton calls attention to the fact that here is buried Sarah Winston Henry, and many are the visitors in the course of a year who pause, perhaps a little puzzled as to why they are intrigued, and find their way to the graveyard.

At the foot of the grave is buried Colonel Meredith. His wife lies at his side, but his lichen-covered headstone faces that of his mother-in-law.

The French have prettier words for the relationship, and they seem more suitable in this case. The words are Belle Mère.

chapter 13

SOUTHSIDE VIRGINIA

Prestwould, Berry Hill, Staunton Hill

In Mecklenburg County, rich in tobacco fields and dotted with small tobacco barns stained by smoke and age to softest brown, on a rise of land overlooking the Roanoke River, there has stood, for nearly two hundred years, a solidly built house, with thick stone walls and ten-foot chimneys, called Prestwould.

Nowadays one must approach it by a long unpaved drive, running between stone walls, and enter through the north or rear entrance hall. But, like so many old Virginia houses, it was designed to have its chief entrance on the south side, facing the Roanoke River, for water, not land, offered the usual and most attractive approach.

The age of the plantation is immediately apparent by the immense oaks and cedars, the great magnolias with polished leaves, the massed clumps of ancient box, groves of smooth-barked crape myrtle, tall hollies and rare ivies. The period which it represents is further indicated by the score or more of small buildings scattered about with cheerful disregard for convenient accessibility. Some of the barns and henhouses and tenant cottages are still used, but most of the little white frame, or stone, smokehouses, icehouses, cornhouses, washhouses, slave quarters, et cetera, are abandoned.

The great house itself, while by no means abandoned, serves chiefly as summer retreat for its present owner, Mrs. Grover C. Kester, of North Carolina. Most of its original antiques had been sold before she bought the place in 1946, and are replaced by more casual furnishings.

The oblong house, with porches on three sides, is built of pinkish ashlar. Slaves quarried the stone on the place, cut it into the large rectangular blocks, and cut the great pines whose wide planks make the waist-high dados and carved cornices. Pine boards, hand-grooved and fitted together without nails, but with wooden dowels, are used for the wide stairway, with simple scrolled step ends, and plain square banisters set diagonally and with square posts. It mounts by easiest risers to a wide and airy upper hall where, doubtless, ladies sat and sewed, and from whose windows they could look out and down over the river below to see if guests were arriving. There is another stair—a so-called secret stair—leading without too much secrecy from one of the upper chambers to the ground.

While the stair has no flowing grace of line, and while there is no paneling from floor to ceiling in the spacious rooms, and instead of marble fireplaces there are only wooden ones—one of them painted in marbleized design—its interior effect, like the exterior, is impressive. The massive doors with their hardware imported from England, are without side lights or fanlights, so that they could have offered protection against Indian attacks. The solid shutters inside the windows would have sealed them completely. The basement which runs under the entire house, and is actually the first floor, is absolutely dry. The whole place was built of the best materials and constructed so well that it is easy to agree with those who claim it is the most substantial house in Virginia.

One of its chief interests is what is left of its scenic wallpapers, which were probably hung about 1800. In the River Entrance hall one wall is covered by a blue sky arching above castle and trees of faded green and brown under which ride ladies and gentlemen. In what was the living room, originally called "South Parlor," the paper is better preserved and there is more of

Photo by Flournoy

FIGURE 49. Prestwould is named after the English home of the Skipwith family. Sir Peyton Skipwith built it about 1770, after his father had won the land on which it stands by three days' card-playing with William Byrd III of Westover.

it, with ladies in directoire gowns and bonnets delicately stepping across rustic bridges, and gentlemen with swelling hips seated on garden benches, with classic pavilions crowning hills in the background, and arches of broken stone framing fanciful seas.

On one wall in the dining room are still left a few pink-coated hunters and dogs gathering in autumnal woods. Over the dining table in this room hangs a pie-shaped fan or punkah, which was kept in motion by a slave during meal times. Around its border is painted the same motif as on the cornice above the paper.

Prestwould plantation was part of the ten-mile tract along the Roanoke River, patented in the early years of the Eighteenth Century by William Byrd II, and later called Blue Stone Castle.

It passed to his son William Byrd III, and to him arrived one fine day a caller—Sir William Skipwith, grandson of Sir Gray Skipwith, who had fled from England to Virginia during the Protectorate. Sir William came by the river in a boat well manned by slaves and well supplied with wines of excellent vintage, and it was an unlucky day for William Byrd III, when he invited the stranger to come ashore and extended to him hospitality which included a few games of cards. The few games became many. In fact, the two men played uninterruptedly for three days, and Sir William won Blue Stone Castle. It was his son, Sir Peyton Skipwith, who, about 1770, built the present Prestwould, taking seven years to do so, and named it after the English home of the Skipwith family in Leicestershire.

Sir Peyton is buried in the small graveyard near the house and on the flat table stone which covers his grave is deeply carved his coat of arms. This includes a conventionalized turnstile which is reproduced on the entrance gates. Above his grave is that of his wife, Lady Jean, who is credited with designing the gardens and whose harpsichord was supposed to have been presented her by the Prince of Wales. Beside him lies his daughter Elizabeth, with more remote family members at correctly greater distances.

Blue Stone Castle burned to the ground many years ago, but the children who race up and down the wide stairs at Prestwould still poke among the charred ruins and occasionally come up with a bit of glass or pottery which was doubtless brought from England in past centuries.

Prestwould, which carries its age so stoutly, also maintained its tradition for the love of gaming which brought the plantation into the Skipwith family in the first place. In the River Entrance hall there stands a huge piece of furniture built by slaves to occupy this particular space. It is the finest cabinet work, and large enough to hold glass and silver, china and books. But it has two special features which are not usual in a piece for an entrance hall. These are two closets, one large enough to accommodate a barrel of whiskey, and its floor cut out in a curve to hold it steady, and the other to hold a barrel of brandy. Thus the gentlemen could sit at the gaming table as long as they pleased, and not have to send to the wine cellar or even step into the dining room for refreshment.

The River Entrance hall is large—as are all the rooms in the house—but evidently it was not large enough for every gaming occasion. At a little distance from the house is a delicious octagonal pavilion, with its narrow cornice nicely carved and its windows neatly shuttered. It is empty today, but it used to hold an octagonal Jacobean card table, built to fit the space, and here the gentlemen could play indefinitely. There is no room in the pretty little place for a cupboard holding a barrel of whiskey and a barrel of brandy, but there is thoughtful provision for refreshment in the wine cellar underneath.

Even in these days of automobiles Prestwould seems far away, not only from the highway but from the world. It must always have been isolated, for we read that at one time when a daughter of the house went to school in Clarksville, across the river, it seemed easier to have her board over there instead of wrestling with transportation.

The Skipwith family, who had such a flair for merry living, were in possession of the plantation until 1914, and since then it has passed through the hands of several owners. Despite the scattering of most of the original furnishings, there are still extant some of the old bills of lading, records showing the genealogy, sale and purchase of slaves, lists of flowers and shrubs planted by Lady Jean, etc., so that someday, if the grand old place should be restored to its original atmosphere and appearance, there will be plenty of data for guidance.

In the meanwhile, there seems no danger of any immediate deterioration of the fabric. The solid doors which could have kept out Indians do still keep out draughts; floors and walls, ceilings, stairs and chimneys are intact.

It is a truly excellent example of good design, good taste and good workmanship. And from gaming pavilion to burial ground it is a testament to the family whose ancestor won the plantation with a turn of the wrist, whose son built the house, and whose descendants enjoyed its spacious amenities for so many years.

Berry Hill stands unique upon its twenty acres in Halifax County. It stands unique in Virginia architecture. For although there are other buildings in the state showing the influence of the Greek Revival, Berry Hill is justly considered the noblest model of its kind.

The transient tourist does not see Berry Hill from the high-way. Indeed, unless he has special permission, he does not see it at all. For not only is the house closed to strangers, but even the long drive from the road is barred. Thus no alien intrusion, inside or out, disturbs the exclusiveness of the templelike mansion.

Those who are fortunate enough to pass the entrance gate are faced by a lofty white portico, topped by a classic pediment, upheld by eight massive Doric columns based upon a flight of steps running the sixty-foot width of the façade. Flanking the entrance, equidistant from the house, and at right angles to it, are two separate and miniature pavilions, completing the majestic balance of the approach.

Even in the time of large houses—Berry Hill was built in 1842—this stately façade must have been impressive. In our present casual and informal age, with eyes accustomed to crowds of "ranch houses" elbowing one another in new "developments," these lofty lines, holding themselves in imperious isolation, are solemnizing. Some of us had almost forgotten that men and women could create and live in such dignity.

From the spacious entrance hall twin flights of stairs curve upward in grace to meet on a landing and continue as one—not the actual measurements but the proportions emphasizing the dignity of the plan.

Neither is it the number of rooms—there are twenty-eight in the house—which maintains the tone of aristocratic calm. This elegance derives from the high-ceilinged proportions. The dining room, with its original wallpaper; the library, with its fine old books and tremendous globe of the world, its curtains the color of sunlight and its oil portraits of previous owners; the drawing room, with its square Steinway piano—both drawing room and library with fireplaces of carved Italian marble and baseboards of the same material—all suggest not primarily wealth, but leisure and cultivated taste.

No detail is mediocre. The hardware on the doors and windows and inside window shutters is of silver. At one time the washbasins and pitchers in the bedrooms were also of silver, but with the installation of modern plumbing many of these have been sent to the Smithsonian Institution. There is a rumor that one very intimate piece, preserved in a mahogany, plush-lined case, was

FIGURE 50. Berry Hill in Halifax County is considered the noblest model of Greek Revival in Virginia. Two separate and miniature pavilions, one at each end, complete the majestic balance of the approach.

given a place in the initiation rites of the Current Events Class of the late Douglas Southall Freeman in Richmond.

Silver is used in another detail which, although not conspicuous, touches a flood of significant reflections. Affixed to the wall of each of the principal rooms are small silver bell pulls, gleamingly polished. In the pantry between the dining room and kitchen hangs a row of bells which are connected with these. A twist of the wrist in any room set jangling one of these bells, each with its distinctive tone, and at this signal maid or butler or boy could fly at once to inquire what was wanted.

In our electric age we have plenty of conveniences and gadgets and labor-saving devices. But where are the smiling servitors to come running—or even ambling—at our slightest signal to attend to our slightest request? These small, finely made bell pulls could be incorporated into a coat-of-arms as a symbol of an obsolete luxury.

If there was an abundance of service inside Berry Hill during the life of its builder, James Coles Bruce, there were hundreds of slaves on the plantation—a plantation on land originally owned by William Byrd of Westover, sold to Richard Bland, bought by Isaac Coles, inherited by Edward Coles Carrington and acquired by James Coles Bruce. It remained in possession of the Bruce family until 1950, when it was bought by Mr. Frederick Watkins, who does not live in it.

A single caretaker keeps the lovely old place in perpetual and immaculate order. The glass as well as the silver gleams. There is no dust on stair or banister: no stain on marble mantel. The old square piano is in tune. Neither do children go to their lessons in one of the pavilions at the entrance, nor gentlemen play billiards in the other. In the pantry the bells hang motionless, and the conscientious caretaker cannot find a finger mark on the silver bell pulls.

There is a legend that sometimes ghostly footsteps are heard on the stairs, and a ghostly knocking in a certain closet. These are echoes of the past, as is suitable for a place where life has receded.

But there is no tinkle or even an echo from the pantry. The elegance which flowed so calmly through these classic rooms has ceased, like the long-silenced vibration of the bells.

A few years after James Coles Bruce built Berry Hill in Halifax County, his half brother, Charles Bruce, built Staunton Hill in nearby Charlotte County. James Bruce modeled his house after the fashion of the Greek Revival. Charles Bruce chose the style which has been called the Gothic Revival, or, even more aptly, Hudson River Tudor.

With towers and battlements, with Gothic arches, stained-glass windows and marble portico, it faces a circular sweep of lawn beyond which the land drops down to the Staunton River and its surrounding fertile plains.

Charles Bruce spared neither money nor effort to make Staunton Hill as imposing as possible, according to the standards of the day. He had the thick brick walls stuccoed, and across the

FIGURE 51. With towers and battlements, Gothic arches, stained-glass windows and marble portico, Staunton Hill is a unique period piece.

front raised a marble porch with fluted pillars and granite steps. The marble was quarried in Italy, cut to specifications in Philadelphia, transported by boat to Albemarle Sound in North Carolina, and thence by bateaux up the waters of the Roanoke and Staunton Rivers to the landing at the foot of the plantation grounds.

In the old days visitors also arrived by water and were driven up the winding, well-graded gravel road from the landing, through handsome iron entrance gates and a grove of oak trees.

They were received in the polygonal hall which remains today as it was then, with its black and white marble floor, and its wall niches holding Greek figures in plaster painted black. The stained glass in the fanlight and side lights of the front door has been allowed to remain, although this once-popular grandiose flourish has been removed from the windows in the middle drawing room and the Gothic library.

The interior emphasizes the same baronial air as the exterior. A double stairway sweeps upward, the dining room extends its polished table, and the formally furnished double drawing rooms and the library are embellished with marble fireplaces and elaborate plaster work on the ceilings and cornices, with long gilt-framed mirrors made to fit the specified spaces.

It is, in brief, a perfect period piece representing the idea of elegance which was admired not only along the Hudson River in New York but in certain exclusive sections of New England.

It would, however, be a mistake to think of it merely as a show place. From the time it was built in 1848 until after the War Between the States, Staunton Hill plantation, with more than five thousand acres of land and half a thousand slaves, was a highly productive enterprise.

Besides furnishing domestic supplies for the family, in some years the farm lands yielded, in addition to wheat, oats, hay and livestock, between four and five thousand barrels of corn and the growth of not less than a million hills of tobacco. Even after the war and the introduction of the new system of hired labor, it continued in tremendous agricultural activity, with all the crops bringing even higher prices than before—a remarkable adaptation to changed conditions.

Today, well-kept roads wind between mile-long stone walls, pass exotic and native trees and forest groves and numerous small buildings which once made the place into a veritable village.

In those days the plantation, divided into three tracts, each a complete and separate organization with its own overseer, resembled a feudal village. Slaves tended the fields, pastures, orchards and gardens, the tobacco barns, stables, henhouses, icehouse and smokehouse. They wove the coarse cloth from which their garments were made. Carpenters, stone masons, blacksmith and superintendent of the granary were all necessary. In and around the house was another army. Three cooks were not considered too many—one to prepare breakfast, one dinner and a third to make desserts. More servants were needed to wait on table and to clean the rooms, tend the conservatory, cut wood, chop it into suitable lengths in the Gothic woodhouse, and keep the many fireplaces supplied and burning. Kerosene lamps and candlesticks had to be cleaned daily. Although there was a hydraulic ram to carry water to the kitchen, drinking water was brought by hand—or rather by head—from the spring; and water for bathing was heated in brick caldrons in the colonnade and carried up to the tin-hat baths in various dressing rooms, although the mansion did boast two marble tubs, one in the master dressing room and one in a bathroom in the colonnade.

Many of the cabins and other buildings are no longer used, but they are kept painted and in repair and what was once called "the Street" retains the old name. The five-room Gothic lodge near the house was the plantation office, billiard room and gun room and accommodated occasional strangers "not entitled to the fullest measure of hospitable consideration."

When Charles Bruce died in 1896, the vast property passed to his widow, and after her death to his son, William Cabell Bruce of Baltimore. Later it became, temporarily, a hunting and shooting week-end club composed of James Bruce, his brother David K. E. Bruce—at one time Ambassador to France—and some of their friends.

Now it has reverted to the private ownership of David Bruce, and is kept in constant readiness for his occasional visits.

When Staunton Hill was built it was a three-day journey by carriage from the capital of the state. Although much slave labor was used, trained workmen had to be brought from Philadelphia. The expenditure of labor, time and money was prodigious, but the very remoteness saved it from the pillage and vandalism of war.

And yet today, with automobiles and good highways, Staunton Hill seems farther than it did then. It is remote, not only in its isolation but in its architectural fashion, and in the whole pattern of existence upon which its prosperity and its ideals of luxurious living were based.

That pattern has been broken and has disappeared forever. No one can prophesy how long the towers and battlements and marble portico of Staunton Hill will remain as a testimonial to an age that has passed.

chapter 14

JEFFERSON'S COUNTRY

A Princess at Home, Monticello, Love and a Cottage, Redlands,
The House that Disappeared

Castle Hill holds a special place in the hearts of Virginians, not only because it has been part of the social and historical scene for almost two centuries, but because it has been the home of people whose remembered charm, like the scent and shadow of its great boxwood trees, is not lost even in the fluctuation of the passing years.

Perhaps the most winning occupant of the place was Amélie Rives, who spent her childhood summers there, and who, after her marriage to Prince Pierre Troubetzkoy, was its mistress for more than forty years.

Amélie Rives wrote novels, stories, poems and plays which were immensely popular in the later part of the nineteenth century. If, to modern taste, they seem a bit overglamorous, her own life must seem even more so. Before her birth, fame and fortune stood waiting to shower her with favors. Her grandfather, William Cabell Rives, was twice Minister to France. Lafayette was godfather to his son, who was born there, and Queen Amélie, wife of Louis Philippe, was godmother to his eldest daughter, conferring on her the name which her granddaughter was to inherit.

It is pleasant to picture the Minister returning from abroad whenever possible to stay at Castle Hill where his wife planned the lawn in the shape of an hourglass and planted the entrance hedges in a style reminiscent of France.

It is pleasant to picture his son, Alfred Landon Rives, who became a Colonel in the Confederate Army, bringing his bride—who had been Sadie McMurdo—back to the place he loved. Pleasant to think of his pretty daughters growing up there, playing bowls on the bowling green and watching the sunlight dappling Walnut Mountain.

When Amélie was two she was riding horseback. When she was tall enough to reach her pony's head she learned to saddle, bridle and harness him, and even when she was grown she would ride with her golden hair floating in the breeze. Before she could write, she was making up stories and rhymes.

She never went to school, but was taught by governesses, who found her busily writing down her stories when most children are learning their letters. Her grandmother, thinking the labors of authorship might better be postponed for a few years, took away pencil and paper, so Amélie wrote her verses on the wide hems of her white starched petticoats. At twenty-five she published her first novel, "The Quick or the Dead," and found herself famous. The sale was enormous for that period—three hundred thousand, due to her facile and fervid style and her bold treatments of subjects then considered taboo, and she continued to write constantly and successfully and apparently with greatest ease during her long and eventful life. She never seemed to lack subject matter and certainly never lacked acclaim.

Today we may not feel that her "A Brother to Dragons," which was published anonymously in the *Atlantic Monthly,* shows "an imaginative power unequalled in contemporary fiction," and we may swallow hard at the pronouncement that her work embodied the "bold yet delicate quaintness which characterized the finest productions of the Elizabethan era."

But the fact remains that long before that phrase was coined, she was a steady best seller and enjoyed all its attendant emoluments.

It was easier for a woman to become a literary celebrity in 1888 than it is now: the mere fact that one was a woman and

Photo by Holsinger Studio

FIGURE 52. The brick addition to Castle Hill was built in 1820, with one-story wings added in 1840. At this time Mrs. Rives developed the hour-glass-shaped lawn and entrance box hedges.

able to write at all was worthy of mention. But it is never easy for a girl who may be acknowledged one of the great beauties of her day to remain beautiful to extreme old age.

We have photographs and sketches of Amélie which sub-stantiate this claim. Not only American artists but European de-lighted to paint and draw her. Lady Granby, who was sought by the Duchess of Marlborough, Mrs. Patrick Campbell and other notables, has left a flattering sketch of the Virginia girl.

That girl passed from one exciting and usually delightful experience to another. During her first season in Newport, just when "The Quick or the Dead" had made such a furor, she met John Armstrong Chanler, like herself born to the social graces and

161

conveniently well supplied with money, and shortly after they were married at Castle Hill.

Two such colorful personalities found themselves incompatible. The young wife remained in Paris, studying painting and enjoying association with artists, and the young husband hied himself to South Africa to shoot big game. Amélie braved divorce when divorces were by no means a matter of course, and lived for a while in England, finding an agreeable welcome from the great and the gifted. It is said it was Oscar Wilde who introduced her to Prince Troubetzkoy, the painter, recently arrived from Italy to fill commissions for portraits.

And now there was another marriage, and like the first, it took place at Castle Hill and for more than forty years it held for both exceptional happiness.

All stories come to an end, and the end came for Prince Troubetzkoy in 1936, but the Princess was to live for almost another decade. Still fascinating, although more and more withdrawn from social contacts, she must have often recalled the days in England when she was quite aware of the sensation she made as she appeared in her dazzling blondeness with the jet-black mammy she had brought with her from Castle Hill. She must have recalled her presentation at the Russian Court, shortly after her marriage to Prince Troubetzkoy, for later she was to give to the Valentine Museum in Richmond the gorgeous gown she had made in Paris for that memorable occasion.

Her last years, like her earliest ones, were spent in the house which she loved so dearly and which, even now, holds a vibration of that charm which is so hard to define and so impossible to forget.

It holds, too, many pictures painted by the Prince and prized by the new owners, Colonel and Mrs. Clark J. Lawrence, who purchased the famous old place in 1947 and who have taken pains and pleasure in restoring house and grounds.

Castle Hill actually consists of two houses—the first one built in 1768 of clapboard, only one room deep and a story and a half high, with six dormer windows and a small porch. This was built by Dr. Thomas Walker, when he married the widow of Nicholas Meriwether and thus came into possession of fifteen hundred acres which had been a grant from King George II.

Photo by Holsinger Studio

FIGURE 53.   Castle Hill is actually two houses. The first one, built in 1765, is a story-and-a-half clapboard structure with six dormer windows. It faces the old Bowling Green and Walnut Mountain.

It was his granddaughter, Judith Page Walker, who married William Cabell Rives, the Minister to France, thus bringing the estate into the possession of the Rives family.

It was they who added the second addition, in 1820, which is really another complete house, facing the entrance drive. It is of brick, with high-ceiled rooms and elaborate interior trim, and from it were extended, later, two one-story wings.

During Princess Troubetzkoy's last lonely years much of the house was closed off and garden and grounds shadowed by the forty-foot boxwood trees reflected the melancholy isolation of the mistress.

Today the hall, which runs the depth of both houses, is cheerfully open, and on the broad stairway guests greet each other in passing. In the drawing room, where once the young Jefferson fiddled for the younger Madison to dance, on gala nights other young people dance until sunup. When they gather in the dining room, perhaps only a few have ever heard that it was here that Jack Jouett, tearing from Cuckoo to Charlottesville to warn Governor Jefferson that the British were coming, ate in a hurry. But Tarleton and his troops, when they arrived, were so delayed by the mint juleps and the prolonged hospitality of Mrs. Walker that Jack Jouett had more than made good his escape by the time they took their leave.

To the guest rooms where Washington, Lafayette, Dolly Madison, Andrew Jackson, Martin Van Buren and John Tyler stayed, come so many visitors that one wonders if the ghost who is credited with recurrent appearances may not be a bit overworked.

This ghost bears a suspicious resemblance to a former member of the household, and is declared to materialize at the foot of the bed occupied by a guest who has outstayed his expected term and whisper insistently, "Go home! Go home!"

One cannot help wondering if there are not similar ghosts in many Virginia houses—and not only in those which are two centuries old. For visitors have a way of lingering under Virginia roofs, and sometimes lingering so long that it might seem a prodding ghost or two would be a useful appendage to the household.

Most houses express, to greater or less degree, something of the person who designed and built them, but Monticello is the actual biography, written not in words but in brick and wood, in mortar and glass, of its brilliant and original creator. To follow its conception, and the gradual development of its planning, to interpret its extensions and refinements, is to understand much about the temperament and versatility of the architect who was also its master. It is to understand, also, many of the events which molded his long and far-ranging life.

This peculiarly close connection between Thomas Jefferson and his house begins when he was a boy, tramping over the hills and through the valleys and beside the rivers in Albemarle County, Virginia, where he had been born, looking for the place for his future home.

FIGURE 54.   More than two hundred thousand visitors come annually to see Monticello.

He decided upon it finally—the top of a low mountain—a little less than six hundred feet elevation, three miles east of Charlottesville, and overlooking a panorama which encircled the entire horizon. In those days, while a bluff above a river was often chosen as a house site, it was not usual to build on a hilltop. Lower and flatter ground near the water was considered more convenient of access and better suited to the planting and care of crops. But Jefferson, even at that early period, selected a site which, although it did not conform to custom, suited his own taste.

And even then he was instinctively attracted by the idea of a circular pattern—as opposed to usual rectangular or square ones —in both house plans and ground plans. This idea was to hold his approval throughout his life and was to influence many of the mansions subsequently built by friends but suggested by him. In these we notice not only certain rooms, but whole houses emphasizing octagonal or circular lines.

He was just seventeen years of age when he went to Williamsburg to attend the college of William and Mary, and his days and nights were pleasantly filled with the usual student activities. But there was one activity—a mental one—which distinguished him from his fellows. He was always aware of the marvelous house he would someday build on his mountaintop. Therefore, when he chanced on some engravings of the Italian architect, Andrea Palladio, he instantly fitted them into his hitherto vague plans.

The principal houses and public buildings in Virginia were modeled after those in England or in the Low Countries. Jefferson, although he had never been abroad, realized that the climate of Virginia is far more like that of Italy than of either England or Holland. He perceived that the pillared portico and immense Palladian windows were suitable for such a climate and that the classic Italian form could well be adapted to the home of a Virginia colonial.

Thus began his affection for Italy—an affection which he expressed in naming his mountain site Monticello, which is Italian for Little Mountain. Years later, during his residence abroad, as he watched the building of the Hotel de Thelusson and the Hotel de Salm, the Palladian idea of a single-story Roman building so appealed to him that when he returned home, he sought to emulate it as far as possible. Thus he removed the upper story of Monticello and built a domed glass room to crown the house—the first of its kind ever seen in America. His *simpatía* for Italy remained throughout his life. In his last noble group of buildings—the University of Virginia—he was to import not only Italian marble for the capitals of its classic pillars, but Italian stone cutters.

His actual contact with Italy was still in the future when, in 1768, he began to level the top of the mountain so that it would precisely accommodate the red brick, white-pillared mansion which he had in mind and which was to change and grow for almost sixty years more.

During his college holidays at home in Shadwell, after the midafternoon dinner, he used to paddle across the river and then climb to the top of his mountain and ponder his plans. When Shadwell burned (1770), he moved to the beloved site, although the house was not sufficiently completed to live in even when he married in 1772.

The wedding day fell during the heaviest snowstorm that had been remembered by anyone then living, but the young couple, nothing daunted, set out in a two-horse chaise for their new home, more than a hundred miles away. They arrived late at night, finding the small cottage which was to be their home until the mansion was ready, dark and cold, and the slaves, who had never dreamed any one would attempt such a journey in such weather, asleep in their quarters.

Legend has it that it was so bitterly cold that the bridegroom played his fiddle and the bride danced to get warm, which seems a rather unnecessarily strenuous procedure in a region where there has always been plenty of firewood and where the virtues of a hot toddy are fully appreciated. At all events, the little brick building which is still called Honeymoon Cottage, did very well until they could move into the mansion which was being constructed with timbers cut from the woods, with bricks burned on the place, and with nails hammered out by pickaninnies in the little building dignified by the name of the nail factory. Later he was to devise a cement which would withstand the damp of the underground passage.

Hard native woods were used for the floor of the drawing room, cut and fitted by hand in parquet pattern. The darker centers of each block were of highly polished cherry, with lighter borders of beech, and after nearly two centuries of use they are still handsome.

Although Monticello was to undergo numerous alterations, it expressed, from the beginning, some of Jefferson's social and economic ideas.

His delight in hospitality was expressed by dedicating the whole first floor primarily for the accommodation and entertainment of guests. It has been said that one reason he omitted a grand staircase leading from the entrance hall to the second floor was that he disliked having groups of people linger to chat on the stairs and thus impede the free flow of movement. It has also been suggested—less charitably—that Jefferson never managed to handle stairways properly. In one of the chief pavilions on the lawn of the University of Virginia the only stair runs directly across one of the front windows. Whatever the reason, the only way to reach the second floor at Monticello is by two steep flights, barely two feet wide, in the wings.

Jefferson's attitude toward slavery was to culminate when, an old man, he took steps for the emancipation of his own servants. This attitude was foreshadowed by his novel arrangements for their accommodation. An army of blacks had to be maintained to care for the barns and stables, woodlands and pastures, crops and cattle. Others were needed to prepare and cook and serve the enormous quantities of food consumed by the family and visitors; to clean and card and spin; to carry the wood for all the fireplaces and water for the washstand basins and tubs that served before the age of bathrooms.

In order that house and grounds should not be continually swarming with black figures and to reduce the hazards of fire, Jefferson placed the kitchens and slave quarters in buildings below the level of the house, at some distance from it and connected to it by underground passages—an innovation which, like his octagonal rooms, was to be repeated in other plantation houses of that period.

The years when Jefferson was American Minister to France took him away from his beloved Virginia, but when he finally returned he had absorbed many French ideas. He had become a judge of good wines, which led to his planting vineyards and attempting to make wine at Monticello. In the dining room one can see the dumb-waiter which brought the bottles from the locked wine vaults directly into the room. In 1953, Dr. Julian P. Boyd of Princeton, an editor of *The Papers of Thomas Jefferson,* which include lists and correspondence concerning old wines, brought back to Monticello old bottles from the very vineyards from which Jefferson stocked his cellar. In the kitchens with their array of cranes and kettles hanging in the huge open fireplaces, French dishes were prepared. In his conservatories were tended plants and seedlings he had shipped to him regularly by his "good old friend Thouin" of the Jardin des Plantes in Paris. His enthusiasm for all things French ranged from his admiration of its landscape architecture, its city planning and the beauty of its public and private buildings to manners, as when he continued, despite criticism, to hold his violin under his chin in what his critic called

FIGURE 55. In the dining room at Monticello, a dumb-waiter was built into the space by the fireplace. This brought bottles from the wine vaults directly below.

"the effeminate European manner" instead of against his stomach in the sturdy American fashion.

His absorption of cosmopolitan culture in no way lessened that ingenuity and inventiveness which is often considered a special American characteristic. Jefferson dearly loved a gadget and Monticello is replete with those of his devising.

Even before you enter the house you can look up and see, perched on the roof, the weathervane which connects with a compass two feet in diameter set in the ceiling of the east portico. There is also a clock face of the same dimensions over the outside entrance door. Thus it was possible for Jefferson, when sitting outside or in, to tell without leaving his chair, the direction of the wind and the hour of the day. In the entrance hall is another clock (controlled by the same works as served for the one outside).

169

When this is to be wound, it is reached by an ingenious "fox and geese" ladder which is folded up when not in use.

Between the reception hall and the drawing room, with its glassed, octagonal bay window extending into the garden in the manner of a French salon, are double glass doors so mechanized that when one panel is opened or closed the other swings automatically with it. We are familiar with such doors in buses today, but these were the first ever devised. All the doors are of solid mahogany and on many are catches which engage automatically as the door swings fully open, and hold it in place. Makers of modern furniture display as innovations pieces which have a double use. But Jefferson designed double-purpose pieces two centuries ago. Standing beside his chaise longue in his study, there is a table whose top circles on a pivot and can be drawn over the leg rest. Another table had hollow legs containing rods which could be adjusted, to raise or lower its height, so it could be used by one while standing or sitting. The top could also be tilted, for writing or reading, and probably served as a drawing board for his architectural work. His polygraph pencil made duplicate copies as he wrote.

He also devised a portable writing desk which, when folded, was no larger than a quarto volume and contained a drawer for paper, ink and quill. When opened, it served as a writing desk and on it he wrote the Declaration of Independence.

In the space between his bedroom and study he fitted a bed which could be drawn to the ceiling during the day to allow uninterrupted passage and circulation of air between the two rooms. But the beds in the chambers were far from mobile. They were built permanently and immovably into alcoves in the walls and must have been airless enough in summer and difficult to make summer or winter.

This fertile imagination did not stop with the interior of the house and its furnishing. He invented the mold-board plough, which was a great improvement over the straight or coulter plough; a self-closing buggy top which was the forerunner of our convertible automobile tops, and a cane which could unfold into a chair.

After almost forty continuous years of public life—as President of the United States, as Minister to France and as Governor

FIGURE 56. Jefferson's bed, in the space between his bedroom and his study, could be drawn into the ceiling during the day to allow circulation of air.

of Virginia—during which much of the work at Monticello was directed by correspondence, he was at last able to retire. Free to direct his dynamic energy into agricultural activities, this final period was one of his happiest.

There was not a detail of farming—he advocated the rotation of crops and contour plowing, grading of roads, timbering of forest land, or planting of orchards—which escaped him. Inside the house his quick eye and nimble fingers were always busy. After his wife's death his married daughter, Martha Randolph, kept house for him. However, the sketches for window curtains which were cut, shirred and hung Empire fashion on rods, are still preserved, and are in his hand and not in hers.

His passion for hospitality overflowed all reasonable bounds. It was usual for distinguished travelers from Europe, such as

Lafayette, the Marquis de Chastellux and Duc de la Roche-foucauld, to begin or end their tour of the country by a visit to Monticello. There was a steady stream of statesmen, soldiers, scientists and musicians, to say nothing of a continual influx of family friends and kinsfolk. As was said, Mrs. Randolph was able to put up fifty people overnight, and if one wonders how this was arranged with only two principal guest rooms—those on the first floor—one remembers that it was possible, although awkward, to climb those narrow, steep stairs in the wings to other bedrooms on the second and third floors, where it was taken as a matter of course that there would be several beds in a room and several people in a bed.

The whole place was designed for entertainment on the most lavish scale. The smokehouse was hung with hams, the icehouse, woodhouse and chicken houses stocked to overflowing, so that the old steward complained that he would "cut up a fine beef and two days later it was gone."

There were bridle horses and bridle paths. On the lawn between the Honeymoon Cottage and the office—the two small buildings which are still standing—visitors strolled and chatted.

The expense of such a household was fantastic and Jefferson died a poor man.

At his death the house which had been so much a part of his thought and affection since boyhood, which had gradually come to be a record of his wide travels and experiences and expanding interests and tastes, passed to James Barclay and then to Commodore Uriah P. Levy and then to the Commodore's nephew. Finally, in 1923, it became the property of the Thomas Jefferson Memorial Foundation, and was opened to the public.

Gradually the original furnishings were located and when possible purchased. The grounds were put in order, the trees pruned and treated, and the flower beds, which Jefferson had designed, were replanted with the flowers he himself had designated.

More than two hundred thousand visitors climb to this famous mountaintop every year to see how a Virginia plantation looked and how it was operated in its opulent heyday. But if Thomas Jefferson himself should return, we may take it for granted that he, who always looked forward instead of backward, would be more interested in practical innovations than in the retention of archaic features. He would wholeheartedly approve of the new boiler plant at some distance from the house with its underground pipes replacing hazardous wood fires and oil stoves. He would approve of structural restoration of the floors and the transparent waterproofing of the old brick walls. He would have been un-qualifiedly delighted with the introduction of air conditioning. He would have been the first to grade the entrance and exit roads and arrange for parking places for the stream of automobiles from every state in the Union.

Such improvements are a truer expression of Jefferson's spirit than a static museum would be. The great man's grave and its tombstone, an enlarged replica of the original obelisque on the campus of the University of Missouri, can be seen from the road which winds past it and down to the entrance gates. The house, however, is not a monument to a dead man, but to the lively ideal of a living one.

Thomas Jefferson loved Italy and France and from these countries he assimilated traditions and tastes. But he loved his own country with even greater fervor and sacrificed almost half his life to its service. Since one enthusiasm sustains another, per-haps he loved most intimately of all the Virginia where he was born, and that spot which he chose as a boy to be his future home.

Toward the end of his life he said, "All my wishes end where I hope my days will end, at Monticello."

His wish was granted, and the house he designed and built and shared with so many others still holds the vibrations of a young man's dreams and an old man's memories.

About three and a half miles beyond Monticello, overlooking its rolling acres, its paddocks and its pastures, bounded and criss-crossed by white fences, is Morven, one of the best-loved and most generously shared of the old places in Albemarle County.

Ever since Mr. and Mrs. Charles Stone purchased the estate in 1926 and began the restoration of the house and the rehabilita-tion of the grounds, many hundreds of visitors have been welcome to stroll through the gardens, with their brick walls, ancient box-wood and extensive flower beds. Many others have come on business, for Mr. Stone, who enjoyed breeding horses in New

England, added this Virginia place for the same pursuit. Since his death, his son, Whitney Stone, has continued to breed thoroughbred horses and has added two hundred Hereford cattle.

Morven seems to comprise everything that one expects from an ideal Virginia plantation. The red brick house, with its white trim, was built in 1820. Probably Mr. Jefferson had something to do with the drawing of its plans, and it is certain that he advised the selection of the Italian marble mantels which were shipped from Leghorn to Baltimore and thence to Virginia.

After various changes in ownership, the fifteen hundred acres —two thirds in woodland and one third cleared—the house, exquisitely restored inside and out, the small brick building with the flagged floor and immense fireplace originally used as a kitchen, the smokehouse (in continuous use for more than a century), the stables, barns, seven farmhouses, and two cottages have been brought by the Stones into working order and immaculate repair.

The casual tourist sees and enjoys this general picture. The architect studies the house; horse breeders and horse lovers and cattle experts come from a distance to bargain and buy.

Many of them glance at the white frame cottage, now used as the estate office, and nod when it is explained that this was the first building on the grounds and that it was used as a residence while the mansion was under construction. Few realize that it is all that remains of one of the most touching and most delicate of international romances.

Morven was originally part of the ten-thousand-acre grant made to one of the sons of that ubiquitous "King" Carter whose holdings spread so widely in every direction. In 1796, William Short bought 1,334 acres called Indian Camp, and on it he erected the small frame cottage so charmingly refurbished today.

William Short was a young man of such winning charm and such sound ability that Jefferson liked to call him his adopted son and was gratified when Short referred to him as his second father. When Jefferson was Minister to France he made Short his secretary—a post which he filled so well that subsequently he was sent as United States Minister to the Netherlands, and then as diplomatic representative to Spain.

It was during his residence in France that Short met the

Photo by Holsinger Studio

FIGURE 57. The old white frame cottage at Morven, used as the estate office, is a reminder of one of the most delicate and touching of international romances.

Duchess de la Rochefoucauld, at that time a matron of twenty-seven, one of the great peeresses of her day, and married to her cousin twenty years her senior.

Americans who are inclined to believe that French society in the eighteenth century was the epitome of frivolity and corruption will do well to consider the story of Rosalie, the Duchess de la Rochefoucauld and William Short, the Virginian.

There is no doubt that almost immediately upon meeting, the two young people fell in love with each other, and there is no doubt that this love, which was never to reach fulfillment in marriage, endured for nearly fifty years.

While there could be no thought of marriage while Rosalie's

husband lived, the several hundred letters which passed between the lovers, and came to light only after their deaths, reveal the scrupulous correctness of their relationship. The letters are extremely interesting, not only because of the ardor of their avowals, but because of their glimpses into the life of a fashionable French noblewoman of the eighteenth century.

It is probable that the young people met through Jefferson, who was a friend of Rosalie's husband. Certain it is that the happiest time in their lives was a week in May, 1791, when Short visited at La Roche-Guyon, the country seat of the Duke and Duchess de la Rochefoucauld. It was then, as they strolled together in the gardens and lingered in the rustic pavilions, that each recognized an emotion never experienced before, one which they were never to relinquish.

Rosalie's letters, after this visit, reveal both her passion and her rectitude. "You know my way of thinking," she writes. "You know how far removed from constraint and deception my life has been, thus you must believe that I would never find peace were I to turn aside from the duties which are marked out for me."

Subsequent letters, while still carrying their message of love, are valuable testimony of an eyewitness of certain events of the French Revolution. She describes the storming of the Tuileries, the arrest and conviction of her brother Charles, the stoning to death of her husband before her eyes, and her own imprisonment.

William Short, completely and irrevocably in love, now dreamed of marrying the young widow and carrying her back to Virginia—back to that very spot which is now named Morven, whose lovely vistas must often have come back to him during his long absences abroad.

But although her husband's death did leave Rosalie free to marry, she was now confronted with another barrier. She was the sole companion of her aged grandmother with whom she had suffered imprisonment for nearly a year. She felt it impossible to desert her, and so once again devotion to duty made marriage impossible. William Short understood and respected her decision. He wrote, "If you insist upon remaining with your grandmother— and I admit that her age and your devotion to her would demand it—I shall never again leave you, but shall ask permission of my government to remain in Paris."

The constant letters testify to the deepness and tenderness of their mutual love, but these long separations, which they seemed unable to bridge, kept them apart. When, at last, her grandmother died, Rosalie was unable to take the final step. It was eighteen years since she and the Virginian had fallen in love, and although her affection and admiration for the only man who ever touched her heart never faltered, her resiliency seemed to have snapped. On Short's departure for America, she ended her letter, "Do not leave me without the hope of your returning to a country where you have friends and above all one who will be that to her dying day, and who, whatever the circumstances of her life will ever be the same."

Short returned, but not to Virginia where he had hoped to bring Rosalie as his wife. He sold the place and the little frame cottage to David Higginbotham, a neighbor and also a friend of Jefferson—who gave it the name of Morven. Short returned to Philadelphia, and there for twenty-five years he continued to exchange letters with Rosalie—letters so poignant and so fond no one can doubt their sincerity.

The last letter from Rosalie which has been preserved is dated two years before her death, and it is not only an acknowledgment of her love which had never faltered, but a blessing and a benediction.

Short never married.

This is the story which occurs to us today as we stand by the small white frame cottage and look out over the fields of Morven —fields which Short was never to return to, and which Rosalie was never to see.

On the same ten-thousand-acre grant of land (made out to one of the sons of "King" Carter) from which Morven was partitioned, is twelve hundred acres which is Redlands, for nearly a hundred and fifty years a social and architectural landmark in the annals of Albemarle County.

Like Morven, Redlands was built with the timbers, bricks, mortar and plaster produced and worked on the place, and, like Morven, it is of red brick with white trim, and far-reaching tranquil views. It was completed fourteen years before its neighbor, but unlike it, it has remained in the same family ever since Robert

177

Carter brought his bride, Mary Eliza Coles, to it in 1808.

It is this continuity of family possession and tradition which gives Redlands a special charm and intimacy. It is placed in Georgian symmetry on a wide lawn shaded by large trees, and the same Georgian balance prevails inside. The entrance hall opens into an oval drawing room with three tall north windows directly opposite the front door, the dining room and library on one side, and two bedrooms on the other. The doorways, cornices and mantels are among the finest examples of Adam design in Virginia. The tobacco leaves, buds and flowers carved into the marble of some of the mantels add a pleasing local touch of decoration. Upstairs is a large hall—actually another sitting room— spacious bedrooms and one of those stairways misleadingly called "concealed." Everything about the proportions, and in the smallest detail, is restrained and graceful.

These features, worthy of conventional classification as they are, are enhanced by being a background for the easy and generous life which has flowed unbrokenly through the old house for nearly a century and a half.

Each generation has left its mementos. There are the marble-topped table and the chaise longue with the rattan seat which came from Monticello; a tea caddy which belonged to George Washington, and on the drawing-room table a pair of black and gold French pedestals. The spinet was imported from England, and the bookcase of ironwood, filling a whole wall of the upper hall, fell into the James River when it was being brought from Washington. The days—or perhaps the nights—of what we call old-fashioned hospitality still prevail at Redlands, for in the big bedrooms are not only antique four-post beds complete with testers, but these are frequently supplemented by a single bed or even two, and also a cradle or crib—a sound precaution against emergency. For children and grandchildren and great-grandchildren are still seen and heard in their ancestral home. Bathrooms have been cunningly inserted in convenient spaces, but on some of the washstands still stand old pitchers and basins of Canton china. Central heating is, at this writing, unknown in the mansion.

It is obvious that no interior decorator or museum expert has persuaded the Carters to discard or rearrange the pictures which are lavishly hung on every wall. Gilbert Stuart painted the ancestor

Photo by Kiraly Studio

FIGURE 58. At Redlands, the oval drawing room with three north windows holds heirlooms of many generations.

who was Governor Wilson Cary Nicholas, and who, incidentally, was such a friend of Jefferson that he was buried at Monticello. Sully has admirably copied the soft tones in the gold-framed portrait which hangs over the drawing-room mantel. Facing it is Charles Willson Peale's portrait of General John Smith, and on this wall several large and decorative St. Memins, including one of that same Governor Nicholas.

St. Memin holds a rather special place in Virginia's affections. A French émigré, who came to America in 1793, he originated a process for producing inexpensive and yet attractive portraits, inventing a device which he called a "physionatrace," by which he drew the profile face, life-size, on pink paper. Then, with a "pantograph" he reduced this to the limits of a small medallion engraving. He delivered the life-size drawing in a frame of his own design, with the copper plate and twelve proofs of the engraving, for twenty-five dollars a set for men and thirty-five for women, whose headdress and laces were more troublesome. He turned out an enormous number of these portraits, and although many of the large profiles have disappeared, there are a quantity of the delightful small engravings and the plates from which they were made. Before St. Memin went back to France, where Louis XVIII appointed him Curator of the Museum at Dijon, his birthplace, he destroyed his "physionatrace" so that his process should never be duplicated.

Besides the large St. Memin "physionatraces" in the drawing room at Redlands, there are, in the upper hall, a number of his delightful medallion engravings. In this same hall is a color photograph of Elizabeth Hill Carter and another of George Washington by Miley, a popular artist of the late 1880's. Miley invented a process by which color applied to a photograph never faded, and although he left a number of these and more than a thousand plates, his process has not been copied. Piranesi engravings, so dear to the hearts of our great-grandparents, fill any space which might otherwise be empty.

There is another picture which is prized by the Carter family —an etching of Andrew Stevenson who was the American Minister to the Court of St. James's a hundred years ago. Mr. Stevenson presented some Albemarle pippins to Queen Victoria, who was so pleased with their flavor that she straightway removed import duty on all American apples. A good many orchards in Albemarle have claimed the honor of raising those pippins, but Redlands is positive they came from there, and to prove the point, cite a letter from Mrs. Andrew Stevenson, the Minister's second wife, who was Sarah Coles and, therefore, a Carter. Mrs. Stevenson wrote home that she had presented the apples in a silver basket and although she was delighted that the Queen appreciated them, she regretted that the basket had not been returned; she asked advice from the family as to how she might diplomatically go about regaining it. (She never did.)

Piranesi and Peale, St. Memin and Sully, old-fashioned lithographs sent from abroad by some youthful Carter on his first voyage in a sailing ship, the last snapshot of the last grandchild—

FIGURE 59.   One of the many guest rooms at Redlands shows how the old houses provided for more than one person to a bed and more than one bed to a room.

here they all are, preserved and placed, not according to chronology or perhaps even according to merit, but according to sentiment.

For Redlands is not primarily a show place. It is an authentic plantation, having been under continuous cultivation since its very beginning. Formerly it produced the varied crops of a general all-around farm, but lately it has specialized in Hereford cattle.

Everything about the place is genuine—the house, the farming and cattle-raising activities, the people. And very real indeed is the long and happy family tradition.

Not many substantial and good-sized houses with a substantial and good-sized history behind them get lost. If they do, few of them are found again. But such has been the rather odd story of Edgemont.

It was in 1787 that Colonel James Powell Cocke, hoping to find relief for his malaria, exchanged his home, Malvern Hills in Henrico County, for sixteen hundred acres of land owned by Thomas Nelson in Albemarle County. He chose the site for the house he hoped to build on a natural hillside terrace, on the south fork of the Hardware River facing Fan Mountain, near North Garden and thirteen miles from Charlottesville.

It was not unusual that his friend Thomas Jefferson should offer to draw the plans, and there is even a story that he contributed his own carpenters and stone masons to do the actual work of building. In any event, the plans incorporate many of Jefferson's pet ideas. Edgemont, which is approximately fifty feet by fifty feet, appears from the front to be a one-story Palladian pavilion, while in the rear it drops down in terraces of seven levels, to a formal garden, a holly garden, a bowling green, two small stone garden houses and a small family graveyard. These features, including an octagonal drawing room, are familiar to everyone who visits the many Virginian houses which were influenced directly or indirectly by the tireless architect of Monticello.

But Edgemont carried the influence even further, for two long underground passages lead from the lower floor of the main house to two matching dependencies, the one on the east containing—in the present restoration—a guesthouse and office, and the one on the west, servants' quarters and a garage.

It is believed that Colonel Cocke built the house between 1793 and 1797 and for more than thirty years pursued there the pleasant life of a country squire, creating the customs and repeating the stories which accumulate whenever a family stays in one spot long enough to consider it a permanent home. The grain mill nearby supplied their income, the water flowing from a spring up on the mountainside only fifty yards from the main building. Whenever Colonel Cocke was thirsty he would send a slave up to the spring to fill his favorite cup and bring it back. He refused to drink from any other cup, and this one is now in the possession of a citizen of Charlottesville.

When Colonel Cocke died, Edgemont passed to his eldest son's widow, and then to her heir, Judith A. Randolph. From

FIGURE 60. The Old Ivy Inn, which was built in 1812, was the home of Senator Thomas Martin for many years. During the War Between the States, it served as headquarters for General Sherman. It has identical porticos in the front and rear.

1862 to 1937 the property was held by a succession of owners.

It was not damaged in any way during the War Between the States, but gold from the Scottsville bank is supposed to have been buried somewhere near the front gate to save it from falling into the hands of the Northern soldiers. After the war, when the bank officials came to reclaim the gold, they were unable to locate it and, for all anyone knows, it is still missing.

The Yates family were in possession of the place for sixty years, twice as long as the Cocke family, and managed to accumulate some stories of their own. The most extraordinary one is about two maiden sisters who were living there when one of them died. The grieving survivor not only put herself in blackest mourning, but had the entire house, inside and out, painted jet black, of which dismal traces were to turn up years after when the restoration was begun.

The dates of subsequent ownerships are duly recorded, including those of a bootlegger who, during Prohibition, set up his still in the old kitchen, with the chimney serving as a convenient outlet for the smoke.

And then Edgemont—with its four porticoes, with its frame construction of eighteen-inch pine timbers filled with brick noggin and surfaced with wide flush boarding which simulated stone; Edgemont, with a fireplace in every room, with its wainscoting and floors of wide heart pine—disappeared.

There were rumors of such a place and an article about the Cocke family which appeared in the *Virginia Historical Magazine* in 1934 mentioned it, but despite the rumors and printed records, no one—not even the students of Jeffersoniana—seemed to know where it was or whether it even existed. It seems incredible that a house whose plans, showing its derivation from the Villa Rotonda of Palladio, drawn in Jefferson's own hand and preserved in the Coolidge collection in Boston, should be thus lost.

In 1935, Mr. Milton Grigg, a local architect, and Miss Frances B. Johnston, a professional photographer, were out hunting for old houses and noticed what appeared to be a ruin on a hill. The building itself was in a state of collapse: a grass fire had erased the gardens except for two box bushes and two oak trees. Weeds covered the yard, erosion had shattered the terraces. It was not until later, with the exploratory digging of trenches in search of original ground lines, that the conformation of the terraces, the ramps and the shallow rise of the bowling green were revealed.

After further investigation and meticulous measurement, it was concluded by experts that the plans had indeed been made by Jefferson—a discovery unnoticed by the general public and remarked by only a few students of Jefferson's life and works.

The house and its history, however, did appeal to one young man, a medical student at the University of Virginia, who bought the place in 1936 and began the restoration of the gardens, terraces, bowling green and garden walls. Work was suspended during World War II, and in 1946 Doctor Clarke was obliged to sell the property.

Now comes the final oddity about Edgemont. The picture of the house which accompanied the advertisement for its sale showed a dilapidated heap, suggesting not only long neglect

Photo by Holsinger Studio

FIGURE 61. The recently restored Edgemont incorporates a number of Jefferson's ideas. The front appears to be the façade of a one-story pavilion, while the two-storied rear drops down into terraced gardens on seven levels.

but almost complete decay. Abandoned and forlorn, it was the epitome of ruin and obscurity.

It was this very dilapidation which proved intriguing to Mr. and Mrs. William Snead. Mr Snead is a descendant of the Virginia family, now living in St. Louis. The Sneads were sure there were many elements which could be salvaged, many original features which could be restored. They bought the property and detailed and delicate restoration brought the house and grounds back to their pristine eighteenth-century atmosphere.

From the west, where the house appears to be only a single story in height, one enters a large wainscoted hall, while the two other side entrances open into a long corridor which divides the house longitudinally. Directly opposite the front door and across

185

the longitudinal hall, a bay projects, forming one side of the octagonal drawing room. This was originally the dining room, and at the entrance one notices a slight hollowed indentation of the floor boards, which is said to have been made by the slaves shuffling their feet as each waited his turn to carry in the covered dishes of hot food or bottles of wine.

The rooms on this floor are all small and all exquisite, and from it an elliptical stairway leads down to the ground floor where the present dining room opens out into the terraced gardens. A modern kitchen, servants' dining room, pantry, offices and storerooms are on this lower floor. The original kitchen fireplace, eight feet wide and five high, is preserved, with its two cranes and various iron utensils.

The other original fireplaces—there was one in every room— have been kept. Necessary structural reinforcements have been made as far as possible with the old wood and woodwork, put together with wooden pegs, and a few hand-cut nails have been utilized. The terraced gardens, with their seven levels and dry stone walls, are in perfect order, and the Sneads have added a swimming pool near the graveyard.

Thus Edgemont, having faded from remembrance and almost from sight, emerged in swift and surprising charm. The fact that it had been so long forgotten added to its appeal. When it was opened for the first time in Garden Week in 1951, a hundred and fifty people rode out to see it. The following year fifteen hundred found their way thither, each one regarding the lovely place with the air of an original discoverer.

chapter 15

HOSPITALITY, HORSES AND MONTPELIER

George Mason, enjoying his serene activities at Gunston Hall, advocated the inherent natural right of men not only to the enjoyment of life and liberty but to the pursuit and obtaining of happiness. The belief that such pursuit was worthy of men's efforts must have sounded Utopian and slightly immoral to those sterner colonies where happiness, to say nothing of pleasure, was regarded with suspicion.

It never sounded anything but admirable to Virginians to whom the joy of living was part of the reason for life itself. They built their homes with the idea of entertaining formally or informally but in either case frequently. They accepted as legitimate the expense of guests who came not for weeks but for months, bringing their own horses and servants—who had to be sheltered and fed.

It was not only in the great houses that pleasure was wooed and won. On a modest plantation in Louisa County the plans for a celebration which was to last several days included a corps of cobblers to half-sole the shoes of the dancers. In North Garden, on the line of Caroline and Spottsylvania Counties, the mistress, as she came downstairs in the morning, frequently saw the walls of the wide hall splashed with feathers and blood from the cock-fights of the night before. John Lee, a merry bachelor of West-moreland County in 1670, entered into an agreement with his neighbors, Thomas Gerrard and Isaac Allerton, to build a ban-queting hall at the point where their estates met and where annually each in turn should make "an honorable treatment."

"Blow high, Blow low, Virginians . . . will dance or die" ran the old saying, and although in many houses two parlors could be thrown together to make a ballroom, in others such a hall was provided for in the original plans. Sometimes a dancing pavilion was built at the same time as the house. Thus John Todd Payne, the son of Dolly Madison by her first marriage, when in 1840 he built Toddsberth near Montpelier, included near the house a circular building about thirty feet in diameter, to be used as a ballroom. Under the dance floor were basement compartments serving as an icehouse and wine cellar—a plan similar to that of the gaming pavilion at Prestwould.

While the moonlight and magnolia school of romanticists like to picture these balls as stately and decorous affairs, a descrip-tion of one by Philip Vickers Fithian—a young Englishman who was a tutor at Nomini Hall—suggests there were various degrees and fashions of jollity.

On May 18, 1774, Fithian recorded in his diary a ball "attended by over seventy persons, of whom forty-one were ladies." With occasional intermission for sleep the party continued for three days. The music "was from a French Horn and two violins. The ladies were dressed Gay and Splendid, and when dancing their skirts and brocades rustled and trailed behind them. . . . There were parties in rooms made up, some at Cards, some drinking for Pleasure, some toasting the Sons of America: some singing 'Liberty Songs' as they call them in which six, eight or ten or more would put their heads near together and roar."

Montpelier, the family homestead to which James Madison returned in 1817 after the expiration of his terms as President, was famous for its hospitality, but, it must be added immediately, this had little in common with the hilarious affairs such as fasci-nated Fithian.

James Madison was the fifth of his family on Virginia soil.

Photo by Dementi Studio

FIGURE 62. For three generations the Madison family lived at Montpelier, which was built by Colonel James Madison about 1756.

For three generations they had lived on the great estate of three or four thousand acres where his father was the richest and most important man in Orange County. The central part of the brick house—two rooms on both sides of the transverse hall on both floors—was built by Colonel James Madison about 1756. His son and namesake, after his marriage, enlarged the building, adding wings, a second story and a classic portico—reportedly suggested by his friend and neighbor, Thomas Jefferson—and changing the appearance of the exterior to stone.

During the sixteen summers while Madison was living in Washington, he supervised the administration of the plantation in Orange County—the tobacco fields which furnished the chief crop, the excellent vegetable gardens, the mills, and the slaves who took care of these things.

When he retired, while still taking an interest in public affairs, he was able to devote more time to the house, garden and land. He made the natural amphitheater in the rear into a large formal garden, following plans drawn by General Lafayette while visiting Montpelier in 1824. The descending terraces, box-bordered paths and geometrical flower beds were kept to perfection by a French gardener. The ex-President, now a country squire, planted with his own hands some of the trees which are still to be seen, notably the cedars of Lebanon considered by many the finest in this country.

While Dolly Madison loved the garden and adored the farm animals, she also took liveliest pleasure in furnishing and decorating the house.

Lighted by tall French windows and warmed throughout by great open fires—Jefferson sent one marble fireplace from France—it was cheerful, comfortable and extremely attractive. The windows were hung with light silken drapery, and there were French furniture, light chairs and gay carpets. Portraits and portrait busts gave a period touch to the drawing room.

Madison was primarily interested in the library and the dining room. And he kept adding to the volumes he had inherited by so many new purchases—not a few from France and England—that before his death he was literally crowded out and had to work in his sitting room.

His interest in the dining room centered around his enjoyment of entertaining. While every dinner was a ceremony, a formal one offered three or four kinds of meat, several kinds of bread, fresh vegetables, fruit pastry, champagne and ice (the ice-house can still be seen). If chance visitors arrived between meals "wine, ice punch and delicious pineapples were immediately brought."

Dolly, who has come down in history as the most accomplished hostess Washington ever knew, did not depend upon her personal glamour to please her guests. She was a most efficient housekeeper, although few realized her unceasing industry or time she devoted to her husband. In one of her letters she writes lightheartedly:

"Yesterday we had ninety persons to dine with us at one table, fixed on the lawn under a large arbor. The dinner was profuse and handsome and the company very orderly . . . we had no ladies except Mother Madison, Mrs. Macon and Nellie Willis. The day was cool and all pleasant. Half a dozen only stayed the night."

Her relationship with "Mother Madison" was entirely in keeping with her generous and tactful nature. When she and Madison came to live at Montpelier, they arranged the house so that the old lady kept her own apartments with her own staff of servants. By opening a door, Dolly could pass from her own light rooms into those where, amid heavily carved and polished mahogany, her venerable mother-in-law pursued the placid tenor of her ways—grateful to be spared the prolonged and ritualistic dinner parties which her son so enjoyed. Dolly took care that her mother-in-law's position should be regarded with respect and that guests should realize it was a favor and distinction to be admitted to the presence of the old lady.

This felicitous arrangement continued for many years, for James Madison's mother lived to be ninety-eight—her illustrious son survived her only seven years—during which time she became more and more dependent upon Dolly of whom she lovingly said, "She is my mother and tenderly cares for all my wants."

Surely one of Montpelier's greatest charms must have been the atmosphere of love and harmony which pervaded it.

As her husband—who was seventeen years her senior—became an invalid, his wife's attentions to him were unremitting.

One of the most intimate pictures of this singularly devoted and companionable couple has come to us from Harriet Martineau who visited Montpelier when Madison was eighty-three and because of his rheumatism confined to one room from nine in the morning until ten at night. Miss Martineau writes: "He was in his chair, with a pillow behind him, when I first saw him; his little person wrapped in a black silk gown; a warm gray and white cap upon his head, which his lady took care should always sit becomingly; and gray worsted gloves, his hands having been rheumatic. His voice was clear and strong, and his manner of speaking particularly lively, often playful. Except that the face was smaller, and, of course, older, the likeness to the common engraving of him was perfect. He seemed not to have lost any teeth, and the form of the face was therefore preserved, without any striking marks of age. It was an uncommonly pleasant countenance."

When the remarkable man died in 1836, his body was carried to the private burial ground, a small brick-walled graveyard not far from the house, and a hundred slaves stood weeping as James Barbour, his neighbor and friend, pronounced a eulogy. Dolly returned to Montpelier where she was to live for another year as a widow before she took possession of the house on Lafayette Square in Washington which was to be her home until her death.

She hoped at that time that she might spend her summers at Montpelier, but—largely due to the prodigality of her son—she was obliged to part with the beloved plantation. But after she died (1849) her body, having lain in the Congressional Cemetery for nine years, was taken back to Montpelier and placed near that of her husband in the brick-walled graveyard.

Madison lies under a gray granite shaft—a big monument for a small body and a great man. Dolly lies under one of white marble.

After having been bought and sold several times, Montpelier was purchased by William Du Pont, who, while carefully preserving the general appearance of the house, modernized and enlarged it to its present size of forty-four rooms. The gardens surpass even their original plan, with the cedars of Lebanon, planted by Madison. There may be seen not far from the house a small circular classical building which most people assume is a summerhouse. Originally it was an icehouse, said to be the first experiment in Piedmont Virginia of storing ice underground.

It is gratifying to those who like to picture the great plantation in its Madison heyday to know that not only the house and grounds, but the customs of hospitality are generously maintained by the present owner, Mrs. Marion Du Pont Scott, one of the foremost horsewomen in this horse-loving state.

Anyone who enters the wide grounds of Montpelier sees, sweeping away on either side of the main driveway, race tracks, with their starting gates, and the great house extending its classic façade as a background.

But once a year the scene is one of excitement, movement, color, hubbub and vivid pleasure. For here is held the Montpelier Hunt Race Meeting with horses being entered from the whole eastern seaboard and sometimes as many as four thousand spec-

FIGURE 63. The ex-President made the natural amphitheater in the rear into a formal garden, following plans drawn by General Lafayette while visiting Montpelier.

tators. Not only from neighboring counties in Virginia, but from distant states, they begin to arrive before noon and participate and picnic until dusk.

There is a grand parade of all the horses in front of the steward's stand en route for the starting point. Number cloths and arm emblems glint in the sunlight. There are steeplechases, hurdle races and flat races climaxing in money prizes (twelve hundred dollars is the highest) and awarding of plates, trophies and cups.

These Montpelier Hunt Races are under sanction of the Hunt's Committee of the National Steeplechase and Hunt Association, whose provisions, rules and decisions are scrupulously enforced. Since the first one in 1933 they have been made possible by the generosity and hospitality of Mrs. Scott, who is hostess and donor of the prizes. The magnificent Hunt Race Meeting at Montpelier is only one in the Calendar of Events.

Horses and everything to do with them bulk large in Virginia life. Beginning in March with the point-to-point races at Warrenton and Middleburg, the circuit shifts up and down and across the state. The Deep Run Hunt Race Meet at Richmond, in April, and the Flat and Steeplechase Race in Middleburg that same month, the Junior Horse Show in Lynchburg, The Stuyvesant School Horse Show at Fort Meyer, the Upperville Colt and Horse Show, the Warrenton Pony Show, the Pony Penny Day at Chincoteague Island and many many more fill the calendar from March to October. Fox hunting takes over from October to March at more than a dozen nationally recognized hunts, chiefly in Northern Virginia.

This is no recent fashion patronized only by the wealthy. From earliest days horses have been bred, trained, shown, raced and ridden on a state-wide scale. Thomas Anburey, a British officer who was a prisoner in Albemarle County wrote in 1779: "Near most of the ordinaries, there is a piece of ground cleared in the woods where there are two paths, about six or eight yards asunder, which the horses run in: this diversion is a great favorite of the middling and lower classes, and they have a breed of horses to perform it with astonishing velocity, beating every other for distance with the greatest ease. . . . It is the most ridiculous amusement imaginable, for if you happen to be looking another way, the race is terminated before you can turn your head; notwithstanding which, very considerable sums are betted at these matches."

There is no reason to think that the horse will diminish in popularity as long as Virginia offers its agreeable climate and terrain. Horse lovers from other states will come to make it their home, and every year there will be born a new and lusty crew of modified Mazeppas.

Photo by Holsinger Studio

FIGURE 64. For seventy years Barboursville was the center of hospitality and elegance. It was designed by Jefferson for his friend James Barbour, with a garden laid in formal squares with grass walks. It was burned on Christmas Day, 1884, and its vine-grown ruins have been permitted to stand in picturesque beauty.

chapter 16

FEDERAL HILL IN FREDERICKSBURG

The Daniels House, The Doggett House, Kenmore, Mary Washington House, Chatham

The ample two-and-a-half-story house of snowy white clapboard called Federal Hill in Fredericksburg is unlike the other houses in that honored old city. It is unlike houses elsewhere in Virginia.

This is not merely because the use of wood for such a large and fine building is unusual in a region where brick and stone are the more familiar materials, but because the uncompromising proportions and emphatic plainness give it an air of aristocratic aloofness, suggesting a Northern rather than a Southern residence.

As a matter of fact, Federal Hill is anything but aloof. It has been the center of everything that has ever occurred in Fredericksburg, where stirring events have crowded upon each other's heels for two centuries.

The precise date is not known when these walls of brick noggins were erected and covered with substantial clapboards, each with its beading, and cut from tulipwood which, while it becomes weatherworn, is almost impervious to decay.

It is generally supposed that it was built under orders from Queen Anne for purposes of state and as an official residence for

Sir Alexander Spottswood, one time Governor of Virginia and later Postmaster General of the Colony. At any rate, there is no doubt that the ghost in a pink coat not infrequently glimpsed—invariably near a sideboard or table with a punch bowl, and invariably raising a glass to drink to someone's very good health—resembles that lighthearted gentleman.

Another Governor of Virginia—Robert Brook, 1794–1796—bought it after the Revolution and named it Federal Hill in recognition of the Federalist Party, of which he was one of the founders.

Since then it has been bought and sold and inherited; lived in, loved, altered, repaired, neglected, forgotten, discovered and elbowed by the encroachment of newer buildings. It has been the scene of births, deaths, balls, banquets, shellfire and capture by opposing forces, and it has served as a wartime hospital.

At the time of the War Between the States, Federal Hill was directly in the line of battle and was bombarded by cross artillery fire from Marye's Heights, held by the Confederates, and from Stafford Heights, held by Union troops.

A hundred and thirty-five direct hits shook the old place—there are thirty-five metal patches over holes left by cannon balls on the north side alone—and only the substantiality of the construction and the thick growth of ivy saved it from complete demolition. Some of the cannon balls are still buried in the thick walls, but the bullets piled up everywhere like autumn leaves. Years after, when a stairway was built to the unused garret and dormer windows were to be inserted, the carpenters sought out Mrs. Wight, at that time the owner of the house, and asked for baskets. Mystified, she inquired why they needed baskets, and was told that when the opening was cut for the first dormer window and the light had poured in, they had seen so many bullets strewn on the lath and plaster ceiling that they had feared their weight would break through into the rooms below.

Mrs. Wight found baskets for them and, finally, after she had listened to the tramping up and down stairs for what seemed an interminable time, decided she would count the basketsful they were bringing down. After she had commenced this enumeration, the carpenters brought down twenty-four more basketsful.

FIGURE 65. Federal Hill, although struck 135 times by artillery fire, captured by enemy forces and used as a hospital, is still serene and distinguished.

The old house did more than serve as a target. A Union doctor, in search of a temporary hospital, found that the drawing room, twenty-one by thirty-three feet, extending the entire width of the house and with six large windows, was precisely what he needed for an operating room. It was, therefore, converted into one, and it is believed that Clara Barton nursed here.

In this same room, most carefully and correctly restored by the present owners—Dr. and Mrs. Richard Nunn Lanier—there is a dark stain on the floor between the two front windows, which scraping and sanding have never been able to erase.

It dates from the time when, by orders of General Lee, the house was evacuated at the approach of the Union Army. Some weeks later, the owner, returning with the Federal authorities, found that the door had been broken open, and at the end of the drawing room the body of a dead Union soldier stood, in a pool of congealed blood. He was leaning against a pilaster, held in this upright position by his arm, which was caught up by a picture frame, from which he had just cut out the portrait. It lay at his feet and on it his sword had fallen.

Bullets in the attic, blood stains on the drawing-room floor, a hundred and thirty-five direct hits on the walls—Federal Hill has survived them all. It has survived the battles which raged around it, when one could not walk on the streets without stepping on the dead and dying. It has survived the encroachment when Burnside's men dug the trenches whose indentations around the curved terrace are still visible.

Today the immaculate white house is composed and serene.

In the drawing room, which was used as a hospital, the fluted pilasters and cornice accentuate the graceful spread of the arches over the window alcoves, and the scrolled pediment over the mantel and the contrasting broken pediment over the door are in unblemished repair.

In the library opposite, the wainscoting, which is one solid piece of pine thirty-three inches wide, has been rubbed down to its basic finish and the cornice above has had restored to it its original rosettes of metal affixed by hickory pegs.

At one time the woodwork in this room was covered with painted murals depicting desert scenes, which were obliterated by a workman misunderstanding instructions. The hanging chandelier is a duplicate of the one which hung in Gadsby's Tavern in Alexandria and is now in the Metropolitan Museum in New York.

In the dining room—the favorite rendezvous of the convivial Sir Alexander Spottswood—the carving is most unusual, the space between the tops of the windows to the cornice being filled with a diamond-shaped latticed carving. The same fine work is repeated over the mantel.

Out of the paneled transverse hall a mahogany staircase sweeps to the third floor, and on either side of the front door are cupboards which once held firearms and ammunition.

Of these the most interesting is a flint-lock pistol which belonged to George Washington. It was made by Wilson of London, with a Queen Anne mask butt and a silver escutcheon.

Photo by Dabney Studio

FIGURE 66. The carving on the windows and mantel in Federal Hill is unusual and pleasing.

FIGURE 67. Kenmore was built by Colonel Fielding Lewis for his bride, who was the only sister of George Washington.

Fredericksburg was the center of the home life of the Washington family for forty-four years, and George Washington himself planted the thirteen horse chestnuts on the property—of which one remains—in recognition of the thirteen original colonies. Therefore it was appropriate that the house of his only sister, Mrs. Fielding Lewis, and the cottage where his mother lived, should have received attention.

Kenmore, built about 1752 by Colonel Fielding Lewis for his bride, is a two-story red brick house between a pair of detached wings. The gabled roof is pierced by built-in end chimneys, the simple framed entrance doors surmounted by rectangular transoms. This plain exterior does not prepare one for the extreme elaboration of the ceilings, and the overmantel panels —the most complicated decoration of the kind in Virginia.

When in 1922 the place was threatened by encroaching commercial interests, The Kenmore Association was formed, and this organization of local ladies went to work with right good will. They engaged the best architects and interior decorators; they acquired a really remarkable array of authentic eighteenth-century furniture, china, silver and glass. When the furnishings were complete and the grounds and gardens were restored by the Garden Club of Virginia, Kenmore could rightfully be claimed as one of the outstanding museums in America.

The white frame cottage of Mary Washington has received the same meticulous care. The middle section, built by her illustrious son in 1772, arises two stories from the simple doorway to the plain gable roof. Other sections were added later. The old-fashioned garden is in the rear with its original sundial and part of the box-bordered brick walk along which Mrs. Washington went for her daily call upon her daughter at Kenmore. It is rumored that Betty Lewis took the precaution of sitting near a window from which she could see the approach of the redoubtable old lady in time to hide behind the folding shutter the novel she was reading.

When the Association for the Preservation of Antiquities took over the cottage, it left the brick-floored kitchen and her sewing stand as they had been during the life of the mistress, and it has gradually added suitable additions.

The value of restoring such houses and opening them to the

FIGURE 68. The decoration of the ceiling and overmantels of KENMORE are the most elaborate and complicated in Virginia.

public is unquestioned. But visitors to Fredericksburg are frequently tempted to hunt out the quiet side streets whose names— Princess Anne, Prince Edward, Princess Elizabeth, George, William, Sophia and Amelia—date from the early days, and speculate about the low brick buildings with sloping slate roofs and dormer windows, and the white frame cottages and half-hidden "quarters" tucked away in the rear of larger buildings.

They will pause to look at the Doggett House, a brick mansion behind a grilled gate, and wonder if the old scenic wallpaper, The Monuments of Paris, is still upon the walls. This paper was printed by Dufour in 1815 and depicts the important buildings of Paris—l'Hôtel des Invalides, Beaux Arts, Arc de Carrousel, Colonne Vendôme, Nôtre Dame and others—move up along the banks of the Seine. It was immensely popular and at the time a set of the first edition sold for fifty francs, which may be compared with the set sold recently in New York for twenty-five hundred dollars. It may be seen in a number of old houses from Maine to South Carolina, but perhaps in no setting more appropriate than Doggett House, where the woodwork in the room on whose walls it is hung is picked out in gold leaf.

A stranger will not need to have the Daniels home pointed out to him, for this little old house—now divided into two littler ones—is so pleasing that it immediately catches the approving eye. It looks as if it might have been antique at the date signed on a certain deed which it preserves with other heirlooms. This deed is made out to George Washington by Fielding Lewis in 1781 and is one of the few signed by him and not by his agent. It states the obligation of "yielding and paying therefor the rent of one peppercorn upon the feast of day of St. Michael the Archangel."

The Gibson house—the oldest in town—suggests Mount Vernon with its high-pillared portico, but as a matter of fact this white frame wing is a fairly recent addition. The original section is that which is made of stone.

If the visitor is accompanied on his stroll by a native of the city, he will not escape without hearing about the soldier who was strolling past Federal Hill with his compass in his hand. There is some variation of the story. One says it was a Confederate soldier—another attributes it to a Union soldier. In either case a shot hit him in the arm and the compass sailed through the air and landed in a tree. He shook his head sadly, and continued on his way, nursing his arm. But thirty years later he thought better of it. He came back, located the tree and found the compass, still pointing faithfully to its designated direction. After shaking his head once more, the soldier again took his departure. Whether these details are accurate or not, the incontrovertible fact remains that the compass is still in the tree, deeply imbedded after almost a hundred years, but still faithful to its original duty.

There are plenty of things to see in Fredericksburg, but it is suggested that one lift one's eyes from the town and look across the river, where the rosy walls of Chatham rise in grassy terraces on the north bank of the Rappahannock. Sun-drenched and charming, it preserves its privacy behind a lawn with a columned summerhouse and gardens edged with box or enclosed by brick walls topped with pineapple decorations.

From the time it was built, some time between 1760 and 1770, it has always been the home of people who have loved it;

FIGURE 69. The entrance to Chatham is marked by unique wrought-iron grillwork.

its last owners—Mr. and Mrs. John Lee Pratt—preserved its original beauty while extending garden, guesthouse and pools. Since Mrs. Pratt's death in 1947, these have been kept as she left them.

One may stand under the well-kept trees and imagine the grace of living which has flowed behind these walls, from which the whitewash, flecking off, reveals the rosy speckle of the bricks below. Washington stayed here; Lee courted his wife beneath these trees. Madison, Monroe, Washington Irving and Lincoln have stood where we are standing looking out over the grassed terraces to the spires and roofs of Fredericksburg.

It is said that William Pitt, Earl of Chatham, commissioned Christopher Wren to draw the plans and then presented them to William Fitzhugh, who had been his classmate at Eton and Oxford and was at that time living in Virginia. Fitzhugh named the place for his friend and although it has passed through other hands since then, the name has been retained and the brick walls and slate roofs, the center doors with trim of cut stone instead of the usual wooden frames, are as solid as when they were built nearly two hundred years ago.

The principal old buildings of Fredericksburg are now so carefully listed and described, and the names of the many famous men who are associated with the town so thoroughly catalogued, that the stranger may wonder a little regretfully if there is a bit of legend left which is not worn smooth with repetition.

There is one such legend and since the place with which it is associated is now torn down and the principals are no longer living, perhaps if it is retold it may reach a new—and probably skeptical—ear.

There was at one time a house near Federal Hill which belonged to an old man, who refused to sell it, although he was by no means wealthy and was being pressed by an overeager buyer.

The old gentleman had fallen into the pleasant routine of strolling every Wednesday evening to the house of a friend and having supper with him. On Sunday mornings he went across the river to his sister's house and breakfasted with her on the porch. Except for these two modest ventures into the world, he stayed at home and took great satisfaction in keeping the place in his possession.

But the old gentleman died, as old gentlemen do, and he was hardly in his grave before the eager purchaser had concluded the deal with his heirs, bought the house and sent workmen early Monday morning to pull it down.

But in jig time the workmen came tearing back, threw down their tools and refused to proceed with the wrecking. They said they had no sooner raised the first pickax before a big black crow flew out of the empty house and attacked them so persistently and savagely that they ran for their lives.

The new purchaser loaded his gun and started toward the house, when he chanced to meet the sister, with whom the old gentleman had been accustomed to take Sunday breakfast; she told him of the most peculiar happening. It seemed that the morning before she had heard a sound and had come out on the porch where the breakfast table was set, and there, on the back of the chair in which her brother always sat, was perched a big black crow. He watched her with bright friendly eyes and head cocked on one side while she ate her solitary meal and then with a flirt of his tail flew away.

Somewhat sobered by this story, the purchaser of the house

waited a day or so, and then once again started out with his gun. This time he met the friend with whom the old gentleman customarily dined on Wednesday evenings. The friend remarked that the night before was the first time the old gentleman had not been with him and he was very depressed. And then, he added, when he went into the dining room he heard a whirr of wings, and in flew a big black crow who perched on the back of the chair where his friend used to sit and stayed with him during the meal.

No one seems to have heard the finale—whether the crow continued the weekly routine or vanished. Ultimately the purchaser must have got rid of him, for the house is long since torn down and a newer one looks across the street at Federal Hill.

chapter 17

BESIDE THE RAPPAHANNOCK

Elmwood, Gaymont

In Essex County, well back from the Rappahannock River and well back from the highway to Fredericksburg, stands Elmwood, splendidly unique among Virginia mansions.

It has stood thus, extending its hundred-foot length along the brow of a hill, overlooking the open meadows and wooded slopes of the valley, since 1774. Built of brick, its timbers and floors and walls so substantial, the rich detail of its exterior brickwork and the carving of its interior wood paneling so solid, that, in spite of vicissitudes, when it finally came into the possession of its present owner, its structural needs were merely some beams in the basement.

It is the design of Elmwood which makes it immediately striking. Its four corners are true to the four points of the compass; its immense length of a hundred feet and its comparatively narrow width of about thirty, assure that every breeze, every movement of air, every exposure of sunlight and shade can be regulated and enjoyed to the fullest advantage. This floor plan is so peculiarly suited to the Virginia climate that one is puzzled that it has not been more generally followed throughout the state, where the square design has been and still is prevailingly popular.

To be sure, Mount Vernon has a similar façade, although a few feet shorter, but being of frame, and shaded by a veranda running the full length of the south, it produces quite a different effect. Although Mount Vernon's wooden sheathing is painted to simulate stone, it is plain indeed compared to these brick walls, laid with unusual regularity in Flemish bond, with finely worked window arches and cornices, belt course and water table. Elmwood suffers from a cumbersome tower added, during the Victorian era of alterations, to the northeast corner, to carry the stairs which were removed from the hall. Although it has extensive farm buildings some distance away—it is at present specializing in cattle—it lacks the intimate dependencies of Mount Vernon. The last such structure—a small schoolhouse—crumbled to dust when confronted by the recent possibility of restoration.

Architects may quibble and measure and compare Elmwood to Mount Vernon and to Blandfield, also in Essex County and of approximately the same period, but Elmwood has nothing to fear from this talk of "scale," shortcomings of design or imperfections of carving. It is not only fundamentally satisfactory to gaze at, but invitingly livable. This is partly, as has been said, because of the way it is placed upon its chosen site, but also because a wide and airy north corridor crossing the central hall obviates the necessity of traversing one room to get to another, as at Mount Vernon. On the second floor a similar corridor extends from chimney wall to chimney wall, with the five bedrooms which open out of it having the advantage of southern exposure, and three of them with additional double exposure.

Elmwood has experienced many changes in its two hundred and eighty years of history. The land on which it stands was acquired in 1768 by Muscoe Garnett, and much of the material required for the house was brought by water from Baltimore. However, the site chosen for the house was not near the river, for rumor had it that malaria lurked along low river lands, and it was therefore decided to place Elmwood on an elevation about two miles inland.

If, in this day of good roads and automobiles, the estate seems more or less remote from anywhere—it is, actually, thirty-

FIGURE 70. Elmwood, a hundred feet long and about thirty wide, assures every exposure of sunlight and shade to fullest advantage. In the old days forty-two servants—not counting farm laborers and artisans—were employed in the house and immediately surrounding gardens and lawns.

five miles from Fredericksburg—it is sometimes assumed that it must have been isolated indeed in its early days. We forget that those were the times of big families, with one generation crowding on the heels of the preceding one, so that even in a house of these dimensions and vistas, there could have been no such thing as loneliness. Neither was there undue crowding. There was plenty of room in the cool upper hall for the ladies to foregather and chat and sew and knit; plenty of acreage for the men to traverse on horseback, supervising the farming operations and, when that business was seen to, to go hunting. Plenty of space in the dining room and ballroom for the entertainment of guests; plenty of room for the children to play in the shrubbery and around the numerous outbuildings and on rainy days to explore those dim

209

attics and the cellar rooms with ponderous doors and gigantic wooden locks and queer niches and grated windows. Even plenty of room, as the oldsters stepped off the stage, for them to be given ample graves in the iron-railed burial ground not too far from the garden on the south side, outlined in holly and box, where the spring flowers come up every year and incredibly tall crape myrtles display their polished trunks and shake out their blossoms.

Besides the family and kinsfolk, besides the visitors who came for a week to six weeks, or six months, there was an army of blacks. Old household records list forty-two house servants—not counting farm laborers and artisans—who were kept occupied (more or less) merely in the house and in the immediately surrounding gardens and lawns.

The Garnett family was a distinguished one, and it intermarried with other distinguished families, so that their names are found not only throughout the annals of Virginia, but of Maryland and Washington. We find them as officers in every war, as statesmen in legislatures and in Congress, on the Board of Visitors of the University of Virginia and as its benefactors.

Neither did they confine their marriages to the South, and one of their Northern alliances precipitated a lively incident during the Civil War. The Honorable Muscoe Russell Hunter Garnett (1821–1864) married Mary Picton Stevens, daughter of Edwin A. Stevens, of Castle Point, New Jersey, who founded the Stevens Institute of Technology. Incidentally, Mr. Stevens was not only an inventor and a man of wealth, but a well-known yachtsman and one of the crew which sailed the yacht *America* to its first victory over the Royal Yacht Club at Cowes, England, in 1851. Later, Mr. Stevens was made Commodore of the New York Yacht Club. He was also a parent of that authoritarian stamp which has become almost as obsolete as the forty-two household servants at Elmwood.

His daughter was now a widow, with two small children—a son of three years and a daughter of nine months—living at Elmwood. The men had all gone and there were left on the place only a few elderly female relatives and some women servants. Mrs. Garnett's Northern father had no intention of letting her remain in such a barbarous region, remote and unprotected, and sent word for her to come home. She declined his invitation and continued to live serenely in the house and on the place which suited her very well. The Commodore went storming to President Lincoln, and arranged to have a gunboat, under Captain Dod, make its way up the Rappahannock and anchor off the Garnett estate during the night. Captain Dod followed directions and after anchoring took an armed escort and proceeded to Elmwood, waited on Mrs. Garnett and delivered her father's ultimatum that she and the children were to come with him instantly. Mrs. Garnett refused with spirit worthy of the Commodore. Finally, Captain Dod compromised. He said Mrs. Garnett might stay until morning, but if she refused to come then, he would be obliged to carry her and the children to the gunboat by force. The lady saw no way out of submitting. She and the children went back North and stayed with the Commodore until the end of the war.

It should be added, however, that as soon as hostilities ceased, she returned like a shot to Virginia and Elmwood. Subsequently she remarried, and when her husband—Edward Parke Custis Lewis, a nephew of General George Washington—was appointed United States Minister to Portugal, she again found herself obliged to leave Elmwood, and she and her children lived abroad.

And then began a period when the great house was to stand empty for nearly seventy years.

It still remained in the Garnett family; the farms were still cultivated and the house itself was supposed to be aired and kept in repair. But it was temptingly filled with valuables and temptingly distant and concealed from the farmhouses. As befitted a house of its magnitude, a robbery was planned on a similar scale. Thieves obtained plans of the house, a description of the furniture, portraits, china and silver, and their exact location in each room. They came with a truck through the garden to the south entrance—the one farthest removed from possible sight of the farm buildings—and with the truck piled high with ancestral pieces drove away absolutely unseen and never to be traced.

After this, a little late in the day to be sure, the house was tightly boarded up. For seventy years it remained unoccupied. The plaster flaked and fell from the ceilings; the somber Victorian colors darkened the rooms and the Victorian porch over the south entrance completed the gloom.

And then in 1943 Elmwood came into the possession of its present owner, Muscoe Russell Hunter Garnett, of New York, the fifth in the line of Garnett ownership.

Once again the doors and windows were flung wide and the breeze blew through the wide corridors. Some of the more distressing Victorian touches were removed. The thirty-by-twenty ballroom, with its medallioned cornice and elaborately carved pedimented overdoors and overmantel, was restored to its original blue. Family portraits look down upon another generation of the same name living in the old place for many months a year. A youthful Mrs. Muscoe Garnett plants young holly trees along old boundaries. Two small Garnett children play in the shrubbery, and on rainy days investigate the same attics and cellars which intrigued their great-grandparents, doubtless puzzling over the discarded old-fashioned bathtubs, homemade shower stalls, round tin-hat tubs, sitz tubs and bidets which form a sort of domestic museum of the seven ages of plumbing.

Suitable furniture is gradually being acquired to fill the pillaged spaces and the eager house owners, like householders everywhere, discuss the advisability of changes. Shall they take out the remaining panes of Victorian stained glass still bordering some of the windows? Shall they tear down the extraneous tower which holds the stair and put the stairs back in their original position? And what was the original position?

Like the best of old homes all over the world, Elmwood is again a new home. Portraits of Garnett ancestors are all very well and should be honored. The tablelike gravestone, decorated with carved corn stalks, which states that James Mercer Garnett who lies beneath was "a staunch republican" is properly respected. But certain modern changes have followed modern needs.

Thus, what was once the dining room has become an up-to-date kitchen, and what was once the library has become the dining room. The books, which for so long lined its walls, had been collected by the grandfather and the father of that Muscoe R. H. Garnett who made a brilliant record at the University of Virginia and later served on its Board of Visitors. He not only pored over the handsomely bound, well-read and well-handled volumes, but added to them, until his scholarly tastes made the library one of the most complete of the period.

FIGURE 71. Gaymont has overlooked the Rappahannock for more than two hundred years. The scenic wallpaper, brought from France in 1815, depicts the Bay of Naples and Vesuvius. The octagonal room, with a convex center, crowned by a cupola, is beyond the hall and projects into the garden.

It was this Muscoe Garnett who, dying at forty-two (1864), left the spirited young widow who, with her son and daughter, was so unwillingly conveyed North by the gunboat. More than half a century was to pass before the boy died and Elmwood came into the possession of his sister, Mrs. Clayton Mitchell. And another quarter century slipped away until, at her death, the library was bequeathed to the University of Virginia, not only as a memorial to her father, but as a valuable representation of the library of a Virginia gentleman.

A special room in the Alderman Library at the University was prepared to receive it, and here the old books and some of the old furniture are again arranged as they were at Elmwood more than a century ago.

Thus the generations pass, but the ancient homestead remains, serenely retaining its tangible and intangible treasures.

Elmwood's neighbor, Gaymont, escaped the malaria of the lowlands by perching itself high above the river. Thus on a clear day one can look out from the long sweeping terraces upon a thirty-five-mile panorama, and see beyond the highway the glint of the river and Port Royal.

After Gaymont was built—the date of the two-story central portion is given as 1725—it saw Port Royal made into a town (1744) trading directly with Old World ports. It saw it become so prosperous that it made a bid as the site for the seat of our Federal Government. It saw it, with the coming of the railroad, slip quietly back into a village, with white frame houses behind white picket fences, and motels flocking to welcome the James Madison Memorial Bridge.

Under its original owners Gaymont was called Rose Hill, but when John H. Bernard, to whom it was left by his grandfather, brought his bride, Jane Gay Robertson, to it in 1815, he renamed it in her honor. It was this young couple who were to become the grandparents of the present owners, the Robbs.

During its more than two hundred years Gaymont has undergone changes natural to shift of ownership and progress of time. But they have been so gradually assimilated that at first glance one cannot be sure what is new and what is old.

It is all old, as a matter of fact. You have only to step up on the six-pillared portico, closed at each end by later additions, and see the dusty white plaster busts of Shakespeare and Milton, Scott, Byron, Napoleon and Washington ranged in a row against the wall, to step into a period of the past.

The original two-story central portion is of frame, and to it were added brick wings with curiously shaped chimneys whose age baffles the architects.

In the entrance hall, with its elliptical arch, still hangs the scenic wallpaper brought from France in 1815, depicting the Bay of Naples and Vesuvius—those views so dear to our forefathers. Beyond the hall is the octagonal music room, which was added in 1830 and projects into the garden. The high ceiling converges into a convex center crowned by a cupola through which filters the golden sunlight, while the antique wallpaper of French gray, suggesting drapery, is caught by pictured golden rings. In this room, which must have been truly elegant in its day, hangs a portrait of Jane Gay Robertson.

In the dining room stretches the long table where seats for sixteen were once customary. On the square piano in this same room is the music box which belonged to Jeb Stuart. He carried it with him on his campaigns and its tinkle was a familiar sound to his companions.

At this writing, Gaymont is closed to tourists, and like a very frail, very old lady seems to be fading away from the world. The firm hand of restoration is still suspended in mid-air.

And yet, despite its threatened dissolution, it is still charming.

Inside, everything is hushed and static. Outside, vigorous English box encircles each end of the wings and in the spring syringa flows like perfumed fountains along the garden walks. And always, always from the terraces the superb view sweeps to the horizon.

Whether the infirm old lady will ultimately submit to having her face lifted, her hair shampooed and waved, and her fingernails enameled, remains to be seen. In the meanwhile, she dozes undisturbed through the passing seasons, breathing gently in repose after two hundred years of gentle living.

chapter 18

STRATFORD

Stratford Hall, massive, low and neighborless, overlooks the Potomac River in Westmoreland County. Its brick walls are ponderous; its two groups of enormous chimneys—four in each group —sustain heavily molded tops. The outside flights of stairs, which march up to the entrances, are monumental.

One reason the mansion does not immediately appeal to certain tastes is because it is entirely unlike others in the South to which they are accustomed, having been built to conform to a plan which was favored in Elizabethan and Jacobean times, but was never adopted in Virginia. This plan is simple enough. It is in the form of the letter H. The bar of the H is a great hall thirty feet square. On either end of the hall, and opposing it at right angles, are four rooms, thus making nine rooms on this main floor.

Braving the steps which make no concession to curves, one enters the heavily paneled hall, with pilasters carrying around the four walls and framing the openings. The importance of this room is further emphasized by recessing the ceiling into the roof space, thus creating a clear height of nearly eighteen feet.

Although the high basement, or ground floor, provides a

number of rooms and, although the attic is vast, the stairways to these upper and lower floors are so narrow and so deliberately inconspicuous that the first impression on entering is of a house built on one floor.

The solidity and forthrightness of the quadrangular mass are heightened by its position on the site chosen for it. It is set in the center of a square parterre, the corners of which are defined by four dependencies. Its box garden to the east is laid out with geometric precision.

This robust and masculine house was the home of a robust and masculine family. Thomas Lee, the only native Virginian to be appointed by the Crown as governor of the colony, built it about 1725–1730. It was a fitting birthplace for thirty-two of his distinguished descendants—governors of the state, members of the Council and of the House of Burgesses, two signers of the Declaration of Independence, the foremost cavalry officer of the Revolution, with the line culminating in the heroic and honored Robert E. Lee.

The history of the house is the history of the family. The history of the family is interwoven with the history of the United States.

It is proper that these records should be starred with the names of men whose personalities and contributions to our country are so conspicuous. Not so well known is the name of one of its women, who sounded an astonishingly carrying note above a chorus dominated by basses and baritones.

Thomas Lee and his wife, Hannah Ludwell, had eleven children, of whom two died in infancy. Eight sons became men of recognized standing. Their third child and first daughter, Hannah, was quite as remarkable in her way.

Hannah (1728–1782) grew up well trained by her mother in household management and encouraged by her father in an interest in reading—her own nature inclining her to books on religion.

That she was competent we know, for besides her domestic accomplishments, she learned to bind books and even to make furniture. That she was independent and courageous must have evidenced itself early, although it did not come to its full testing until later.

When she was twenty, Hannah was married in the great hall

Photo by Thomas F. Scott

FIGURE 72. This front view of Stratford shows the distinctive H form, unusual in Virginia, and also the high basement, its bricks laid in Flemish bond with decorative glazed headers. Tradition says Philip Ludwell Lee built a promenade on the roof, the two groups of chimneys serving as two summer-houses, with musicians playing in one of them.

at Stratford to Gawen Corbin, and thereupon became mistress of his home, Peckatone Plantation, twenty miles away—at that time not an inconsiderable distance.

Peckatone was one of the landmarks of lower Westmoreland, and, judging from its inventories, had its full share of comforts and luxuries, including family portraits, a harpsichord, mahogany furniture and heavy silver plate engraved with the Corbin arms.

Hannah not only managed the house efficiently, but found scope for her practicality in improving the plantation and in assisting in the development of other Corbin properties. When her husband died, she felt fully competent to take over their management.

She was to show her initiative along other lines when she left the Church of England and entered the Baptist Society, fully aware of the unpopularity of that sect. Although she was presented to the Grand Jury "for not appearing in her parish Church for six months past," she refused, from the time of her conversion, to attend any services at the Established Church and until her death remained a fervid upholder of the Baptist Society.

Her ability in practical affairs and her independence of thought and action increased her self-confidence, which was sharply challenged by her husband's will. He left her all his estate, both real and personal, only if she remained a widow and continued to live in this country.

Hannah was indignant.

She had long resented the fact that women, and particularly widows, were obliged to pay taxes when they had no hand in the framing of laws or any voice in the election of officers who disbursed such sums. Briefly, Hannah believed in women's rights and was one of America's first suffragists.

By her husband's will she was confronted with a double injustice. If she did not remarry, she would be forced to pay taxes on property without being permitted to vote. If she did remarry, she would forfeit two thirds of the estate, in whose improvement she had so large a contributing part. Her husband's will insulted her principle as to women's rights, and included what she felt was a curtailment of her personal life.

She refused to appear in court as co-executor with her brothers, Richard Henry, Thomas Ludwell and Francis Lightfoot Lee, and apparently refused to pay the fine imposed upon her for not appearing.

She could not escape taxation without representation, but she could manage to keep the entire estate while living her life as she saw fit. She was only thirty-two—a widow with one daughter. She had fallen deeply in love with Dr. Richard Lingan Hall, a physician of highest standing and a man of highest integrity. Two years after her husband's death she arranged for him to come to Peckatone to live, while she continued to enjoy and manage the Corbin estate. She signed herself Hannah Corbin, Widow, and even gave the name of Corbin to the two children she had by Dr. Hall, although in some of her last papers she does allow the name

FIGURE 73.   The austerity of the east façade of Stratford Hall is softened by the planting of the Garden Club of Virginia.

of Hall to appear. Dr. Hall recorded approval of her decision when he made a formal deed of gift to his daughter whom he calls "my dearly beloved daughter Martha Corbin, youngest daughter of Mrs. Hannah Corbin."

It is true that by her refusal to change her legal status as "widow" Hannah did not forfeit two thirds of her husband's estate, and this might seem a sufficient reason. But another less materialistic fact may have influenced her. At the time she decided upon the step, the Baptist Society did not have its own form for the solemnization of marriage. Hannah would have had to subscribe to the ritual of the Church of England and this she positively refused to do. Later, when marriage ceremonies by dissenting ministers became valid, there is no record that she availed herself of the opportunity to legalize her position.

For nearly eighteen years she and Dr. Hall lived together as man and wife, never losing the affection of the Lee family or the respect of their friends. The doctor died in 1778 and four years later Hannah was buried in his grave.

The great hall at Stratford which had been the scene of Hannah's marriage to Gawen Corbin was to be the stage for eighty years of gaiety and tragedy, hopes and humiliations.

It is pleasant to think of the happy periods when the immense fireplace, twelve feet wide, six feet high and five feet deep, in the kitchen building (now restored) prepared the daily dinners and the feasts for holidays. Pleasant to remember the tradition that on the roof Philip Ludwell Lee built a promenade and that the two groups of chimneys served as the columns for two summer-houses, and in the evenings a band of musicians played in one of them, while the ladies and gentlemen strolled or danced on the cool and airy promenade.

On the river there was a pleasure barge, and from here, too, the music could be heard. In the long brick stables the horses of the horse-loving family were groomed, and in the carriage house the chariots and carriages brought from England, the harnesses, saddles and bridles were kept polished and ready to be used at a few minutes' notice.

Nothing was too good for his two pretty daughters, Matilda and Flora, and their indulgent father engaged a dancing master to instruct them. The classes were attended by girls and boys from the neighboring plantations, and there was never lack of company or fun.

This hall must often have been traversed by General Henry Lee—Light-horse Harry—intrepid and dashing general of Washington Cavalry and Governor of Virginia. The popular young man married his cousin Matilda—she who loved to dance. When she died, leaving a son—sometimes called Black-horse Harry to distinguish him from his father—Light-horse Harry married again. He was Governor of Virginia at this time and Ann Hill Carter of Shirley, seventeen years younger, was quite swept off her feet when he courted and married her and took her back to Stratford.

And now the shadows began to slant across the great hall.

General Lee was brilliant on the battlefield, successful as Governor, tender as a husband and father and charming as a host.

Photo by Thomas F. Scott

FIGURE 74. The Great Hall at Stratford is heavily paneled and thirty feet square. Its importance is further emphasized by recessing the ceiling into the roof space, thus creating a clear height of nearly eighteen feet.

But he was not fitted for the intricate business of running the great plantation at Stratford, with its farms and gardens; its mills, smithy, smokehouse and meat house and springhouse; its wharf, stables and dairies with all their equipment and their hordes of Negroes, some of whom labored and some of whom loafed, but all of whom had to be supervised and supported.

It was not only the burden of the plantation which was crushing. He had never received or even asked for a return from the government of the many thousands of dollars he had spent from his private purse in 1776 to equip cavalry troops with arms, ammunition, horses and provisions. Even more than its indebtedness to him, he was apprehensive about the state of the country for which he had sacrificed his fortune and many years of his life. These were anxious years for him, and lonely years for Ann when he was away, leaving her alone with the children.

Every year the situation became worse. General Lee's high

political offices had always brought him more prestige than cash, but they had meant some sort of a regular income, even if a small one. Now there was not even that, and when Ann and the children went to visit her mother at Shirley the carriage in which she had come from Stratford broke down. It was the last of that once glittering array in the old coach house, and she was forced to prolong her visit to an embarrassing length while her husband tried desperately to procure some sort of a vehicle to bring her back home.

The best he could do, at long last, was to procure an open carriage, and when the family arrived they found the house so deathly cold that they made no attempt to heat it, but bundled themselves as best they could into the cramped quarters of the east wing for the rest of the winter. Maybe the wintry rains that beat against the windows seemed like tears to Ann, with four young children, and terrified by the continually threatening clouds of financial disaster.

Perhaps there was a momentary burst of sunshine when her fifth child was born, and she named him for her two favorite brothers, Robert and Edward Carter of Shirley. Perhaps, like all mothers, she hoped he would become a great and good man.

If the wolves of fear prowled ever closer and closer around Stratford when little Robert E. Lee was growing up, he was oblivious to them. He did not wonder about his father's mysterious absence and equally accepted the family's move to Alexandria (1811) leaving Stratford Hall to his older half brother, another Henry Lee. He remembered his birthplace through the haze of childhood joys, and its garden as a place where he had chased butterflies. Like any child, he was delighted when his father rejoined his family, not knowing that for nearly two years he had been imprisoned for debt. It would be a long time before he would appreciate that during those years his father, like Sir Walter Raleigh in similar circumstances, triumphed over physical humiliation and distress. Like Sir Walter, Harry spent much time in writing and his *Memoirs of War in the Southern Department of the United States* became the source book of the American Revolution in the South.

Ann had been glad enough to leave Stratford and move to a scene unassociated with the family's distress and humiliation, and

Major Henry Lee was ready to take over the estate which was legally his.

The son of Matilda and Light-horse Harry, Black-horse Harry was a man of immense charm. He enjoyed hunting and sports of all kinds and the company of attractive women, and he chose one of the prettiest when he married Anne McCarty. Anne was one of two sisters, both of whom were accomplished, lively and extremely wealthy. She brought with her silver and linen to refurnish the shabby and depleted house, and when her sister Elizabeth joined the young couple a little later, she, too, brought her own maid and turned her fortune over to her brother-in-law, who became her guardian.

This brief period of love and laughter was not to last, and was never again to be repeated. Disaster followed disaster. Black-horse Harry, like his father, was unfitted to handle so large an estate. He was accused, among other things, of misappropriating the funds his young sister-in-law had entrusted to him as her guardian. Furthermore, the relationship between the two gave rise to a scandal which Elizabeth strove to expiate by wearing black the rest of her life, and Anne, the betrayed wife, was sent to a sanitarium to recover her shattered health.

Later the court gave Stratford to Elizabeth as compensation for her money, and she lived out her days there as Mrs. Storke. At her death the estate passed to her relatives, the Stuarts, who are buried in the garden. From them the Robert E. Lee Memorial Foundation, Incorporated, purchased it in July, 1929, and since then its gardens have been restored by the Garden Club of Virginia.

Light-horse Harry had listened to the wolves of apprehension howling ever nearer his home. His son heard actual wolves from the forest and, so reduced was he, he wrote to his friend and neighbor, Robert Carter at Sabine Hall, asking for the gift of three or four dogs to keep away the murderous marauders.

The dark period in the life of Colonel Harry came out into a brighter one when, rejoined by his wife, he redeemed his reputation by a brilliant diplomatic career abroad.

Stratford Hall is an austere building. But the somberness of its heavy walls is relieved by variations in the brickwork. On the ground floor or basement, the large bricks are laid in Flemish bond, with decorative glazed headers. The first floor is pinkish red without glazed headers. The windows and the corners of the building are bordered by rubbed red brick. Thus across the stern walls there plays a pattern of light and shade, and across the crowded family history are discerned figures of brilliance, of frailty, of courage and despair.

The room at the right of the entrance is called the Mother's Room and in it were born an unparalleled number of distinguished men of the Lee family. In one of its darkest hours, on January 19, 1807, here a child came into the world who was to be acknowledged as one of the greatest generals and one of the noblest characters this country has ever known.

Stratford Hall is a supremely masculine house. The events which stemmed from here and the deeds, good and bad, of the men who called it home were masculine deeds. The women who were brought here as wives or were born here as daughters seem to have had especial fortitude and courage.

But there is one room where all the associations are soft and relaxed. This is the small one adjoining the Mother's Room, and here Robert E. Lee slept in his swinging cradle. He heard no howling of wolves, figurative or literal. He was oblivious of the mountains of perplexity and pain which had beset his kinsfolk before him and were, in time, to beset him. On the fireback in this room is a reminder of that brief babyhood. On it are the heads and wings of cherubs.

chapter 19

THE EASTERN SHORE

Eyre Hall, Kerr Place, Seven Gables, Corbin Hall, Wharton, Hills Farm, Warwick, Elkington, Arlington

The Eastern Shore of Virginia is the end of the peninsula which lies between Chesapeake Bay and the Atlantic Ocean. Although it was one of the original shires of Virginia, created in 1634, an astonishing number of Virginians have never braved the ferry trip across the bay to make its acquaintance.

The loss is all theirs. For three hundred years the Eastern Shore has managed to get along without undue dependence upon the Western Shore. It has managed its business and built its delightful small houses and its fine mansions, embowered in fruits and flowers, surrounded by waters dancing with succulent fish, and by shores which are the chosen habitat of oysters and scallops, clams and crabs.

The charms and wealth, actual and potential, of this region were early recognized by men who chose it as a place to build their homes. While many of the smaller houses and some of the larger ones have disappeared, there are more than enough left to illustrate the history and culture of this part of Virginia.

Eyre Hall, although it dates from 1775, is not the oldest of the great houses, but it typifies many of their characteristics and attractive features, besides having the distinction of having been kept in the same family and in loving repair since it was built.

It is in Northampton County—the Eastern Shore is divided into two counties, Northampton occupying the southern one third and Accomack the northern two thirds—and it is reached by a long, tree-lined driveway, and framed by a great green lawn sweeping down to the water. Indeed, on this peninsula, which varies from twelve miles to four in width, a house does not have to be old or costly to enjoy a setting which includes great trees, verdant lawns and view of creek or cove, bay or ocean.

Those visitors who are convinced that the Eastern Shore is most inconveniently isolated, find their conviction strengthened by the distance of Eyre Hall from the highway and by their first sight of the long clapboard house, out of sight of all immediate neighbors.

It is gleamingly white and the finely detailed wooden fence which surrounds it is white; the roofs are of varying elevations and with many chimneys. With its additions and outbuildings, it steps down through the centuries and up and down through architectural periods.

It may seem far from the highway, but once it is reached it is accessible and friendly. A sign cordially inviting the public to visit the gardens at all times is a further hospitable token.

The moment one steps into the white paneled hall the hospitality is verified. Everything is spacious and cheerful, fresh with light colors and breezes from the water. To be sure, it is an old room. Its cornice is heavy and the furniture stands where it was placed a century or more ago. This small barrel organ with gilded dummy pipes was made in London at the time of the Regency. That game table has corner pockets of polished wood which often held kernels of corn instead of poker chips.

The entrance hall is spanned by a wide arch and beyond it becomes almost another room, out of which the staircase rises. For in contrast to the tranquil white paneling of the entrance, this section is animated by scenic wallpaper, full of movement, light and shade. Hung not in strips but in squares, the soft, perfectly clear colors reveal scene after scene along the banks of the Bosphorus. Pleasure boats gleam on the water, and on the shore rise minarets and domes, and tropical trees wave feathery branches.

FIGURE 75. Eyre Hall, on the Eastern Shore, has been kept in loving repair by the same family since it was built in 1775.

Palanquins are passing, figures wearing turbans or clad in burnooses kneel or stand. Fishermen work over their nets, the rug seller displays his wares, and the glint of the fabled water on the papered wall seems a slanting reflection of the familiar water of Cherry Stone Creek lying just beyond the windows. This paper, which was recently removed and repaired and replaced upon properly restored walls by experts from the Metropolitan Museum in New York, is now in flawless condition. Manufactured by Dufour about 1816, and sometimes called the Rug Seller or Lallah Rookh, it makes the hall a fitting prelude to the other rooms which are maintained in similar authenticity and good taste.

In the dining room, for instance, are many pieces of Lowestoft which were first brought from England and later shipped to China to be given the Eyre crest, and which now, after so many journeys on far oceans, have come to rest, one hopes in perpetuity, in Eyre Hall.

In this same room there is a large silver bowl called the "Morning Star Bowl," after a favorite horse. Morning Star won a race in 1672 and did it so magnificently that his jubilant owner filled this bowl with champagne and with his own hands carried it out to the winner, who is supposed to have quaffed it with relish. As to the effects, legend sayeth not. At any rate, here is the bowl, quite modern in design and certainly of most generous proportions.

The present owners, Mr. and Mrs. Henry Du Pont Baldwin, have not spared research, patience or money in the affectionate preservation and necessary remodeling of the place. In the paneled library hang gold brocade curtains which were made, not for this house, but for that of a kinsman, in honor of the reception for Lafayette. They have been miraculously cleaned and repaired.

In spite of such meticulous preservation of antiques, there is nothing of a museum atmosphere about Eyre Hall. Severn Eyre, whose portrait by the younger Hesselius hangs over the mantel in the parlor, with a signed copy by Sully in the library, may have found a washbowl and pitcher sufficient for his needs. But Severn Eyre died in 1773 and his present descendant, Mrs. Baldwin, has seen to it that bathrooms—one very cozy with an open fireplace—have been cunningly and plentifully inserted. A modern kitchen replaces the one which filled a separate brick building, now vanished. Even as recently as Mrs. Baldwin's childhood, it was the custom, during hot summer days—although not so hot on the Eastern Shore as on the Western—to close all the windows, pull down the shades, and shut the four doors which open into the hall, and sit in the airless dark. Now doors and windows are opened wide, and although the old marble steps still lead from the west entrance to the lawn and to the water, the porch is screened against mosquitoes.

Similar steps lead to the garden on the north, where sanded walks, neatly raked, thread the green gardens of box and yew, holly and magnolias, fringe trees and laurel. The ruined walls of what was once an orangery cast a romantic shadow across the pristine freshness of the garden, confined by a picket fence set above a brick wall—a garden to which the public is always welcome.

Eyre Hall is far enough away from the highway, and the Eastern Shore is far enough away from the Western Shore to preserve its air of isolation. But it must have seemed as remote as another world to the little sixteen-year-old bride who was once brought here from Baltimore. She was a wife, to be sure, but she was hardly out of childhood and she was homesick. So her husband brought her a pair of roller skates and she skated up and down the wide hall—under the arch, past the Regency barrel organ, with gilded dummy pipes, past the game table, under the arch again, and past the rug seller on the banks of the Bosphorus, and back again under the arch and past the barrel organ. The little mistress of the great house is long since dead—she died within a year in childbirth—but in a paneled cupboard in the paneled hall are her skates—small black wooden skates, each with four little wooden wheels painted red, and fastened one behind the other, down the middle.

People who live on the Eastern Shore like to say that nobody here is very rich and nobody very poor—a claim which is, however, refuted by the fact that until about twenty years ago Accomack County was the richest county per capita in the whole United States.

While this is no longer the case, a drive down the Ocean Highway passes level, fertile pastures and truck gardens, cultivated to finest tilth, passes storage plants and produce exchanges close to the railroad, threads its way through industrious villages, with comfortable white houses behind wide lawns, all testifying to today's prosperity.

Many of the houses—of an extremely pleasing architectural proportion distinctive to this region—are of frame, some of the oldest being frame with brick ends. Many have been added to again and again, until they are far from small. All are trimly kept and attractive, with flower gardens whose colors are intensified by the sea air, in bloom for weeks longer than those on the Western Shore.

The people on the Eastern Shore who are proud of not being purse-proud are confronted with other contradictions. How, for instance, did Kerr Place come to be built, enlarged, and continue to be maintained if no one is rich? For Kerr Place is a large and handsome Georgian mansion which takes a rightful place beside any of the large and handsome Georgian mansions of Virginia.

It is set far back in a green lawn and approached by a circling drive, in the town of Onancock. Since 1779, when it was built by John Sheppard Kerr, it has stood thus, the finely carved detail of its front door, the paired modillions under the eaves and about the pediment, immediately stating its age and elegance.

The classic proportions belong to any architectural period, but the ivy mantling the two-story façade could attain such thickness only with years, and when we step into the airy entrance hall, our eye is caught by an old-fashioned detail which has been retained—in spite of such modern innovations as coat closets and powder rooms.

This is a coat rail, shoulder high, with handmade pegs, which in the old days of lavish entertaining were hung with the coats of the gentlemen and capes and bonnets of the ladies as they came trooping in to attend a party. In the high-ceilinged parlor hangs the crystal chandelier which illuminated such gatherings; it bears evidence of having held candles, kerosene, gas and finally electric bulbs.

The hand carving, which is one of the chief beauties of the house, is seen on the mantel of this same room, where, between each of the delicate dentils, is a tiny pine cone. On the mantel face in the library is a pineapple—that symbol of hospitality often found in the great houses along the James River, but only in this one on the Eastern Shore. The open, four-petaled flower of the dogwood is used as a decorative motif throughout the house, appearing over the windows and over the doors and on the stair ends.

Such elaborate decoration was merely the embellishment for a structure of great substantiality. It has been discovered that no less than a foot of sawdust was used between the ceilings of the first floor and floors of the second to insure insulation from sound and heat.

George W. Powell bought the house, with seven acres of land, in 1872 after it had passed through several ownerships.

Mr. Powell was a member of the Powell Brothers, a firm of

FIGURE 76. Kerr Place is a large and handsome Georgian mansion which takes its place among any in Virginia.

merchants and maritime agents, for this has always been a seafaring as well as a farming region, and Onancock was once a customs port. Mr. Powell built a glass-inclosed cupola on the roof from which he could watch the vessels, his own among them, as they passed into the mouth of Onancock Creek to and from Chesapeake Bay. The cupola when it was no longer of practical use, and of no architectural value, either, was removed in 1936.

Mr. and Mrs. Robert Oldham, who live in the old house, have inserted certain modernizations with greatest skill. Mrs. Oldham and her sister, Mrs. Donald J. Parsons, of Lorton, Virginia, are granddaughters of Mr. George W. Powell.

While the Eastern Shore has its share of brick Georgian mansions, a great deal of its charm derives from the white frame houses, some of them one-story cottages with brick ends, and others of two stories, with a narrowness of depth and a steepness of roof characteristic of the region. Many, as families increased, added first one section and then another to the original unit, so that the rambling structures of many elevations, many chimneys and many angles are sometimes called "the little house, big house, colonnade, kitchen."

Such houses have been lived in by the same family since they were built a century or so ago. Their acreage and farmlands may be less, but their family burial grounds are companionably close and are respectfully preserved.

Such a homestead is Seven Gables, the oldest house in the town of Accomac, it's front entrance close to the village street and its rear door opening out into a clutter of smokehouse, doghouse, pigeon house, dairy, office, so dazzling under their thick patina of whitewash that they seem a miniature village of snow houses.

The roofs of Seven Gables go up and down, and so do the floors. You step up and step down into rooms which have been added, and you step up and step down into rooms which were built a hundred years ago. On one side the kitchen is lined with modern equipment; on the other a mammoth fireplace hung with ancient utensils fills a whole wall, and its brick hearth fills half the floor space of the room. Beside the fireplace under a brick arch between two chimneys is a deep ingle nook, where the slaves could lounge in comfortable warmth while the fowls turned on the spit. This is the oldest part of the house and was built in the year 1786 by Matthias Outter in order to qualify for his deed.

In houses like this lived men of substance who farmed for profit and boated for pleasure—or vice versa—and whose descendants do the same, surrounded not only by family heirlooms, but by unbroken family traditions.

In the courthouse in Eastville in Northhampton County, from whose doorway on August 13, 1776, was read the Declaration of Independence, are the oldest continuous court records in the United States. In the first volume, which covers the years from 1632 to 1640, may be read, among the lively lawsuits and long-winded wills, names which appear today among the doc-

Figure 77. The oldest part of Seven Gables was built in 1786. In it is the original kitchen with a brick arch between the two chimneys, forming an inglenook where the slaves could lounge in comfortable warmth.

tors, lawyers, farmers and exporters of seafood and of orchard and garden produce. It is a deep-rooted and indigenous culture so that it is customary to call anyone who was not born on the Eastern Shore a foreigner. If such persons settle in Accomack or Northampton County, it may be asked, "Wonder what they did so they couldn't stay home?"

It is rather surprising that such an entrenched provincial society should have seen a performance of the first play in what is now America—"The Bear and the Cub," in 1665. The performance was followed by an arrest of some of the actors who were to appear in court "in those habiliments that they then acted in and give a drought of such verses or other speeches and passages which were then acted by them." It was further ordered that the "Sheriff arrest the Body of William Darby for his appearance . . . being artour (author) of a play commonly called "The Beare and Cubb." Censorship was evidently strict on the Eastern Shore and no chances were taken in encouraging gatherings which might become disorderly.

Comfortable privacy was insured by both land and water. The road from Maryland was so rough that the mail coach could cover only six miles before it had to change horses—which is the reason one still finds small settlements six miles apart. It was not only cheaper but quicker to send produce north by water instead of overland, until in 1882 the railroad laid its first single track down the length of the peninsula.

This enforced isolation contributed to the distinctive flavor of the Eastern Shore, although nowadays it is difficult to keep alive the suspicion of "foreigners." For it is to the foreigners that some of the most attractive places owe their renaissance.

The long narrow peninsula of the Eastern Shore makes a distinction between the Bay Side and the Sea Side, a distinction implied in the reference to gossip as rumors which are "told from Sea to Bay."

Water infiltrates the edges of both Accomack and Northampton Counties with a fringe of irregular inlets, coves, creeks and bays, so it seems entirely logical that sea gulls should glean in the fields and gardens and that the driveway from the highway to Corbin Hall should be surfaced with crushed oyster shells—that white and durable material typical of seaside roads in many parts of the world.

The driveway, between its tall trees, is a fitting introduction to the Georgian mansion solidly and splendidly preserved for more than two centuries. It is built of locally burned brick laid in Flemish bond, the water table having a beveled brick top course and a three-brick belt course along the second-story level. The bricks above the window lintels are rubbed, the modillions under the cornice have an ogee shape on the lower edge and below them is a row of dentils. Two palladian windows open out of the hall on the second floor. It was an extremely handsome house when it was built—the date is usually agreed upon as 1725—and it is extremely handsome today.

The interior is as dignified as the exterior with paneled walls, hand-carved details and recessed cupboards—some of them lighted by outside windows—on either side the principal fireplaces.

When the present owners, Mr. and Mrs. Raymond C. Mackay, bought the property in 1948 they found that it had been so well constructed, with even its interior walls of brick twenty-four inches thick, that the only radical structural repairs needed were in the floors of two rooms. The original panes were in most of the windows. On the graceful stair of solid walnut there was not a broken spindle.

This is more remarkable since the property has changed hands a number of times in its long history. The land has changed not only in ownership but in size, since the original three-thousand-acre tract was patented to Colonel Edmund Scarburgh in 1664 and sold in 1669 to Mrs. Ann Toft for "9101 pounds of Mevis Sugar in Cask and 708 pounds of Indigo." To keep in step, the name changed, too, from Chincoteague Farm to Wolfridge to Corbin Hall. And now architectural changes are being skillfully incorporated, not only with modern lighting, plumbing and a service wing, but with most patient duplication of the original paint on the walls. By careful investigation the Mackays ascertained that the original pastel colors were softer than those commonly used at that period—which interior decorators now tone down with white to suit current taste. An untouched panel has been left in each room to set the correct key, and the finished effect is very charming.

In its well-bred exterior and formally arranged interior Corbin Hall is not unlike other imposing Georgian mansions. But its furnishings are entirely dissimilar, for the present owners have lived long in China and have brought back their treasures with them. Chinese rugs are spread upon the floors, Chinese lanterns are suspended from the ceilings, Chinese screens stand across the walls. Bronze and jade objects are discreetly displayed in the recessed cupboards.

Such articles find an appropriate setting in a house which stands not on the bay side but on the ocean side—opening into that distant world from which seafaring men used to bring back the furniture, shells, porcelain and pewter which their wives and daughters placed in their parlors from New England to Florida.

The Mackays have built a great living room with an old brick floor and an immense fireplace, and connected it with the main house by an enclosed colonnade. Through its windows one looks across Chincoteague Bay to Chincoteague Island. White houses line its shore and small fishing boats hug the little wharves which jut out from amongst the piles of oyster shells along the beach. Nets are drying, boats are being built or repaired and all the year round the fishermen follow their trade, and in season clams and oysters and crabs are sent to market.

Chincoteague Island, although seven and a half miles long and one and a half miles wide at its extremity, cannot be considered large. It is, nevertheless, the largest inhabited island in the state of Virginia. And although its daily routine is tranquil, on one day in the year there is great hustle and bustle with thousands of visitors finding their way thither. This is on the last Thursday in July when the Pony Penning takes place.

The ponies are small half-wild little creatures which have been born on the nearby island of Assateague and have fed upon the sea grass there. Just how the first ones arrived has never been agreed upon. Some people claim they are descendants of horses which strayed or were abandoned in early colonial times. Others like to believe that their ancestors were Arab mounts which swam ashore from a Spanish galleon wrecked off the coast. At all events, on this day of carnival color and stir, they are driven from Assateague Island and forced to swim the narrow channel between it and Chincoteague Island, where they clamber up the beach. Here they are herded and penned up until the buyers can see them and choose what ones they want and carry them off—sometimes in automobiles quite as if they were oversized dogs instead of small-sized horses.

From the great window in the living room of Corbin Hall you can look out across the wide green pasture which lies between the house and the water, out across the bay to the beach, lined with white houses glittering in the sunlight.

It is not far away—only four miles—but there is a sense of distance, of space and of time. It comes from the consciousness that yonder stretches the Atlantic Ocean. And merging with this consciousness, as you stand among the richly gleaned treasures of the East, you are aware of another ocean, stretching over the rim of an unseen horizon, and washing the shores of China, far away on the opposite side of the world.

The wealth of the Eastern Shore has always been derived from the water as well as from the land, but at one time that from

FIGURE 78. Wharton, though standing in open country, seems more like a city house than a country one. John Wharton, who built it in the early eighteenth century, may have found his architect in Philadelphia.

the former source was often somewhat deviously acquired.

The Englishmen and descendants of Englishmen who had settled here resented the English laws which forbade them to trade with any but British ships and ports. Before the forests were cut down and erosion set in, lessening the depth of the water, there were, besides the recognized ports of entry, plenty of hidden coves where boats could unload their cargoes unobserved. It was easy to do what was called "evade the restrictions"; in other words, to engage in smuggling, and respectable planters did not hesitate to take advantage of this opportunity. Legitimate goods might be safely unloaded in daylight, but it was safer to handle contraband after dark, and once it had been slipped ashore, it was wise to have a windowless closet built in the brick ends of the old houses, where the unlawful goods could be concealed.

Many of these otherwise law-abiding citizens considered such "evading of restrictions" entirely permissible, and in boats which a modern yachtsman would hesitate to take across the bay plied back and forth between the Eastern Shore and the West Indies. They carried grain and beans and peas and meat and turkeys and brought back sugar and molasses and rum. While it is not suggested that such "evasion" was akin to privateering, it is said that Blackbeard the Pirate was a familiar caller up and down the Eastern Shore. Thus the bucolic records of crops of potatoes and tomatoes are dashed with the piquant sauce of activities at sea which had nothing to do with fishing and gathering oysters and clams.

The true stories and the fabricated ones cluster most thickly about the head—or rather the house—of John Wharton who, in the first decade of the eighteenth century, built the big square, hip-roofed brick house overlooking Assawaman Creek, out to the barrier islands and to the ocean itself.

Although it stands in the middle of open country, Wharton does not seem like a country house, but a city one. Neither does it belong architecturally to the Eastern Shore, but to Philadelphia, where John Wharton maintained certain business interests and where he may have found his architect.

The front door faces the lovely twisting creek, reflecting the trees which border it and the sky which arches above it. The rear door faces the garden and the family burial plot. The two doors are identical in their fanlights and in the reeding and fishtail carving at the sides. Neither of them had the porches typical of Eastern Shore houses, but could appropriately face the sidewalk of a street in Philadelphia.

One enters the house by a large square hall, with a graceful stairway at the left extending to the third floor, with the rooms opening out of the hall symmetrically placed and the bedrooms finished in the same style as the rooms downstairs. The wood mantels—four of them are autographed—are carved with Biblical and patriotic subjects, including the landing of the Pilgrims and the Sacrifice of Isaac, Mr. Wharton apparently being unaware of any incongruity of such moral subjects in a house associated with smuggling and gambling on a scale which was high, wide and handsome. There are paneled walls in all the rooms, those in the

FIGURE 79. Four of the carved mantels in Wharton are autographed. The paneling was imported from Philadelphia or London.

drawing room, as well as the other woodwork, imported from either Philadelphia or London.

Throughout the house there is no duplication, the woodwork and the plaster work on the ceilings differing in each room and yet blending harmoniously with the others.

Such decoration was so highly valued that the center of the design is signed with the name of the maker, R. Wellford. Robert Wellford was a Philadelphian, who listed himself in the directory as an ornamental composition manufacturer. The composition was "a paste of plaster, resign and size, squeezed into metal pottery or box wood moulds" and applied to walls, ceilings and mantels. At Wharton such decoration was also applied to the exterior, as one can see from flush board-paneled aprons between the first and second floors, which once bore an ornamental plaster swag.

John Wharton is supposed to have watched for his ships as

they slipped into the inlet of Assawaman Creek, loaded with their rich cargoes from Holland. It is believed that underground tunnels connected the house and stables with the water and, although these have not yet been wholly uncovered, the discovery, during some recent landscaping, of a brick arch large enough for a bull cart to pass through indicated the existence of such underground passages. Depressions and fissures in the lawn give further credence to the story.

While John Wharton was not the only one engaged in surreptitious activities, he did things on a grander scale than most of his neighbors. His house was more impressive than most of theirs—with 7,568½ acres he was the largest landowner in the county. His underground tunnels, if there were such, add glamour to his memory.

So reluctant is the Eastern Shore to relinquish its legends of smuggling and pirates that there was a good deal of excitement in 1953 with a report of newly discovered buried treasure. The Ocean Highway was being widened with earth brought in from the country, and as some of the truckloads of this were dumped, old coins tumbled out. The search was on, and newspaper reporters and photographers hastened to the scene to get stories and pictures about people grasping bags bulging with antique foreign coins. The skeptical declared the whole thing a publicity hoax, but others made the most of the brief excitement.

It is gratifying that the present owners of Wharton, Mr. and Mrs. Charles R. Busch, have taken the greatest pains to restore the house in authentic detail and that Mrs. Busch, in planning the garden in the rear, used the design of one of R. Wellford's plaster ceiling decorations.

In this garden, according to Virginia custom, is a small family burial ground and two of the tombstones give further information about John Wharton and his wife Elizabeth. From the inscription which marks his grave we learn that he was born in the County of Accomack in 1767—which accounts for his building his home here—and that he died in Philadelphia in 1814. His Philadelphia associations may account for some of his wealth and his choice of an architect, but the inscription on the tombstone adds that the body was brought back here for burial.

The inscription on the gravestone of his wife tells more. For

Photo by Hutchinson Studio

Figure 80. Hills Farm, one of the earliest formal brick houses built in Accomack County, is surrounded by fertile acres, with a sparkling creek in the rear.

after the usual facts and dates it says that she was "born in Accomack County Virginia and always resided there."

Here is testimony that John Wharton, whatever his travels in the great world, was true to the Eastern Shore and chose for his wife no "foreigner," but a girl who was born here and stayed here all her life, and that both were proud of their common birthplace.

Hills Farm, one of the earliest formal brick houses to be built in Accomack County, is today the home of Mr. and Mrs. Henry J. Richardson, who came from Washington to make it their home.

The natives of the Eastern Shore have always had a predilection for privacy, and as long as they could place their houses near some creek or bay or cove, they have been quite reconciled to being without immediate neighbors.

The thousand acres on which the original house was built

were patented by Richard Hill in 1663 and inherited by his grand-son, Richard Drummond, who built the main part of the house on a high foundation and with a tall gable roof, and who obviously preferred a delightful site to an easily accessible one. Even today, with excellent roads, a long and devious drive of twists and turns lies between it and the Ocean Highway. Any drive through Northampton and Accomack Counties gains interest by the names on the signposts. The old Indian ones are legion and their mean-ings are frequently interpreted. Accomack means "Other Side of the Water Place," Assateague, "Stony Water" and Chesapeake, "Great Salt Bay." Chincoteague is well named, for the word means "Beautiful Land across the Water," Onancock, "Foggy Place" and Pungoteague, "Sand-fly River."

But there are other names which the stranger finds equally fascinating. Who named Modest Town and Temperanceville— and was it in hope or derision? Bird's Nest and Hawk's Nest ex-plain themselves, but Horn Town, Cat's Bridge and Frog Stool offer food for speculation.

At all events, the drive to Hills Farm may be confusing, but it is never dull, and comes to its climax when, at the end of a long *allée* of tall trees, the rosy house is revealed with white sheep nibbling green grass at the side and white boats dotting the blue waters of the creek in the rear.

Certainty as to the exact date of its erection seemed to be confirmed when on a brick found in the end wall of the original main house in the course of reconstruction, was discovered the date 1697. Another date, 1768, penciled on a rafter may account for later alterations. As if to complete the documentation as far as possible, a penciled notation on the back of a mantel removed from the parlor produced the following rather miscellaneous information:

"August 2, 1856. This work was doen in 1856 was Wm. H. White, boss: Lemuel N. Windsor, joiner; and John W. White and Jesse Shield prentis [apprentices]. Done for John R. Drum-mond and Elishe Ann his wife and its very hot summer and the boss is [boss's] had her tenth child while we were at work here. This mantel was made by me in my 46th year, W. H. White: Wm. Mears, Bricklayer; Henry J. Carmine, Plasterer."

Marked bricks and penciled boards were not enough for the

Photo by Hutchinson Studio

FIGURE 81. Warwick, overlooking Upshurs Bay, carries its two hundred and fifty years with special grace.

Richardsons. The house itself was coaxed into still further revelation.

At the beginning of their restoration, the cross hall in the center and the two rooms—one on each side—had plain plastered walls and a millwork trim of that period chronologically fixed as when the boss's wife was having her tenth child. When this interior finish was removed, it was found that the parlor had been handsomely paneled, and behind the plaster some of the old woodwork had been used as braces. Thus it was possible to make accurate reproduction. As woodwork of this type was not likely to have been installed in 1697 it may have been done later, in 1768, at the time of the addition of the dormer windows.

So eager were the Richardsons to bring the house back to what it probably was during the last quarter of the eighteenth century that they sacrificed certain personal preferences. With the architect they decided that the room on the right of the hall had originally been two small rooms, each with a corner fireplace. Although a good-sized dining room would have suited them better than a small dining room and a small library, nevertheless the Richardsons restored the two small rooms, and when necessary, set a dining table in each.

Every detail has been studied carefully. Every change has been made handsomely, with the best possible materials and workmanship, so that today the proud and pretty house is at its charming best.

The railroad brought great changes to the Eastern Shore, but perhaps the automobile brought greater ones. For the Ocean Highway, which, avoiding large cities, runs from New York to Florida, passes down the center of the peninsula, and over it, day and night, skim pleasure cars, trucks and buses.

Now the fresh tomatoes and potatoes and peaches which grow so bountifully on this fertile soil, the seafood and the canned and frozen fruits and vegetables can reach Washington, Baltimore, Philadelphia and New York in a few hours. Now it is possible for people to commute between their winter homes in the north to summer ones on the Eastern Shore.

Thus it is that Warwick, a delightful early American house, has come into its second—or perhaps its third or fourth—blooming. From the highway one approaches the original section built of old bricks laid in Flemish bond with glazed headers, and possibly part of a larger brick house which was burned.

While there is disagreement as to the exact date of this building—whether shortly before or shortly after 1700—there is no doubt that it carries its years with special grace. While it is probable that the frame section was added later, the whole house is mellowed into tranquil unity as, surrounded by its hundred acres, it overlooks the wide waters of Upshurs Bay.

It has changed owners and changed names, and had its periods of deterioration and restoration, but some of the stories associated with it do not seem to change. Some are printed in the local histories, and others exist only through word-of-mouth repetition, but altogether they are as much a part of the old house as the staunch boards in the floors and the old bricks in the walls.

Such a story is of Arthur Upshur IV, who was away from home when a report was brought him that the British had landed on his property and were destroying everything. Hurrying back, he saw the enemy re-embarking in their barges and ordered his men to fire upon them, which they did, inflicting a number of casualties. After they were out of range, Upshur then went to the house where his wife told him that the British had merely asked permission to fill their water casks and to purchase some meat. Realizing that they might return and retaliate for the treatment he had given them, Upshur removed what he could from the house, but the British, who had been entirely peaceful on their first visit, returned the next day and carried off everything of value they could find and set fire to the house.

There is another story about Warwick which is not only told but illustrated by a dark stain on the steps leading down to the back yard. On a December night in 1749, Abel Upshur and his wife Rachael heard a suspicious disturbance in the fowl house and went out to investigate. They found nothing and were returning to the house when a fox darted out and attacked Rachael, and the blood which gushed from her foot is still ineradicable upon the steps. If such an encounter sounds more like a wild night on the steppes of Russia than a mild night on the steps of a Virginia farm, the sequence is even more violent. For nine days later the unfortunate lady developed hydrophobia, and tradition has it her agony was so frightful that to ease her pain and quiet her shrieks, her family muffled her in feather beds. From this highly unscientific treatment she died. The rabid fox disappeared, but the stain remains to prove the tale.

A good many people have laid their hands upon Warwick. A daughter of the actress Anna Held built the picturesque outside chimney. Ralph T. Whitelaw, who spent many years compiling the definitive history of the Eastern Shore, lived here, and with his wife made carefully authentic restorations. Mr. and Mrs. Richard Hollerith, of Riverton, New Jersey, have carried their restoration to a pleasing livability. Old wood has been salvaged and re-used; the walls are fresh with pastel paint or suitable paper, and in the room overlooking the water a picture window frames the lovely sweep of Upshurs Bay.

The tombs of Mary and Arthur Upshur, who built the house

and are buried nearby, carry the dates 1703 and 1709 respectively. But if visitors are inclined to cast only a cursory glance at these mementos, there is hardly one who does not part the box bushes which crowd the steps and stoop over to hunt for the dark stains, and nod triumphantly when they are revealed.

It would take many pages to describe the houses on the Eastern Shore and relate their histories. Mr. Whitelaw's two thick volumes contain more than fifteen hundred pages. But there is one house which should be mentioned, not only because of its attractiveness, but because it reminds us that despite the traditional cautious attitude toward "foreigners," one foreigner arrived early and his descendants have stayed late.

This foreigner was a thirteen-year-old boy named Thomas Savage, who came to Virginia in 1608 with Christopher Newport and so caught the fancy of Powhatan that it was arranged that the English boy should be exchanged for an Indian one. Young Savage must have been an attractive lad, for when Powhatan's brother saw him, he too coveted him. Thereupon Powhatan, who chose to call the boy Newport, sent him to live with Debedeavon, the "Laughing King" who was chief of all Accomack. Once again young Savage found favor, and Debedeavon gave the south side of Wissaponson to his adopted son, Thomas Savage.

A patent for this tract of nine thousand acres—the largest patent then on record—was issued in 1664 to Captain John Savage, the son of Thomas, and since then the name has been kept alive through numerous descendants.

John Savage's first wife was Ann Elkington, and in her honor the present house was built in 1799 and named Elkington.

It stands in a large grove of oaks, pecans and mahogany trees and the present owner, Mr. Quinton G. Nottingham, is restoring the gardens and the seventeen acres of lawn which slope to the Gulf.

The white frame house stands behind a white wooden fence and its various extensions give it the rambling length characteristic of this region. The hall, with its three massive doors paneled on the outside and diagonally battened on the inside, is hung with a scenic wallpaper of French workmanship, unique in the county. It is hand-painted in strips and its story begins under the

Photo by Hutchinson Studio

FIGURE 82. The rambling white house of several elevations is characteristic of the Eastern Shore. It is sometimes called "the big house, little house, colonnade, kitchen."

stairs with a hunting scene. From here it proceeds without duplication around the hall up the stairs and comes to an end at the landing where the stag stands at bay.

In the parlor and library the paint has been removed from the paneling to show the fine old heart-pine woodwork. On the second floor each room is painted in a soft color typical of the colonial era, and hung with reproductions of old wallpapers. It may be mentioned that Mrs. Evelyn V. Willing, of Pennsylvania, who bought Elkington in 1927 and did so much toward its restoration, was a descendant of Thomas Savage, and that the scenic paper was repaired and retouched by Miss M. Kate Savage. Thus the first "foreigner" is recalled in names of many families, entrenched in the pride of being natives of the Eastern Shore.

In the trim white houses settled comfortably behind their deep green lawns, the front door is often directly opposite the rear door which opens to another lawn sloping down to the water. Breezy in summer, with a living vista summer and winter, many of these houses have been lived in for generations, and such is the fidelity of families there seems no reason to doubt they will continue to be homes for generations to come.

There is, however, one famous house which no longer exists, but should be mentioned since its name is perpetuated in the Arlington estate near Washington, by George Parke Custis who named it for his ancestral home on the Eastern Shore.

The part played by the Custis family is an important one, not only in Virginia but in the history of our country, but visitors usually stop not to see the possible site of a house but a tomb, and to smile over an inscription which commemorates not valor but vindictiveness.

John Custis IV had been gay enough and devoted enough when he married Frances, the daughter of Daniel Parke, Governor of the Leeward Islands. But the two quarreled so furiously that they finally reached a stage where all communication passed through Pompey, a slave, whose duty it was to stand near and relay necessary conversation, word by word.

One day Colonel John sent an invitation, through Pompey, to his wife to take a drive with him, which she rather astonishingly accepted. Without a word her husband handed her into her seat and resumed his own and then silently turned the carriage and drove straight into the bay. Since there was no intermediary present, the lady addressed herself directly to her husband and asked, "Where are you going, Colonel Custis?"

"To hell, madam," he replied.

"Then drive on," she returned. "Any place is preferable to Arlington."

Thereupon the Colonel turned the carriage around and drove home.

Before alighting he said to his wife, "I don't think you'd be afraid of the devil himself."

"No, indeed," replied his lady, with spirit, "I've lived too long with you."

This incident apparently cleared the air somewhat, for afterward they signed an agreement in court settling property differences and had several children.

But the Colonel had the last word. On his tomb he had engraved the following inscription:

"Under this Marble Tomb lies ye Body of the Honorable John Custis, Etqr. of the City of Williamsburg and Parifh of Bruton; formerly of Hungars Parifh and the Eaftern Shore of Virginia and County of Northampton the Place of his Nativity. Aged 71 years and Yet liv'd but Seven Years which was the fpace of time He kept a Batchelers houfe at Arlington on the Eaftern Shore of Virginia."

The gravestone is of white marble, massive and elaborate, with a stout iron railing around it for protection, a tree above it for shade and a cornfield nearby for sociability.

Every visitor reads this remarkable record of matrimonial strife, and only a few bother to look at the other gravestone in the enclosure marking the burial place of John Custis II, who was "one of the Council of Virginia, Colonel and Commander in Chief of the Militia on the Eastern Shore of this Colloney," and, as far as is known, lived amicably with his wife.

chapter 20

RICHMOND AND ROAST BEEF

Virginia House, Agecroft Hall, Ampthill, Wilton, John Marshall House, Wickham–Valentine House, White House of the Confederacy, Linden Row, Pratt's Castle

Richmond has always loved England, admired England, and to a certain extent endeavored to follow and maintain English customs and manners. To be sure, in colonial days, all Tidewater Virginia was closely knit to the mother country by social and economic ties. It was quicker and far more comfortable to take a boat across the Atlantic than to plod and plug with horse and coach through the muddy roads to sister colonies to the north and south.

Since Richmond is a definitely definable area, in it we can readily trace the English influence. It is immediately discernible in the homes which their owners modeled as closely as possible after their ancestral seats and upon which they bestowed nostalgic names.

It is, therefore, peculiarly appropriate that Richmond possesses two authentic English manors—both of them built and used for centuries on their original sites, one in Warwickshire and one in Lancashire, before they were taken apart, stone by stone, brick by brick, and timber by timber, and brought to the places where they stand today, overlooking the James River.

The materials in the older of the two—now called Virginia House—came from the ancient Priory of the Holy Sepulchre at Warwick, England, where it had been built in 1125 by the first Earl of Warwick and had been known through the centuries as The Priory. After the dissolution of the monasteries it was rebuilt by Thomas Hawkins—in about 1565—as his residence. Nearly four hundred years later—in 1925—when it had been purchased by a house wrecker, it was bought and shipped to this country by the Honorable Alexander Wilbourne Weddell, our Minister to Spain, who took great pride and pleasure in its restoration and who, at his death, left it to the Virginia Historical Society.

Unlike a toy building cut out of a single block, Virginia House includes portions of three historic English houses. The main body is after the Tudor portion of the Priory; the wing west of the main entrance is a copy of the principal part of Sulgrave Manor, home of the ancestors of George Washington. The entrance tower is a reproduction of one at Wormleighton, another English home, associated with the Washingtons through their intermarriage with the Spencers.

Virginia workmen preserved and reconstructed and combined these plans with greatest success. Despite the proverb that rolling stones gather no moss, on some of these sandstones which have rolled or been rolled a considerable distance, may be seen soft living flecks which had first become green under English skies. On some of these same stones may be traced the guild emblems of the original masons. The roof slabs, irregular in size and shape, were hewn by hand. A stone set in the front wall, just above the second-story window at the west, bears the arms of Queen Elizabeth in commemoration of a visit she paid the Priory in 1572.

The interior of the house is equally authentic: the carved-oak stairway and balustrades originally in the great hall of the Priory, and wall paneling and exposed beams, are still resolutely solid.

The great lovely manor is set in nine and a half acres of grounds landscaped with terraces, garden, pool and stone stairway down to the James River.

One such transportation and restoration might seem sufficient treasure for any city, even for one with such worshipful veneration for England. But Richmond has two.

FIGURE 83. Richmond has always loved England, and Virginia House, transported stone by stone from Warwick, is especially treasured.

Next door to Virginia House is Agecroft Hall, built a couple of centuries after the Priory (about 1393) and, like it, taken apart piece by piece and brought to Richmond and reconstructed the same year as Virginia House, 1925.

Unlike the sandstone walls of its neighbor, those of Agecroft Hall are of black timber and white plaster. The roof is of gray stone, the chimneys of red brick. The garden which surrounds it and slopes down to the James River is patterned after the one at Hampton Court in England.

The interior, with its great hall, minstrel gallery and carved-oak screen, has oak paneling throughout and stained-glass windows which once bore the coat of arms of John of Gaunt.

There are many exceedingly fine architectural details: an oriel timber window surmounting the service courtyard, with its bracket carved in Gothic tracery; its overhanging gables, its heavy, nail-studded doors with their original wrought-iron fastenings.

Agecroft Hall had stood for about six centuries on the bank of the Irwell in Lancashire, the ancestral seat of the Langeley family which was a branch of the royal Plantagenets. Gradually its proud seclusion was encroached upon by industrial developments—cotton spinning mills, coal works, calico printing and dyeing factories. It might have been demolished to make way for further commercialism, or it might merely have been engulfed by its environment. In any case, there is no question that its purchase and removal by the late Thomas Williams, Jr., has preserved a specimen of medieval times which would otherwise have been lost, and preserved it in a setting where it is assured of care and appreciation. It is owned by Mrs. David C. Morton, and under the terms of Mr. Williams's will, will eventually become a handsomely endowed art museum for the city.

Moving large buildings four thousand miles and placing them in new and advantageous locations did not stop with the two tremendous transportations of Virginia House and Agecroft Hall, although the subsequent ventures were on a more modest scale.

There were two fine houses near Richmond which had been built in the middle of the eighteenth century and, like their counterparts across the sea, found their charms and values threatened by an environment which had changed from rural to industrial.

Ampthill originally stood on the southwest bank of the James River, about five miles below Richmond. It is believed to have been built in 1703–1732 by Henry Cary, Jr. His father, Henry Cary, son of Miles Cary, was the first owner of the land, having acquired it from William Byrd of Westover. Both father and son were experienced builders who had tended the erection of many of the principal buildings at Williamsburg.

On the death of Henry Cary, Jr. (1749) the plantation passed to his son, Colonel Archibald Cary who named it after Ampthill Castle in England.

After various changes in ownership and after years of neglect, it fell into disrepair, and the land surrounding it was acquired by industrial interests. Hundson Cary, a collateral descendant of Henry Cary, acquired it in 1929, dismantled it and moved it, with its dependencies, to the present location on a bluff on the north

Photo by Dementi Studio

FIGURE 84. Agecroft Hall, which had stood in Lancashire for six centuries, is a medieval building which will eventually become an endowed art museum.

Photo by Dementi Studio

FIGURE 85. Of all the major eighteenth-century Virginia houses, Ampthill alone has walls of English, rather than the usual Flemish bond. Named after Ampthill Castle in England, it was moved from five miles below Richmond to its present site.

bank of the James River in the western part of Richmond.

There had been changes in the original plan. Between 1750–1760 the court between two wings was roofed over. The stairway was moved to make the hall larger and to give access to all four rooms on each floor. The roof was developed into the present hip on hip.

Antiquarians still puzzle over the fact that of the major eighteenth-century Virginia houses, Ampthill alone has walls of English bond rather than the more usual Flemish bond. Glazed headers are used in the belt course, which was laid in Flemish bond and unmolded. The cornice has modillions and dentils.

During the time of the 1750 alterations, two dependencies were erected—one a kitchen and one a ballroom. When the house was moved to its present site, these dependencies were connected with the main house.

The entire first floor is paneled to the ceiling; each room has its large fireplace with marble facings, two of them originals. Ampthill is not a shrine or a museum, but a home. It was built to give comfort to a family and pleasure to guests. Today, under the livable modernization of its present owners, Mr. and Mrs. Tennant Bryan, it continues to uphold that tradition.

By now Richmond was fired with the determination to save what she could of her valuable old houses. To be sure, Wilton had not been built in England any more than Ampthill, but it was as fine an example of the late Queen Anne style as could be found in Virginia, both in exterior and interior, and it would have fitted perfectly into an English landscape of 1700.

It had been built in 1753 six miles below the pioneer village of Richmond on the James River in Henrico County. William Randolph II of Turkey Island had acquired the land and the house was built for his son, William Randolph III. It was so remote from any settlement it was called Land's End and, therefore, it must have been surprised when, after passing through a succession of ownerships, it suddenly found itself surrounded by mills, railroad yards and factories.

The Society of Colonial Dames of America in the State of Virginia took advantage of the situation. They recognized it as a historic house, associated with the Randolphs, Carters and Harrisons. Washington, Jefferson and Lafayette had stayed here

Figure 86. Wilton originally stood six miles below Richmond. It was moved to its present site and reconstructed precisely, to serve as an example of late Queen Anne for architects and interior decorators. Every room, including closets, is paneled from floor to ceiling.

and many other notables of the colonies. And, always the final accolade, nobility from overseas had been entertained here.

The Colonial Dames recognized more than the historic and social prestige of the old place. They saw that Wilton was a first-rate example of Virginian domestic architecture and, properly restored, would be of ever-increasing value to architects and interior decorators. Thereupon they had it taken apart—numbering each piece of wood, each brick, each window pane and bit of hardware—and put together in exact reconstruction.

So here it stands, on a bluff five miles above Richmond, over-looking the James, its two stories above a high basement floor and under a slate roof.

The bricks are a deep rose, made and burned on the original site, and where they are rubbed around the windows and corners they stand out in interesting contrast. Two wide halls, one downstairs and one upstairs, run the depth of the house—the upper one, although it was called a "passage," actually an informal sitting room with a view of the river. Out of each hall open four large high-ceiled rooms—two on each side—of great dignity. Every one of them is paneled from floor to ceiling—even the chimney-breast closets are paneled—an elegance unique in Virginia and one which gives an air of unity and substantiality to the mansion.

The marble fireplaces, the deep-silled windows with rich hangings and heavy inside folding blinds, the carefully chosen and placed antique furniture, portraits, silver and china and glass—many of them purchased, others being gifts or loans—are kept carefully within the prescribed limits of the period.

Not only the principal furnishings have been selected with taste and tested with authenticity, but there are many small details which add to the intimate convincingness of Wilton.

What are called closets, for instance, are actually recessed alcoves on either side of the fireplaces, entered through archways and lighted by narrow side windows. In one such closet off an upper chamber stands a copper trivet holding a curious copper caldron with a tightly fitting lid and a long spout. This, we are told, is a still, in which used to be distilled the perfumes, herbs, elixirs and medicines and cosmetics used in the household.

In old-fashioned English novels we sometimes read of the "still room," but probably this is the first opportunity we have had to see the actual article for ourselves. Speaking of closets, clothes were not usually kept in these, but in bulky movable pieces of furniture called wardrobes. It may be added that such wardrobes seem to have been appropriated by the gentlemen of the family, while the ladies packed their more meagre possessions in chests—a division of convenience typically English.

The paneling which gives such distinction to the interior is painted, the soft colors determined by scraping off many superimposed coats which had been applied during the years, until the original was reached, and this is what has been precisely duplicated. Very different are these delicate walls to the dark rubbed oak of Virginia House and Agecroft Hall, although both are authentically English. For during the period represented by Wilton heart pine was invariably painted and never left in the natural

FIGURE 87. John Marshall's house, designed and built by himself, is as forthright as the roast beef of old England.

finish, and the wood used here, except for the stairway with its walnut handrail and twisted newel post, is of heart pine.

The various dependencies which used to cluster about the old houses—kitchen, laundry, smokehouse, meat house, et cetera, and slave quarters—making them virtually self-supporting, have not been reproduced. The grounds are surrounded by a brick wall with iron entrance gates, and terraces with brick steps are laid in both the front and the back of the house. The Garden Club of Virginia has planted the boxwood, the holly hedges and the entrance *allée* of willow oaks.

Among the many shrines in Virginia, Wilton holds a place of enjoyable distinction—large enough to be impressive, small enough to be seen and studied and enjoyed in its entirety and in its detail.

The house of John Marshall, the great statesman and jurist,

which dominates the corner of Ninth and Marshall Streets, differs from Ampthill and Wilton in its proportions and plan, but like them expresses the British tradition. Not for John Marshall the Palladian curves and French touches which his cousin Thomas Jefferson incorporated into Monticello. John Marshall's house, designed and built by himself, is as forthright as the roast beef of old England.

John Marshall bought the land, and the deed in his own handwriting hangs on one of the walls and so does his application for fire insurance, dated in 1796. This covered not only the house but the dependencies—kitchen, stable, "Landra" shed, and a brick office—a clutter of dependencies characteristic of all Virginia houses of the period, now swept away and the space occupied by the John Marshall High School.

The house is two stories with pedimented gables, and three simple porches, one on the north, one on the south and one on the east, two of them opening directly into two of the important first-floor rooms, there being no street entrance into the hall. The stairway leads to the second floor where there are two halls, a dressing room and three large bedchambers. Originally the main floor held only this stair hall and three principal rooms, but twenty years later Marshall added a one-story library.

This comfortable residence was the great jurist's refuge from Washington. Here he was happy with his beloved wife and family and friends. Here he lived during the time he presided over the spectacular trial of Aaron Burr, walking to and from the Capitol. From here he buried his wife, and to this house his body was brought after his death in Philadelphia in 1835.

Among the original pieces of family furniture and china which have been collected there are a number of personal belongings, such as Marshall's judicial robe and Mrs. Marshall's wedding gown, and also articles associated with other famous men. If it seems paradoxical that Henry Clay's cradle should nudge Patrick Henry's punch bowl, the juxtaposition is not clarified by a chandelier which belonged to John Randolph of Roanoke. This introduction of other people's possessions does not in the least diminish the personality of the man who designed and built the house and who saw to it that the "peace button" was duly inserted in the newel post. This wooden peg was a symbol that a house had been

FIGURE 88. When the Wickham-Valentine House was built in 1812, it was rightfully considered the handsomest residence in Richmond. Today it is part of the Valentine Museum.

paid for, and it was carefully preserved and when necessary parted from with sorrow.

With the death of Justice Marshall the house passed to his daughters and then to his granddaughters and in 1909 became the property of the City of Richmond and was used as a public school. In 1913 the city placed the property in the custody of the Association for the Preservation of Virginia Antiquities, which maintains it as a museum.

When the Wickham-Valentine House was built in 1812 it was considered the handsomest house in Richmond. Now, in its old age, it may again lay some claim to that distinction. But between these two periods it was equivocably termed "one of the finest examples of Victorian rooms and furnishings in America."

Of that period two rooms have been kept intact and very amusing they are to twentieth-century eyes. They were created by Mr. John P. Ballard who bought the house after Mrs. Wickham's death in 1853 and redecorated it in frenetic Victorianism. Gilt cornices hang deeply over draped windows and top a mirror which stretches from a ceiling suggesting an agitated meringue, to a floor heaving in convulsions under a rug of monstrous figures. Under chairs on which one could only perch in discomfort are footstools embroidered with beads which would be rubbed off if a shoe inadvertently touched them. Jigsaw whatnots display china which might have emerged from a volcanic eruption. Putting her blessing upon the chaos stands young Queen Victoria herself, a full-length copy by Sully of his original portrait, with a sweeping train and a tiaraed head—the unwitting perpetrator of an era in interior decoration which bears her name. Upstairs one of the bedrooms retains its Victorian furnishing, with draped lambrequins and the thousand and one ornaments which were apparently created and purchased and placed for the sole purpose of giving occupation to a maid with a feather duster.

With this final acknowledgment of fealty to the British Crown, the Wickham-Valentine House calms down and returns to serenity. So pleasing is this embodiment of the classical revival introduced by Jefferson that we admit that the house can afford to be indulgent in preserving the two Victorian rooms.

It was built for John Wickham in 1812 and the square plainness of the street front conceals an interior of unusual beauty. A graceful Palette stairway rises from the circular hall and the woodwork is delicately and imaginatively carved. The rear is bowshaped, with a carved and pillared portico facing the walled garden, where a terrace repeats the same curves. A magnolia tree and a yew, both planted before the house was built, rise above the fountain, the marble figures and the box-edged walks.

When Mann S. Valentine, who was, among other things, an art collector, bought the house in 1882, he left both the residence and his collections, with a generous endowment, to become a public museum, which opened in 1898.

Today the Museum occupies three adjoining buildings and the house and its furnishings illustrate the architecture, the social life and the decorative arts of an earlier Richmond.

G. G. Valentine, son of the founder, restored the fine old place to its original simplicity and elegance, and the James River Garden Club took over the restoration of the walled garden in the rear. Facing the garden and in back of the newer Museum buildings is the studio of the sculptor, Edward Valentine V, the sculptor whom all Virginians love for his recumbent statue of Lee. This studio was formerly a carriage house a few blocks away on Leigh Street, and when it was threatened with demolition was given to the Museum and moved to its present location by the City Council of Richmond.

Two other houses built about this time are the Governor's Mansion (1813) and the White House of the Confederacy (1818). This latter, an angular white stuccoed building, now the Confederate Museum, was from 1861–1865 the home of President Jefferson Davis. To it came his generals to confer and his couriers to report. His daughter Winnie was born here, and from one of the high terraces his little son Joseph fell to death. It may be remembered that Lincoln's son died at the same time and the two fathers exchanged letters of sympathy.

The mansion is today a Confederate shrine and in it is a room set aside for each of the Confederate States, holding the worn uniforms and faded letters, the swords and money and tattered flags of a lost Cause.

With its shallow-roofed portico in Roman Doric style, with its barred windows—a protective measure installed twenty-five years ago, when the character of the neighborhood changed—it is not a cheerful place. But because of its human as well as its historical association it is dear to Richmonders, who think of it as a house and a home as well as a museum.

It was natural that the early homes of any pretension in Richmond should have followed English models. From what other source would the colonists have formed their taste?

But as time went on and the English settlers became American citizens, that taste was inevitably modified. The climate and conditions of living were not identical on opposite sides of the Atlantic.

Even the Revolutionary War, which definitely severed certain ties between the new country and the old, did not wholly uproot the Richmonders' veneration for the birthplace of their ancestors. Without deliberate intention, new buildings caught a reflection of the past.

Linden Row is an example of this. Originally there were ten of these brick houses built between 1847 and 1853—all identical with their narrow façades, Greek Revival white pillars, sunken areaways and small front lawns behind wrought iron railings. They were built as residences. Mary Johnson was living at No. 10 when she wrote *Lewis Rand,* and the first of those Monday Germans which are the zenith—or sometimes the nadir—of the Richmond debutante's season, was started in the basement of 106. But as the city pushed closer to their restricted lots, they were adapted to other uses. Here, in the high-ceiled rooms with their marble-faced mantels and long windows, are antique shops and studios, art galleries, and stamp and coin shops. What was the slave quarters is now a millinery salon, at 100 East Franklin Street.

The counterparts of these decorous shops and studios may be seen in many a London Mews, but these are entirely indigenous to Richmond. Their resemblance to similar blocks in the older metropolis is no imitation but a spontaneous choice of a city which is content to be Virginian and not British.

Virginia, for all her passionate interest in politics, was a long time providing a home for her governors. From 1788 to 1811 they lived in a two-story wooden structure derisively called "The Palace." Legend has it that Jefferson, when he was Governor, paid for his rent out of his private purse. If this was afterward refunded, there is no record of the transaction.

However, from the time when the present Governor's Mansion was completed in 1813 until the present, it has been the social center for the city and the place where distinguished visitors from our own and other countries have been entertained. Here the Governor gives his reception to the members of the General Assembly at the beginning of each session, and a special reception is given by each incoming governor.

It stands in restrained composure on the northeast corner of Capital Square, in the early Federal style, with a single-story Doric portico and four chimneys rising from the ridge corners of the deck roof.

A few days after Christmas in 1925 it caught fire from the

FIGURE 89. There were originally ten identical houses on Linden Row. Each had a narrow façade, sunken areaways, small front lawns behind iron railings and Greek Revival white pillars.

children's Christmas tree and the interior, the furnishings and the pictures were badly damaged, to be refinished and refurnished in the same quiet and excellent taste.

Despite its delay in getting started, it is today the oldest executive mansion in the United States.

A stranger, visiting Richmond today, sees the usual business district lined with the usual shops: glimpses the industrial regions on the outskirts: passes along residential boulevards with rows of apartment houses.

There are still left some of the old residences with iron lace framing their porches, but native Richmonders regret the passing of many landmarks which, whatever their architectural value, were precious because of sentiment.

Comparatively few houses from the eighteenth and nineteenth centuries remain, but these seem to have affected the choice of types most often preferred today. One cannot help observing, in the newer residential sections, where houses are rapidly rising, that Queen Anne, Georgian, half-timbered Elizabethan, Modified Federal, Greek Revival and replicas of Williamsburg colonial cottages—some satisfactory and some not so satisfactory —are the favorites. Only occasionally does the ranch house or the flat-roofed, picture-windowed home of the style vaguely called "modern" get a toehold in the scene. Obviously Richmond has been nurtured too long in the traditional to fling herself wholeheartedly into experiments and innovations, in spite of her influx of "foreigners."

This has always been so. To be sure, in 1853 William Abbot Pratt built a "castle" in Gamble Hill Park—a Tudor kind of contraption, turreted and battlemented and towered and terraced with suggestions of half-hidden passages and twisting stairs. Incongruous as it is, it has been allowed to remain, adapted to accommodate studios and apartments, and is regarded with indulgence. After all, William Pratt was an Englishman. To be sure, in 1853–1854 he built what purports to be a French chateau, and this, too, has been permitted to stand on Arch Street, rather lost in its un-Gallic environment. But, taking Richmond as a whole, there are very few bizarre experiments to be found in its domestic architecture.

Possibly Virginia House and Agecroft Hall have acted as

deterrents to rash experimentalism. Perhaps Wilton and Ampthill serve to hold the English standard firm.

At all events, it looks as if it would be a long time before the traditional bows out before the modern in Richmond, a long time before the roast beef of old England will be replaced by canned, frozen, dehydrated substitutes, a long time before the voice of the prefabricated dwelling is heard in the land.

Fruit punch may have replaced the toddy which once wafted its permeating perfume through legislative sessions, but the bowl used at the Governor's receptions in the Executive Mansion is not yet made of plastic. It is of Lowestoft, without a chip or a crack, genuine and honorably old.

chapter 21

ALONG THE JAMES RIVER

Westover, Carter's Grove

Each of the great colonial plantations which line the James River has its individuality created by long family history and by certain architectural features. Each has its coterie of admirers; each is described in brief summaries for the tourist to read as he rides, and in scholarly books by architects for architects, in novels, memoirs, portfolios of drawings, etchings and photographs. As they sink into shabbiness or blossom forth into "shrines," or are painstakingly restored into holiday homes for "foreigners," new facts are presented and old ones are retold, so there is no lack of available information dealing with this fascinating region.

Since the purpose of this book is to touch on houses throughout the state as a whole—many of them unknown even to Virginians who happen to live in a county on the other side of a mountain or a river—it has been thought best to choose only two of the famous Tidewater mansions, regretfully omitting the other two score.

While such selection is always difficult, it has seemed that Westover might be considered as most splendidly typical. It is not only the architect's delight and the historian's source book, but it

268

is a frame for a vivid picture of everyday life on a great colonial plantation.

The vividness of this record is largely due to the discovery in 1939 of the secret diary in shorthand of William Byrd II, the first gentleman of Virginia during his life.

Born in Virginia in 1674, an heir to a name already given distinction by his father, and to an ancestral fortune, he was educated in England and returned to his birthplace to fill a long life not only with private pleasures and profits, but with public duties. He was the official agent of the colony in London for three separate and extended periods, and enjoyed high civil and military honors in Virginia.

History recalls these events, but it is Westover itself which, through the detailed diary of its master, makes them vivid for us.

The mansion is little changed from the date of its completion in 1730. Unlike many of the others which were built to face the water, its main entrance is from the north or land side, through iron gates hung upon historic piers whose finials, in the forms of birds, are a rebus of the owner's name. On the south side, the lawn, with ancient tulip poplars, sweeps down a hundred and fifty feet to the water's edge. The exterior walls are of brick, laid in Flemish bond, and each of the two façades has a superb doorway of carved Portland stone and is reached by a broad flight of steps in pyramidal form. Dormer windows pierce the finely graduated slate roof.

The interior is worthy of the exterior. From the richly paneled hallway a stairway ascends to the third floor, an unusual feature in houses of the period, as is the habitable attic. From this central hallway open large rooms, their walls paneled, their ceilings ornamented with elaborate plaster work, their deep fireplaces framed by elaborate mantels of marble or carved wood, their massive doors with huge brass locks. Briefly, in its formal Georgian stateliness and its exquisitely executed detail, it is in all its attributes the most complete of the Virginia mansions of its period.

Although it has changed owners many times since it was occupied by William Byrd II, and came into the possession of its present owner, Mrs. Bruce Crane Fisher, the house which was so proudly built, proudly maintains its high distinction. Such maintenance was not supported by moonlight and magnolias.

Photo by Flournoy

FIGURE 90. Westover is little changed since its completion in 1730. Unlike many of the James River mansions, its main entrance is on the land side.

Contrary to nostalgic fiction, the life of William Byrd, like that of other successful planters, held a minimum of days of dalliance and nights of romance. It was a tremendous administrative job to run such a plantation. The planting and care of crops and orchards and gardens demanded the owner's constant supervision, for the overseers were frequently ignorant and unreliable, the servants black and white, incompetent and rebellious.

The usual vicissitudes which beset all farmers did not spare the Tidewater planter. Storms destroyed his crops, livestock escaped, mill dams broke, marshes had to be drained, trees planted, brickmakers and carpenters and blacksmiths given instructions, horses bred, cattle slaughtered, hams cured. River sloops arriving from Appomattox with hogsheads of tobacco, and shallops bringing hides and tallow, must be unloaded and reloaded for England. Seamen must be paid and the great ships from abroad, sailing up the river, must be met, their cargoes of household and agricultural goods sorted and recorded, and sold to friends and neighbors. Sacks of letters must be opened and their contents read and their replies dispatched.

Such activities outside the house were paralleled by others within. We read how the master of Westover mixed his homemade medications—sage and saffron and snakeroot tincture—to dose his family, his army of slaves and his not inconsiderable circle of friends.

The slaves seem to have been more trouble than they were worth. They fell sick with exasperating frequency and died at the most inconvenient times. They ran away and escaped, or were found and brought back and punished. Byrd's diary is peppered with notations of having this black girl whipped and this black man thrashed. He admits that he whipped the cook for not broiling the bacon properly, and kicked one of the maids for lighting a candle in the daytime. He ordered a slave who malingered to be fastened with a bit in his mouth and tied up by the leg. His wife was more violent than he. Her husband reprovingly jots down that she beat one of her maids with the tongs and branded her with a hot iron. Byrd considered himself a kind master, but modern historians agree that such severity was the exception rather than the rule.

It would be a mistake to think that all his time was absorbed by the practical details of managing his plantation and household. He not only had a truly splendid library but thoroughly enjoyed it. Regularly and methodically he read Hebrew, Greek and Latin, and at intervals turned to French, Italian and Dutch. He appreciated not only the classics, but had excellent taste regarding contemporary writing, never forgetting his friendships in London with Congreve, Swift and Pope. The latest new publications were in the Westover library as soon as ships could bring them. He was a creditable naturalist, hunting for birds' nests and collecting seeds for the Bishop of London, keeping up a brisk correspondence with English scientists and maintaining his membership in the Royal Society.

His sense of obligation toward his public duties was equally keen. He attended court in Williamsburg conscientiously, drilled

FIGURE 91. The grounds and gardens of Westover are worthy of the splendid old mansion.

his troops in preparation for a rumored invasion by the French and marched against the Tuscarora Indians.

Besides his diligence in managing his own private affairs and making a generous contribution of time and effort to public demands, he seems to have been a charming host.

Hospitality at Westover, as on other plantations, was lavish and constant. Guests came in hordes and stayed indefinitely. Food and wine were plentiful and people were not overly fussy about one bed to a room or one person to a bed.

Whether there were guests or not, there was plenty of time for a game of billiards or cards, for shooting pigeons. Everyone loved to dance. It is pleasant to think of Byrd and the wife he quarreled with so frequently coming to one of their brief reconciliations as they stepped through the measures of a minuet.

272

Few planters in colonial Virginia equalled Byrd in versatility, in fortune and accomplishments. But his life is typical in many ways of the customs and standards of the time. It was necessary for the owner of even a modest plantation to understand and supervise its management and to be something of an importer and exporter. While perhaps only a few had genuinely scholarly or scientific tastes, most of them made an effort, through books and pamphlets, to keep up with what was going on in England, and not deteriorate into provincial squires with no interest beyond the boundaries of their own lands.

Most of them shouldered public duties and filled appointed offices to the best of their abilities. And most of them were more or less pleasure lovers. Dancing, drinking, racing, feasting, flirting and gaming, balls, parties, picnics and house parties were the order of the day. Fun and frolic were part of Virginia life. Such gaiety was heightened at Westover by William Byrd's bevy of pretty daughters. His favorite was the oldest, Evelyn, who, as a child, was given her own corps of black attendants, and when she went visiting up and down the James River was transported by specially stalwart Negro oarsmen. She never dined without a certain page standing behind her chair.

When she was eight years old, her father took her to London to receive the best possible education, and when she was sixteen she was presented at Court. King George II, seeing the graceful young creature, exclaimed, "Are there any other as beautiful birds in the forests of America?"

Possibly it was this play on words which suggested to Sir Godfrey Kneller the idea of painting a bird in the background of his portrait of the colonial belle.

Besides being beautiful, wealthy and favored by her father, Evelyn further followed the current vogue by being crossed in love. There has always been speculation as to whether the suitor to whom she gave her heart was Daniel Parke Custis, who later married Martha Dandridge, or whether it was to the old Earl of Peterborough, who was forty years her senior, a roué, and who, once a friend of William Byrd, had become his enemy. There is some evidence that it was not the Earl but his grandson and heir, Charles Mordaunt, who, being young, handsome and aristocratic, would have seemed a more suitable choice.

Whichever it was, William Byrd forbade any alliance with this branch of the English nobility. In his own sailing vessel he brought his daughter back to Virginia and there, in Westover, where she had been born, she sighed her life away, dying unmarried at twenty-seven. Here she was buried, bequeathing a much-prized ghost to the family annals, and the tap of her high-heeled slippers and the swish of her silken skirts on the stair are still heard by the properly accredited.

Another Westover ghost is that of Elizabeth Carter of Shirley—Betty, the wife of William Byrd III. Among her five children were two boys who, while they were still very young, were sent to England to be educated—a by no means unusual procedure in the colonies. She never saw them again and never ceased to grieve for them, a grief augmented by other troubles. She was suspicious of her husband's faithfulness and plagued by her mother-in-law who had the hateful habit of punishing her by hiding her favorite trinkets. No one knows whether poor Betty was hunting for love letters which would incriminate her husband, or for her trinkets spirited away by her mother-in-law, when she determined to search the top shelf of a high wardrobe. At any rate, it toppled and fell upon her and crushed her. Less than a year later her husband married again and the couple seems to have been so remarkably happy that it is hard to imagine why he committed suicide. The crash of the wardrobe which fell on Betty and the shot which killed William Byrd III, are both heard at appropriate hours by occupants of the room where the tragedy occurred.

These diaphanous shades, although frequently reported and solicitously cherished, fade beside another ghost who is not a ghost at all, but a substantial figure. By his own hand he revealed himself with remarkable clarity and intimacy, and put a still recognizable stamp upon the social and political history of Virginia.

William Byrd II, is, like other members of the family he founded, buried at Westover, but he rests undisturbed in his tomb. His step is not heard on the stair and his invisible return is not heralded by crashes or inexplicably misplaced objects. This vigorous and fascinating personality has been content to relinquish the flesh whose pleasures and demands he by no means underestimated, and to continue his existence through printed words and the record of his deeds.

Among the handsome old plantations which line the James River, Carter's Grove has, for two hundred years, held a prominent place.

This is not only because of its architectural distinction, but because the various owners who acquired it and the families who lived in it enriched it with legend and sentiment.

On an eighty-foot bluff terraced to the river bank and looking down toward the broad expanse of Burwell's Bay, the central unit of the mansion stands very much as it did when, in 1753, Carter Burwell, who had watched its building for two years, at last moved into it. Carter Burwell was the grandson of that Robert Carter who was called "King Carter" of Corotoman because of the vast estates he acquired for his services as agent for the proprietors of Northern Neck. Among his holdings, which approximated three hundred and thirty-three thousand acres, were seven thousand acres in Martin's Hundred, which came to be known as Carter's Grove. King Carter gave this property to his daughter Elizabeth when she married Nathaniel Burwell, and it was their oldest son who built the Georgian mansion.

Old records show that David Menetree of Williamsburg was paid one hundred and forty pounds for "building a brick house according to agreement" and in addition received a present of twenty-five pounds. The entire cost of the house was five hundred pounds, which included not only the timber, brought from a distance, the bricks, made on the place, the five hundred and forty squares of glass at two and a half pence a square, but also the magnificent woodwork which remains the glory of the interior. The great hall and the formal rooms facing the river are paneled to the ceiling, where they join elaborate cornices. An arch supported on each side by fluted pilasters spans a wide staircase with carved balustrades, the step ends decorated with foliated carving. No owner has missed the opportunity to point out to visitors the gashes on the handrail, made by the sabers of Tarleton's troops who occupied it during the Revolution. The mantels and fireplaces are of fine craftsmanship and these, like the paneling, are probably the work of Richard Bayliss, a master

FIGURE 92. For two hundred years Carter's Grove has stood upon an eighty-foot bluff terraced down to the James River.

joiner whom, with his family, Carter Burwell brought over from England for this purpose.

Carter's Grove has changed hands many times during its long life, and has not always been maintained in the grand manorial manner. In 1876, when Dr. Edwin Boothe went to look at it with the idea of buying it, he found the previous year's crop of wheat dumped for storage on the floor of the parlor.

Dr. Boothe was in no way daunted by this temporary degradation of a stately room. He bought the place and for many years it was the home for his family of three sons and four daughters. Happy years they were, when in the evening Mrs. Boothe played the square piano which had been a wedding present and everyone lined up for the Virginia reel or took their places for square dances. Sometimes they essayed the schottische and if Dr. Boothe

FIGURE 93. Carter's Grove has held a place of distinction among the James River mansions for two hundred years. On the rail of the balaster are scars made by the sabres of Tarleton's troops.

were in a good humor, he might dance a jig solo before an admiring audience.

There were so many visitors that the double beds, sometimes two in a chamber, were all occupied and so was the double bed which stood in the upper hall ready for an overflow.

After the death of Dr. Boothe, Carter's Grove was bought by Mr. Archibald M. McCrea, who brought his bride there, and the old mansion underwent its first radical renovation. Like most of the plantation houses of the period, the two-story house was originally flanked by two separate story-and-a-half dependencies —one of which was a kitchen and the other the office. In 1927 the McCreas enlarged these two buildings and connected them with the central unit. They raised the roof and put dormer windows in the third floor. The paneling and interior woodwork were restored —of course care being taken to leave the saber gashes of Tarleton's soldiers.

277

All these alterations have been done with the greatest skill and taste and today Carter's Grove, in its dignity of scale and substantiality, stands forth as an example of the best Virginia colonial housebuilding.

It is not hard to understand why it has attracted so many owners and still attracts so many visitors, for everything about it suggests hospitality, a suggestion which at one time became an amusing actuality. It was in 1876 that Dr. Boothe was returning home after a short trip and on the train fell into conversation with an elderly gentleman who mentioned that he had long wanted to see Carter's Grove.

"Why, come along with me," invited the hospitable doctor. "Come home to dinner and I'll show you around. Plenty of room for you to spend the night of course."

The old gentleman accepted with pleasure and spent not one night but two, exploring every nook and cranny of the house he had heard so much about, and making himself most agreeable both to the older people and to the children. In fact, he made himself so agreeable that everyone was happy to have him linger a while, although perhaps not prepared for this lingering to be quite as prolonged as it ultimately became. He was exceedingly fond of children and the Boothe children became exceedingly fond of him. He entertained them with stories, he taught them to play whist and euchre, and fitted without a ripple into the happy routine of the large household. He was without funds, but what did he need money for, with his needs supplied with such open-handed generosity? He was without family, but the Boothes supplied this lack with good measure pressed down and running over. He stayed and he stayed and no one kept track of the time. When he died, the household mourned him as one of themselves. He had lived among them for twenty years.

chapter 22

A PALACE IN VIRGINIA

In 1930 the Virginians began to build a palace.

This was to be, and now is, not an ordinary or even an extraordinary house, but a real palace—not so large as Buckingham or Versailles or the Pitti, to be sure, but nevertheless worthy of the grandiloquent title.

It was completed in 1934 and on Memorial Day, May 30, 1952, 3,117 people came to look at it, to walk through it and to gaze at its gardens and terraces and dependencies.

The desire to build a magnificent dwelling, the instinct for an impressive name, the touch of nostalgia for all things British which have lingered in the Tidewater section from early times, have all been gratified at last in the Governor's Palace in Williamsburg.

The Palace is, as the dates show, comparatively new. But it has been constructed on the site and even on the foundations of the original edifice, and as nearly as possible in exact duplication of the one built about 1720 to serve the dual purpose of a residence and official headquarters of the King's Deputy in a great agricultural colony.

After the State House at Jamestown was leveled by fire, the capital of the new colony was moved from the mosquito-ridden place to Williamsburg—which was at that time a stockade settlement called Middle Plantation—in 1699. A few years later the Assembly was prevailed upon to set aside three thousand pounds for the erection of an official mansion for the governors, who were appointed by the Crown, and since this required additional levies the colonists viewed the project rather sourly. Henry Cary, the master builder who had supervised the construction of the massive capitol at the other end of the town, and Alexander Spotswood, Governor from 1710 to 1722, devoted their enthusiastic personal attention to the construction.

After Spotswood, six other royal governors lived in it, the last being the Earl of Dunmore, who fled from it one dawn in June, 1775, thus ending for all time British rule in Virginia. With the formation of the new commonwealth, the mansion served as the executive mansion for the first two governors, Patrick Henry and Thomas Jefferson.

The colony provided the "standing furniture," but the rest was the personal property of the governor then in residence, imported by him from England or purchased from his predecessors. When a governor died, a careful accounting was rendered, and from these inventories the reconstructed building has been furnished.

Alexander Spotswood set the pace when he arrived as Governor in 1710 and found his official home started but not completed, and pushed through the work in such dashing style that when the Palace finally stood forth furnished and burnished amid gardens and terraces, it had cost so much that a complaint was sent to the King remonstrating against the "lavishing away" of the country's money.

During the occupancy of the next Royal Governor, Hugh Drysdale, repairs and improvements were paid for from the 'two shillings revenue' collected on each hogshead of tobacco, and before the arrival of his successor—Sir William Gooch—it was 'further ordered that the great Dining Room and Parlor thereto adjoining be new painted, the one of pearl color and the other of cream color.' By the time Governor Dinwiddie arrived (1751), he had to purchase and lodge temporarily in what is now known

Photo by Thomas L. Williams

FIGURE 94. The Governor's Palace in Williamsburg has been constructed on the foundations of the original edifice. While comparatively new, it is a duplication of the one built about 1720, to serve as a residence and official headquarters of the King's Deputy.

as the Carter-Saunders House, while the ballroom and supper rooms were added to the Palace.

They needed a ballroom, for on the King's Birth-Night the double row of 'noble catalpas' which bordered the Palace Green were hung with coloured lanterns, and the planters and their families 'up for the season,' as well as the gentry of Williamsburg, arrived in coach and chariot, chaise and berlin, to dance and gather round the punch bowls and to enjoy 'as good diverfion and fplendid entertainments' as Hugh Jones, who was the first professor of mathematics at William and Mary and a self-appointed chronicler of events, had 'feen anywhere elfe.' They needed a 'great dining-room' too, since Governor Botetourt notes casually that 'fifty-two dined with me yesterday and I expect at least that number today.'

Social formalities were maintained by Francis Fauquier and the other Royal Governors who held their receptions and received their subjects in the grand manner, standing under the portraits of the King and Queen, the brilliant court costumes of the Virginians vying with the even more brilliant ones of a few Indian chiefs also paying their respects. This instinct for splendour was augmented by the last Royal Governor—the Earl of Dunmore —who brought to the Palace much of his own private furniture. It persisted after Virginia had separated from Great Britain. Even Patrick Henry, who fashionable folk had feared might be too plain for his high position as Governor of the new Commonwealth, appeared in a 'suit of fine black cloth, and a cloak of scarlet adorned his shoulders, while his wig was as big and fine as any worn upon the streets of Williamsburg.' As for Thomas Jefferson, the last to occupy the Palace, a measured plan of it and a plan for alterations drawn up by his own hand and subsequently located in the Huntington Library in California is evidence, if evidence were needed, that the indefatigable statesman-architect-agriculturist-president expended his liveliest ingenuity upon his official home.

An invitation to the Palace was a distinction and might indicate a political purpose as well as the personal pleasure of the Governor and his lady. To the formal dining room food was carried in great covered dishes from the service area west of the building. Entertainment was costly. Governor Gooch noted that

FIGURE 95. The Colony provided the "standing furniture" but the rest was the personal property of the Governor then in residence, imported by him from England or purchased from his predecessors.

FIGURE 96. Entertainment was costly at the Governor's Palace. Governor Botetourt notes that "fifty-two dined with me yesterday and I expect at least that number today."

a celebration of a royal "Birth-Night" drew one hundred guineas from his private purse. Besides the expense of the food, the "Binn Cellar" had to be replenished with hundreds of gallons of imported wines.

In the Upper Middle Room, the Governor could be at ease with a few friends, perhaps enjoying a hot drink seasoned with spices which were kept in a rosewood box like the one standing on the center table—or could find time to read the latest books arrived from England. Appropriate editions of all the books listed in Governor Botetourt's library have, after a long search, been brought together in this pleasant room.

Other rooms tell other stories. In the east flanking building, with its Chinese Chippendale chest and gilt birdcage, was the

284

Photo by Thomas L. Williams

FIGURE 97. In the family dining room in the Palace, as in all the other rooms, interior decorators have collected or had made suitable furniture, chandeliers and wall coverings. The composition and application of paint is a superb example of the best colonial taste.

Governor's office. The opposite flanking building, furnished as a guardhouse, is a reminder that Lord Dunmore once felt it necessary to station marines there for his protection—a precaution which would never have been dreamed of by such popular predecessors as the Governors Fauquier and Botetourt.

During the Revolution the Palace served as a military hospital for the wounded of George Washington's army at Yorktown, and later excavations discovered the unmarked graves of one hundred and fifty-six Revolutionary veterans and two women believed to have been nurses.

In 1781 the Palace burned to the ground. The small buildings which flanked the forecourt survived and were used as private residences until they were destroyed by the Union army.

What, then, is the present Palace? Since the original superstructure was obliterated almost a hundred and seventy-five years ago, how can we consider this anything but an approximate duplication?

The art and science of restoration was perhaps never more thoroughly discussed than in this project. Should only old materials be used, or should new materials be permitted, if treated to look like old? Or should new materials be used and left to weather? Compromise of all three methods was made, and all three used.

When the advisory board and the architects could not agree as to the location of the stables and carriage house, instead of choosing one guess or another, these buildings were entirely omitted.

"The reconstruction of the Palace and the redemption of the grounds, gardens, canal and planting besides being an artistic satisfaction is a fascinating record. It is the record of scholars who unearthed old maps and plans; who searched through endless inventories, books of accounts, files of correspondence, contemporary records, advertisements, and manifests for every possible item bearing on the original interior and exterior appearance. It is the record of archeologists who traced the outlines of foundations, who uncovered bits of wall revealing the type of mortar, and quality and bonding of the brickwork; who sifted the earth to retrieve fragments of stone carving, marble moldings, hardware and utensils, anything which would add a clue

Photo by Thomas L. Williams

FIGURE 98. Landscape architects have planted precisely the trees and hedges which existed, or might have existed, when the Palace Garden was considered the best on the continent.

to their investigations. It is the record of architects who, when they could not be certain of details, followed English precedent or contemporary Tidewater Virginian examples; of interior decorators who collected or had made suitable furniture, draperies, chandeliers, wall coverings and mirrors, and whose studies of the composition and application of paint in the colonial period has resulted in as superb an example of painting as can be found in America today. As for the park and grounds—the Holly Garden, the Ballroom Garden, the Tree Box Garden, the Green Garden where a hundred and fifty-eight Revolutionary soldiers are buried —the landscape architects have, with equal meticulousness and imagination, followed the outline of the original walls and terraces. They have excavated brick steps, paved areas, drains, the foundations of outbuildings; they have rebuilt the canal and, with infinite exactitude, planted precisely the trees, the hedges, the fruit, vines and flowers which actually existed or might have existed in that exact spot at that exact period when the Palace Garden was considered 'the best on the continent.' They have, of course, preserved the mound, originally the icehouse, which served as a place to view the general scene, and is the only one *in situ* known to have been built in America.

"The Governor's Palace with its regiment of outbuildings— quarters for guard and chancellory, bathhouse, smokehouse, salthouse, laundry, were all under separate roofs—was the fore- runner of the Virginia mansions of the first half of the eighteenth century whose beauty and dignity so enriched the pleasure and prestige of life in the South. That it should have risen from its ashes not only in accurate dimensions and structure but in its colour and ineluctable charm is a twentieth-century miracle."

The Palace is, of course, merely part of the project generally known as Colonial Williamsburg—a project concerned with noth- ing less than the restoration and, in necessary cases, the recon- struction or demolition of the buildings of an entire town.

The Reverend W. A. R. Goodwin, the late Rector of Bruton Parish Church, had long nursed the idea of bringing the old capital back to its original appearance, and in 1926 he won the interest and financial support of John D. Rockefeller, Jr.

All the principal buildings of the colonial capital—the Capi- tol, the College of William and Mary, the Raleigh Tavern—have received the same meticulous study as the Palace. Eighty origi- nal buildings are still standing in the restored area, and more than six hundred modern buildings have been removed. Three hundred and twenty-five colonial residences and public buildings, gardens, streets and greens have been restored or reconstructed.

What is now presented to the public is a sort of outdoor museum similar to those displayed in some European cities, but up to this time, unique in the United States. Guides, books and book- lets and pamphlets, direct the tourists and explain the purpose and accomplishment of the project, with specific information as to what is genuinely old, what is duplicated and what is simulated.

Therefore, every visitor to Williamsburg understands that the Palace is not an old but a new building.

FIGURE 99. The Palace Gardens follow the outline of the original walls, terraces and formal flower beds.

Not so many, perhaps, realize that the original Palace, after which it is modeled, was not the oldest residence in the capital. There are three rival contenders for this distinction.

The Ludwell-Paradise House, now one of the exhibition buildings of Colonial Williamsburg, holds Mrs. Rockefeller's collection of folk art. The Nelson-Galt House, residence of Major and Mrs. V. Lee Kirby, has recently been restored by Colonial Williamsburg. The Timsom House, unrestored, is privately owned and occupied by Mr. and Mrs. Rutherford Goodwin. All of these were built between 1700 and 1718, and the Palace was not completed until 1720.

Neither does every visitor appreciate that most of the dwellings in that first colonial capital were modest frame cottages, one or two rooms deep, surrounded by a clutter of outbuildings and looking out over streets where chickens wandered, pigs wallowed, and through whose summer dust and winter slush ploughed heavy coaches and carts. To be sure, at this time conditions were no better elsewhere. Bathrooms and screens were as unknown in London and Paris as in Williamsburg.

The inhabitants of that first colonial city, if they should return, would be astonished at the wide clean streets and neat yards. But if they were properly loyal Virginians, they would not blink an eye but merely imply that this was the state of affairs they were used to, and would point to the Palace to prove that not only in bricks and mortar but in its immaculate elegance it is a precise duplicate of the original.

And yet it may be queried if Virginians regard their wondrous palace with the intimate affection they give so freely to hundreds of lesser houses. They can see it is beautiful and they know it is a valuable historical and educational exhibit, and they cheerfully admit it is a financial asset.

With their flair for impressive names, which leads them to title quite ordinary places Manors and Mansions, Parks and Lodges and even Castles, they enjoy the high-sounding syllables of "The Palace."

But admiration is not love. The Governor's Palace is a new building and it makes no pretense of serving the purpose of the original, for it is neither the official residence nor official headquarters of the Governor. It is merely one item in the truly splendid outdoor museum which is Colonial Williamsburg, not the home of any one person.

The ambition which spurs a man to build or acquire his own house and the sentiment which sustains him in holding on to it in spite of inconveniences, financial and otherwise, is common to many people of many races. If Virginians seem to emphasize this ambition and sentiment, it may be because the usual ancestral ties are shot through with a golden cord of happiness and pleasure, both of which in this sunny land have always been regarded as praiseworthy pursuits.

There were taverns in the early days, of course; Gadsby's in Alexandria, The Rising Sun in Fredericksburg, the Raleigh in Williamsburg.

But the accepted place for fun was in the home.

When people wanted to give a ball, they threw two parlors together and made a ballroom. When they wanted a dinner party, they pulled out the dining table until it could seat twenty-five. By putting beds, cradles, cribs and even trundle beds in the big chambers, they could extend hospitality to a score or more of house guests. They leveled out a race track in the pasture in front or in back of the house, and contrived a bowling green and not infrequently a maze somewhere on the grounds for the entertainment of the household and its guests. Houses and grounds had been planned with these things in mind, and no one grudged expenditure of time and money in the pursuit of pleasure.

Today, many of these diversions once enjoyed at home are pursued elsewhere. One dances at the Country Club and pays to bowl in a bowling alley and an overnight guest is lucky if he is given a day bed in the living room. Such changed conditions only serve to enhance the affection Virginians feel for the homestead they have inherited or otherwise acquired.

These homesteads include the formal Georgian residences of brick which line the streets of Alexandria, and the story-and-a-half cottages of clapboard in the district of the old Port. They include the magnificently restored country seats in Loudoun and Clark and Fauquier counties, and the houses in and around Winchester which suffered shellfire and repeated capture in the Revolutionary War and the War Between the States. They include the substantial rock houses in the Shenandoah Valley whose design and material are reminiscent of the settlers of German descent who came pioneering from Pennsylvania. They include the log houses, some of them now faced with clapboard, which were built as forts against the Indians in the Southwest, and in that same spacious region, the century-and-a-half old handsome brick farmhouses, set amid their prosperous acres. They include the Eastern Shore, where the large houses of ivied brick, and small frame houses with roofs of different levels, face the water of the bay or the sea. They include the famous old plantations up and down the James River, about which so much has been written in the past and will doubtless be written in the future. They include the transplanted and the indigenous dwellings in Richmond. They include Fredericksburg, distinctive with its white frame dwellings, with quaint little places once used as schools as well as dwellings, tucked away in back and side yards, and the huge white Federal Hill which was shelled one hundred and thirty-five times and was used as a hospital in the War Between the States.

Only a hundred of these varied and widely scattered homes have been mentioned in this book. There are hundreds of others of equal significance. It is astonishing how, after centuries of shifting tenancies and fashions, they still seem able to evoke a jealous devotion in the breasts of their owners, who may or may not be descendants of the original builder.

For this reason they possess a quality which gives them an intimacy and warmth. Some of them are architecturally noteworthy; some are not. Some are brave with historical associations and others have only the legends of the families which have occupied them.

In any case, they seem to have a way of attracting strangers, and of possessing their possessors, who make no pretense of judging them impartially, but are content to garland them with pride and praise.

These are the houses Virginians have loved.

BRIEF SELECTED BIBLIOGRAPHY

Adventures of Telemachus—Fénelon, François de Salignac de la Mothe. Translated by Dr. John Hawkesworth. Hurd and Houghton, Boston, 1859

Alexandria Houses (1750–1830)—Deering Davis, Stephen P. Dorsey, Ralph Cole Hall. Architectural Book Publishing Co., Inc., 1946

Cocke, Charles Lewis—W. R. L. Smith, Richard G. Badger. The Gorham Press, Boston, 1921

Colonial Interiors, Second Series—Edith Tunis Sale. William Hepburn, Inc., New York, 1930

Dolly Madison. Her Life and Times—Katharine Antony. Doubleday & Company, Inc., Garden City, N.Y., 1949

Great Georgian Houses of America. Published by the Editorial Committee of the Great Georgian Houses of America. Kalkhoff Press, New York, 1933

Historic Harrisonburg—John W. Wayland. McClure Printing Co., Staunton, Va., 1949

A History of Rockingham County—John W. Wayland. Ruebush-Elkins Co., Dayton, Va., 1912

A History of Shenandoah County—John W. Wayland. Shenandoah Publishing House, Strasburg, Va., 1927

History of Southwest Virginia, 1746–1786. Washington County, 1777–1870. Lewis Preston Summers. J. L. Hill Printing Co., Richmond, Va., 1903

Historic Virginia Homes and Churches—Robert A. Lancaster, Jr. J. B. Lippincott, Philadelphia, 1915

Historic Wall-Papers—Nancy McClelland. J. B. Lippincott, Philadelphia, 1924

Historical Collections of Virginia—Henry Howe. Babcock & Co., Charleston, S. C., 1845

Homes and Gardens in Old Virginia—The Garden Club of Virginia. Edited by Frances Archer Christian and Susanne Williams Massie. Garett & Massie, Inc., Richmond, Va., 1950

Interiors of Virginia Houses of Colonial Times—Edith Tunis Sale. William Byrd Press, Inc., Richmond, Va., 1927

Jefferson and Monticello—Paul Wilstack. Doubleday Page & Co., Garden City, N.Y., 1925

Journal and Letters of Philip Vickers Fithian, 1773–1774. Williamsburg, Va., 1943

Legends of Loudoun—Harrison Williams. Garett & Massie, Inc., Richmond, Va., 1938

Legends of the Skyline Drive and the Great Valley of Virginia—Carrie Hunter Willis and Etta Belle Walker. Dietz Press, Richmond, Va., 1937

Lexington in Old Virginia—Henry Boley. Garrett & Massie, Inc., Richmond, Va., 1936

(The) Mansions of Virginia, 1706–1776—Thomas T. Waterman. University of North Carolina Press, Chapel Hill, 1946

Memoir of Miss Margaret Mercer—Casper Morris. Lindsay & Blakeston, Philadelphia, 1848

Mt. Vernon. Its Owners and Its Story—Harrison Howell Dodge. Lippincott, Philadelphia, 1932

New Roads in Old Virginia—Agnes Rothery. Houghton Mifflin Co., Boston, 1929, 1937

North American Review. Vo. 223—471—William Short, Marie Goebel Kimball, New York, 1926

Popular Lectures on Ethics of Moral Obligations—Margaret Mercer. Edmund and Julian C. Ruffin, Petersburg, Va., 1841

(The) Secret Diary of William Byrd of Westover, 1709–1712. Edited by Louis B. Wright and Marion Tinling. Dietz Press, Richmond, Va., 1941

Stratford Hall—Ethel Armes. Garett & Massie, Inc., Richmond, Va., 1936

Thomas Jefferson, Architect and Builder—I. T. Frary. Garett & Massie, Inc., Richmond, Va., 1950

Tidewater Virginia—Paul Wilstack. Bobbs Merrill Co., Indianapolis, 1929

Virginia's Eastern Shore—A History of Northampton and Accomack Counties. Ralph T. Whitelaw. Virginia Historical Society, Richmond, Va., 1951

Virginia Ghosts and Others—Mrs. Marguerite Du Pont Lee. William Byrd Press, Inc., Richmond, Va., 1932

Virginia. A Guide to the Old Dominion—Virginia Federal Writers Project. Oxford University Press, New York, 1946

Virginia, The New Dominion—Agnes Rothery. Appleton-Century, New York, 1940

Wallpaper. Its History, Design and Use—Phyllis Ackerman. Tudor Publishing Co., New York, 1923

GLOSSARY OF ARCHITECTURAL TERMS

Apron: An area of projecting brickwork or stonework below a window.

Architrave: The finish surrounding a door or window, or the lowest member of an entablature.

Ashlar: A facing of squared stones.

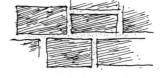

Belt course: A projecting course or courses on the exterior of a building, usually at the floor or window-sill line.

Cartouche: A scroll-shaped ornament used as a feature in a design.

Chair rail: A molding on a wall around a room at the height of a chair back.

Clipped gable: A gable of which the apex is cut back in hipped roof form.

Corbel: A projection from the face of a wall designed to support structural or decorative elements.

Cornice: The uppermost part of an entablature usually used to crown the wall of a building.

Course: In masonry construction, continuous horizontal ranges of brick or stone.

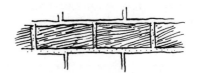

Dado: A plain or paneled field, defined at top and bottom by moldings, that traverses the lower part of a wall surface.

Dentils: Oblong blocks spaced in a band to decorate a cornice. (Common in the bed mold of a Corinthian entablature.)

English bond: A method of laying brick wherein one course is laid with stretchers and the next with headers, thus bonding the double thickness of brick together.

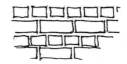

Entablature: An assembly of three parts of a Classic order, cornice, frieze, and architrave, forming the member carried on the column.

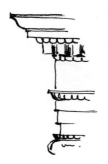

Façade: The front of a building.

Fenestration: The arrangement and proportioning of windows.

Finial: A terminating ornament used on the apex of gables, pediments, roofs, etc.

Flat arch: A series of wedge-shaped stones or bricks over an opening which, though simulating the appearance of a lintel, performs the arch function.

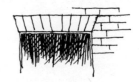

Flemish bond: A method of laying brick wherein headers and stretchers alternate in each course, and vertically headers are placed over stretchers to form a bond and give a cross pattern.

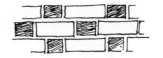

Fluting: The surface of a pilaster or column which is enriched with vertical channelling.

Frieze: The portion of the entablature between the architrave and cornice.

Gable: Often called an "A" roof; a roof section triangular in form.

Gambrel: A roof having its slope broken by an obtuse angle.

Glazed brick: Header brick bearing a gray or green transparent glaze on its surface.

Header: End of brick; a brick laid across the thickness of a wall.

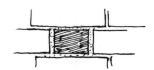

Jamb: The reveal or lining of a doorway or other aperture.

Lintel: The horizontal top piece of a window or door opening.

Lunette: A half-round area in an arch or in the penetration of a vault. The French term for circular opening in the groining of the lower stories of towers, through which the bells are drawn up.

Mansard roof: One having two slopes on all sides, the lower one being steeper than the upper.

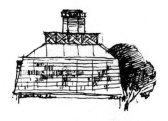

Modillion: An ornamental block, applied to the underside of the projecting members of a cornice.

Mullion: A narrow wood or stone division between window openings.

Muntin: The horizontal or vertical members in sash, used to divide the glass. The horizontals are sometimes called bars.

Newel: The principal post at the foot of a staircase.

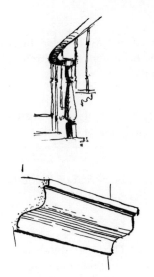

Ogee: A molding, in section concave in one termination and convex at the other.

Palladian motive: The arrangement of an arch flanked by lower square-headed openings and separated from them by columns or piers, which was much used by the architect Palladio.

Parapet: A low wall along a roof or terrace, used as a protection or decoration.

Parterre: A flower garden having the beds disposed in some formal form or pattern.

Pavilion: A projecting motive on a façade to give architectural emphasis.

Pediment: A crowning motive of porticoes, pavilions, doorways or other architectural features, usually of low triangular form, sometimes broken in the center to receive an ornament and sometimes of segmental, elliptical, or serpentine form.

Pier: A square supporting member; also the wall space between windows or other apertures.

Portico: A covered colonnade at the entrance of a building.

Portland stone: A limestone from the Isle of Portland in England.

Quoin: A squared stone at the corner of a building or of architectural features.

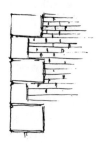

Reeding: A small convex molding, the reverse of fluting.

Reveal: The depth of an opening in a wall or other structure.

Riser: Upright piece of a step from tread to tread.

Rubbed brick: Brick, usually selected for an even, light color, and rubbed to a smooth surface on two vertical faces.

Spandrel: A triangular space, especially between the shoulder of an arch and a vertical member; also the space between the shoulders of two adjoining arches.

Stretcher: The long face of a brick when laid horizontally.

String course: See Belt course.

Stringer: The oblique structural member of a stair; also the finish piece.

Topiary: The clipping of shrubs in ornamental form.

Volute: A scroll form as in an Ionic capital or scrolled terminal of a stair rail.

Water table: A projection of the lower masonry or brickwork on the outside of a wall, usually at the first floor line.

index